SERENITY

SETTING NEW BOUNDARIES

Mark MacDonald, Kevin Brown
Ray Mitsch

*Daily Devotions
for Those
in Recovery*

A
JANET
THOMA
BOOK

THOMAS NELSON PUBLISHERS
Nashville

Published in Nashville, Tennessee, by Thomas Nelson, Inc.,
and distributed in Canada by Lawson Falle, Ltd., Cambridge,
Ontario.

Unless otherwise noted, Scripture quotations are from the
NEW KING JAMES VERSION of the Bible. Copyright © 1979,
1980, 1982, Thomas Nelson, Inc., Publishers.

Scriptures marked (NIV) are from The Holy Bible: NEW
INTERNATIONAL VERSION. Copyright © 1978 by the New
York International Bible Society. Used by permission of
Zondervan Bible Publishers.

Library of Congress Cataloging-in-Publication Data

Mitsch, Raymond R.
    Setting new boundaries : daily devotions for those
in recovery / Raymond R. Mitsch, Kevin J. Brown,
Mark MacDonald.
        p.   cm.
    ISBN 0-8407-3338-0
    1. Alcoholics—Prayer-books and devotions—English.
2. Devotional calendars.   I. Brown, Kevin J.
II. MacDonald, Mark.   III. Title.
BV4596.A48M57   1991
242'.4—dc20   91-23578
                                                    CIP

Printed in the United States of America
2 3 4 5 6 7 — 96 95 94 93 92 91

Introduction

Recovering from dysfunctional relationships takes work. As therapists at the Minirth-Meier Clinic we have had the opportunity to assist many like you begin the difficult journey toward health. The process is slow and results often take longer than anticipated, but the goal is worthwhile.

Each of us brings different experience to the recovery process. Trained in chemical dependency treatment, Mark MacDonald has closely worked with the families of individuals whose lives were impaired by alcohol and drugs. Ray Mitsch daily counsels individuals and families who have become stuck in unhealthy patterns of abuse and communication. I have worked extensively with families torn apart by abuse and other severe problems.

We all share two beliefs. First, true change requires looking at the whole system. When an individual in a relationship makes a commitment to recovery, it will have a profound impact on all those involved in their life. This, to a great extent, is what makes recovery difficult.

We also believe that it is impossible to neglect the spiritual dimension of change. Recovery requires a total commitment of mind, body, and spirit. Unless one is willing to submit their lives and wills to God, dysfunctional patterns are certain to remain solidly in place.

It is our prayer that the meditations you are about to read will be beacons of light illuminating the path upon which you have embarked. While no book can ever substitute for therapy and professional guidance, books can provide encouragement and inspiration. We hope that *Setting New Boundaries* will do just that for you.

Mark MacDonald
Kevin Brown
Ray Mitsch

Therefore you also be ready, for the Son of Man is coming at an hour when you do not expect Him.

—MATT. 24:44

A new year stands before us. What an overwhelming opportunity! A year filled with possibilities, with disappointments, joys, and satisfaction. How will you spend it? How will you prepare for the year ahead?

The Scripture passage for today suggests what is crucial to assuring success for the year ahead: being prepared! But how does one stay prepared? The process a farmer goes through gives a very useable analogy. First, break up the ground that has been unplowed from last year. Maybe there are areas that haven't been attended to over the last year that have grown hard and unresponsive to change. Identify what these are and begin to plow!

Next, sow the seeds of healthy behavior. Start now to renew healthy relationships with others and God.

Finally, prepare to harvest the fruit of growth in your life: unfailing love for your God and love for others that is as unconditional as possible. It is indeed time to be ready for the Lord and renew your commitment to plow, sow, and reap.

Father help me to seek you anew and to be prepared for this year!

> *Direct my steps by Your word,*
> *And let no iniquity have dominion over me.*
> —PS. 119:133

You are not alone. You have begun a strange, new process that will take you from dysfunctional choices and boundaries to health. It may be long, it certainly will be hard, but you are not required to know the entire route. God is your guide.

In your travels, you will go to places you have never been before. Getting lost is normal; that is to be expected when you are in a new place. Sometimes you must stop and ask directions. This is not failure.

However, you have a constant traveling companion who knows the route. God has been there with many other individuals in recovery. Allow God to direct your journey, trust him to lead you down the correct road, and remember to thank him as you near your destination.

Guide me as I walk down this foreign road to recovery.

*"Do not fear the reproach of men,
Nor be afraid of their revilings."*
—ISA. 51:7

One of the reasons we make poor choices in life is because we base our decisions on how others might respond, rather than on what we know to be right. We have learned, mostly in childhood, that even seemingly healthy choices may meet with significant resistance. When setting limits with our parents or spouse we may fear angry criticism or the cold silence of rejection. As a result of this fear, we often retreat and change our choices to suit the desires of others, rather than making decisions that are healthy for us.

A woman stopped attending church because her handicapped husband insisted on it. Prior to dropping out, she had been actively involved in various church functions. As her husband's health worsened, however, he demanded that she stay home and care for him, even though they had hired a nurse for these occasions. When confronted by a friend for not taking care of herself, the wife replied cautiously, "Well, his handicap is bad, you know. . . . Besides, I really don't want to make waves; he can get pretty mad."

In order to free ourselves to make new choices and establish new boundaries, we must not "fear the reproach of men" or their insults. Unfortunately, family members and close friends do not always have our best interests in mind.

Lord, give me courage to make healthy choices even when others insult or criticize me.

> *Therefore let him who thinks he stands take heed
> lest he fall.*
> —1 COR. 10:12

Just when you think you are doing better, something happens and things go sour. This principle is so well accepted that I often predict to the people I work with that as soon as they begin to make progress, something will happen to slow them down. The person will come back amazed at my insight! Of course, it isn't my insight as much as it is God's.

It is part of our human nature to begin to ease up in our efforts when we think we have the world by the tail. It is at this point that we drop our defenses and begin to let old behavior creep back in. At first we simply don't notice. But then with a flood we come tumbling down from our mountaintop and realize that we have lost our footing.

So what is the solution, you ask? The key is to keep a creative tension and skepticism about yourself. That means that you should never lose sight of your ability to create new ways to make poor choices. Be on the alert! Keep a watchful eye on how you interact with people. Use others to help you maintain perspective.

Father, help me to be on the alert even when things are going great.

*For God has not given us a spirit of fear, but of
power and of love and of a sound mind.*
—2 TIM. 1:7

Codependency is a dysfunctional pattern of reacting
to life's situations based on fear of change. To allow
others in your life to continue abusive patterns, first
you must become blind to their part of the problem, and
then you must continue in this denial. Although this
takes considerable energy, often fear of the consequences keeps the pattern going.

You see, there are negative consequences of change
as well as the obvious positive ones. Furthermore, it's
easy to become accustomed to life as usual, while the
future is uncertain and frightening.

When God becomes part of the equation, fear and
timidity need not coincide with change. In fact, God's
spirit offers power, love, and self-discipline, all of
which are necessary components of the change process. While changing dysfunctional patterns of codependency can be frightening at first, it is very helpful
to acknowledge that a caring and loving God will give
you the tools needed to finish the process. God will not
allow fear to subvert the new you that is developing.

---

*God, help me to accept the help you offer in my recovery and to
persevere in spite of my fear.*

> *Trust in the LORD with all your heart,*
> *And lean not on your own understanding.*
> —PROV. 3:5

Once we acknowledge that God certainly does exist, the next step is to realize that he is in control of our lives and we are not. Frequently we sabotage our ability to make healthy choices by taking matters out of God's hands and into our own. We are particularly likely to attempt to take a situation into our own hands when we feel out of control.

Jody, a thirty-eight-year-old Christian woman, was commiserating with a close friend about how difficult it was to be married to her husband, Nick. Jody described Nick as physically and verbally abusive; frequent arguments were the norm, rather than the exception. When asked why she had married Nick, Jody explained, "I thought I was doing the right thing. I was eighteen years old, and I worried that God would not allow me to get married, and that if he did, it would probably be with someone I didn't like. Then I met Nick. I thought he was the perfect man for me. My plan was to sacrifice my virginity, get pregnant, and we would be happily married. What a mistake!"

The choice Jody made at eighteen years of age will affect the rest of her life. Although Jody knew God, she did not allow him to control her life. How are you allowing God to be in control of your life? Are there areas that you are still reluctant to hand over to God?

God, help me to give uncontrollable situations back to you.

Be completely humble and gentle; be patient,
bearing with one another in love. —EPH. 4:2 (NIV)

In many families there is often one person around whom controversy swirls, often because of the person's inability to be flexible. This inflexibility prompts the other family members to concentrate on meeting the challenge this person presents. They end up expending a lot of energy attempting to change this person, rather than concentrating on what they can change in themselves.

In order to begin to address this kind of problem it is important to remember what you have the ability and control to change. You don't have the power to change another person's attitude. However, you have the full ability to change your own attitude and approach to someone who is different from you. The key is to change about yourself what you are asking the other person to change. For example, if you think they are rigid and intolerant, check yourself with regard to these faults. You might be surprised what there is to change! That is the essence of bearing with one another.

Father help me to bear with others as they bear with me.

> *"Behold, God is great, and we do not know Him;*
> *Nor can the number of His years be discovered."*
> —JOB 36:26

I once heard Paul Meier, cofounder of the Minirth-Meier Clinic say that if we took *all* the intelligence of all mankind and put it into a massive supercomputer, it would still be like a tiny speck in God's eye. Unfortunately, we often see God as vengeful, overly demanding, rigid, or like our parents who did not do an adequate job of caring for us. We then reject God as an aid in times of trouble and instead look to our own solutions, the very ones that got us into our rotten situation in the first place.

This is especially true when it comes to choices we make. Boldly we jump into old patterns, believing that "this time it will be different, this time I will make it right!" Later, looking over our situation, we wonder where God was. We then blame God for being too small to help us. We need to look at God as someone who is all-powerful, all-knowing, always available no matter how helpless we feel about our lives.

God, help me to see you as you really are, too big for me to imagine in my limited human experience.

*Immediately the father of the child cried out and
said with tears, "Lord, I believe; help my unbelief!"*
—MARK 9:24

A very important part of the growth process involves
believing that God wants to give us the ability to make
correct choices and to set healthy boundaries. For
most of us, this belief does not come overnight; it takes
time to mature and develop. The idea that belief is a
process can be a new concept for many. We tend to
think that any individual either believes completely or
doesn't believe at all. Life experience, however, generally tells us otherwise. Many of us have experienced
situations in which faith was mixed with doubt.

Belief often starts with the acknowledgment that
God exists, and for some, it will take time just to be
able to agree with this truth. It's all right if the beginning steps of belief take time. The concept of God
should not be taken lightly.

Brent is a good example of the idea that belief needs
time to grow and develop. When I first met Brent, he
stated that he was an atheist. He angrily told me that
he had been taught about God as a child, but now he
did not believe. Over time, however, as Brent actively
got to know others who believed in God, he began to
change his mind. Brent now acknowledges that God
exists, but he is still in the process of learning about
who God is and how God can bring about change in his
life.

What part of the belief process are you in?

> *Bearing with one another, and forgiving one*
> *another, if anyone has a complaint against another;*
> *even as Christ forgave you, so you also must do.*
> —COL. 3:13

Forgiveness is an incredible act of vulnerability. You make yourself open to be hurt again when you forgive someone.

I am surrendering my connectedness to someone when I forgive them. What I mean by this is that if I choose not to forgive someone I inadvertently remain connected to them. Sometimes this can turn into dependency, but not dependency in the sense of accommodating and being walked on. Rather, I am waiting for that person to ask for my forgiveness in order to feel fully justified and then forgive them. If I choose to work my forgiveness this way, I have managed to place myself once again in a dependent relationship where I am making my actions dependent on someone else's.

It is important to note that God expects us to forgive because he has forgiven us. This does not mean to forgive only when someone asks us. God forgave us even before we asked him. We gain more personal independence by forgiving in spite of how vulnerable we become, and we follow the model he has established for us.

Father, give me the strength to forgive even when I am not asked.

The LORD is on my side;
I will not fear.
What can man do to me?
—PS. 118:6

A fearful person will catastrophize situations, blowing them out of proportion until the anxiety becomes far bigger than the problem. An objective person observing such an individual will wonder how he ever arrived at some of his conclusions.

Often such anxiety has its roots in childhood. If the person grew up in a family where he was often afraid and not protected by his parents, he will be fearful even in situations that are minor crises, "making mountains out of molehills." The result is a certain sort of paralysis as the anxiety he feels renders him unable to make the most routine decisions.

In therapy it is helpful to have such an individual visualize the crisis he is experiencing and all the possible outcomes, even the most drastic. Usually a few others are added to make the situation even more dire than the fearful person originally imagined. Then the question can be asked, "Is this impossible for God?" You see, with God on your side even the most catastrophic consequences are within the scope of his ability to intervene and keep you safe.

What things that you fear are beyond God's ability to keep you safe?

> *My eyes are ever toward the LORD,*
> *For He shall pluck my feet out of the net.*
> —PS. 25:15

Many of us have our own particular net in life. It may be money, alcohol, food, addictive relationships, drugs, rage, or even pride. Whatever the net, we cannot progress until we give it to God and look to him for strength and guidance. However, we often want to try it our way before we admit defeat and allow God to help us with our struggles.

Ted, an alcoholic in early recovery, began to worry about his family, job, and finances. He became so consumed by his worries that he began to miss his support group meetings and he failed to keep in close contact with his sponsor from A.A. His sponsor soon contacted Ted and challenged him to let go and let God control his life. Much to the sponsor's surprise, Ted stated emphatically, "Oh no, I'm not giving up yet." Ted didn't give up. In fact, within three days, Ted had relapsed, and he lost his job and family as a result. Ted found himself in the same old net again, except this time it had a tighter grip.

Sometimes giving up is the best thing we can do for ourselves. We cannot fix our problems on our own, because God states clearly that he is the only way out of them. Are you allowing God to help you on your path to recovery? Or are you like Ted, trying to release your feet from the net on your own power?

Lord, help me to trust in your power rather than my own.

> *"Only take heed to yourself, and diligently keep yourself lest you forget the things your eyes have seen, and lest they depart from your heart all the days of your life. And teach them to your children and your grandchildren."*
> —DEUT. 4:9

Maintenance is an exercise in vigilance. It means being a student of the process of growth and not forgetting the basics. A good example is athletes who watch videotapes of their opponents in order to prepare for the game ahead. They study their opponent, watching their reaction to every situation.

To maintain healthy behaviors you must become intimately familiar with your dysfunctional behaviors, so that you can foresee when they are most likely to occur. Then you can prepare for almost anything. It takes continuing effort to maintain healthy behavior. If that effort is not expended, the dysfunctional behaviors can slip back into your patterns of interacting with others.

Another aspect of the vigilance necessary for maintenance is the element of teaching others. There is no more efficient means to retain information than teaching that information to others. It becomes a part of you as you explain and help others to understand the process of growth and maintenance.

Father, help me to be careful and watch for dysfunctional behaviors.

> *Deliver me out of the mire,*
> *And let me not sink.*
> —PS. 69:14

I sometimes tell this story to patients who are having difficulty motivating themselves to change.

A man was walking along a path and fell into a pit. It was a deep pit with clay walls that were slick, and the man, despite much trying, could get neither a foothold nor a handhold. After hours of struggling, he quit.

As the hours passed, the man became increasingly despondent, resigning himself to a fate of eventual starvation, dehydration, and then death. Suddenly another man fell into the hole. The first quickly convinced this man that escape was impossible, so both gave way to depression and despair.

After several more hours a third man fell into the miry clay pit. This man would not believe escape was impossible. After some thought, he figured an escape plan: each of the men would stand on the others' shoulders and the top man would just be high enough to climb out.

When life seems like a muddy hole from which there is no escape, we need to remember that God has a rescue plan.

When was the last time you gave up because the solution was not immediately obvious to you? God may provide help through others.

It is better to go to the house of mourning
Than to go to the house of feasting,
For that is the end of all men;
And the living will take it to heart.
—ECCL. 7:2

We live in a society that says, "Eat, drink and be merry!" "Don't worry about tomorrow, just live for today." This attitude toward life offers little value to the person struggling with setting healthy boundaries and making appropriate choices. Realizing the consequences of our previous choices in life is one of the most important aspects of being able to make healthy choices in the present.

A recovering alcoholic attended her annual work party. Many of her colleagues there were consuming large quantities of alcohol. She saw how much fun they were having, and soon she asked herself the question, "Why can't I have just a few?" Without much more thought she joined in with them. She never made it home that night. The next day, she was found passed out in her car at the side of a road. She had no idea how she got there or who she might have been with the previous evening. One week later, her spouse filed for divorce and custody of the children. This was a consequence of relapsing for a third time.

If only she had taken the time to consider the devastating consequences of her decision to drink, she might have a family to return to today. All of us need to keep in mind the question, "How will my choices today affect me tomorrow?"

Lord, give me the wisdom to look ahead before I make a decision.

> *But now you must also put off all these: anger,*
> *wrath, malice, blasphemy, filthy language out of*
> *your mouth.*
> —COL. 3:8

How does someone get rid of anger? Do they finally realize they don't have to get angry to get their way? Do they give up and it goes away? Of course, none of these ideas are the route to effective anger management. Even after you have begun to look and change regarding your boundary issues, the area of anger is probably the most difficult one to change. This is because we can never get rid of our anger. It *is* important, though, not to fall into the trap of denying the anger.

What can you do when you get angry? First, be honest enough to admit that you are angry. This is the first step in dealing with your anger in a healthy way. Second, act as quickly as you can to do something about it. Be specific and concrete about what you are angry about. Own this feeling as yours alone. The greatest difficulty in dealing with anger while in recovery is figuring out what its presence means. Work to put it in the proper perspective and keep up-to-date with your feelings.

Remember that anger is an expected hurdle while in recovery.

Therefore, putting away lying, each one speak truth.
—EPH. 4:25

Denial is a word used in therapy to describe when a person refuses to see the facts of their situation.

Bob was a thirty-three-year-old heroin addict who lived with his parents. He had been in treatment for years but had never been able to break the chains of his addiction. Just when he was about to graduate from therapy, he would relapse. The solution seemed quite elusive to him and to a number of frustrated therapists.

Bob's parents were brought to therapy, at the suggestion of his newest therapist. It became clear that the parents constantly rescued him, enabling him to remain addicted. Both parents were quite addicted to Bob, unable to cut the apron strings. While they professed a strong desire to see Bob change, both were frightened of what would happen to them if their only child suddenly became competent and left home.

Once Bob stopped denying his family's codependent relationship, he was forced to look at his role in the family. Then he was able to begin the change process.

Lord, help me to see the truth about destructive relationships in my life, and why I really hold on to them as I do.

Then I returned, and I saw vanity under the sun:
There is one alone, without companion.
—ECCL. 4:7–8

I am so tired of making the wrong choices. How can I ever do it right? I'll never be able to do it!" These are the words of a frustrated woman in early recovery from her codependency. Sally had married and divorced three times and was about to marry for a fourth time. However, she realized during the engagement period that she was about to repeat another bad choice.

Her fiancé was a needy and dependent person whom Sally would have to take care of throughout their marriage. Taking the role of caretaker was the very thing Sally was trying to change. This role had caused significant problems in all three of her previous marriages. Upon this realization, Sally broke off the engagement and began to berate herself with the above words.

The mistake Sally made was not necessarily her decision to marry again, but that she made this decision without consulting with others who knew her. She tried to make an important decision by completely relying on herself.

God tells us it is meaningless to live life alone. We need to find a support network of friends who will guide us and encourage us in the choices we make. With help from others we can learn to make the right choices.

Lord, help me to remember that you do not value isolation from others.

> *Beloved, do not think it strange concerning the*
> *fiery trial which is to try you, as though some*
> *strange thing happened to you.*
> —1 PETER 4:12

There are times in the process of recovering from co-dependency that you can feel despair because you're just not sure if you are moving ahead or falling behind. I once had one young female client ask me, "Is this normal for me to go into a tailspin so easily when I don't do so well?"

The time that I find clients being so critical of their progress is when they fall short of their expectations. These expectations become increasingly high with each success they experience in their recovery. So, when a relapse occurs and they stumble in their journey, they are sure they are losing miles of ground. This tendency is a leftover from the criticalness they developed to be sure they didn't lose the person who was so important to them.

It is important to view problems in the appropriate light. Problems and stumbles are to be expected. When (not if) they happen, evaluate honestly what happened and decide what you can do to prevent them next time. Remember it is a process, not a project that will be completed any time soon.

Evaluate problems realistically without turning them into catastrophes.

> *God raised up, having loosed the pains of death,*
> *because it was not possible that He should be held*
> *by it.*
> —ACTS 2:24

What is the worst that can happen? This is a question we often use in therapy to help pessimists realize that the worst is usually not as bad as they thought. As you can see from the above passage even the ultimate tool of the evil one, death, is no match for God.

Depression brings a tremendous sense of hopelessness, helplessness, and worthlessness. When suffering in very codependent relationships an individual feels these and then begins to consider all the awful possibilities for the future. Sometimes, when labeling these beliefs as pessimistic and counterproductive is not helpful, a therapist will parody these beliefs, suggesting even more hopeless scenarios until the client begins to see the futility of believing this way. Then the client may see humor in her stubborn clinging to such a negative view.

Frankly, nothing is impossible with God. On several occasions even the finality of death was overturned with God's intervention. What consequences do you see for your future? Is intervention too difficult for the all-powerful creator who is able to reverse the consequences of death?

God, help me to understand your vast power.

Your word is a lamp to my feet
And a light to my path.
—PS. 119:105

Seth knew he had to set clear boundaries between himself and the women with whom he worked. In the past he had allowed these boundaries to blur, and it had nearly cost him his marriage. His present desire was to remain committed to his wife and to God. Seth wanted to be faithful to God's commands, since he was learning that God is trustworthy. But how could Seth follow through on this commitment?

Looking back, Seth was aware that his decision making had often seemed arbitrary. He had often stumbled through life instead of heading toward a goal.

This time, however, the situation was different. Seth had a clear sense of the direction he was taking. He made the decision to follow God's plans for his life, rather than his own. For the first time, Seth was learning how to rely on his Bible for direction. Although it didn't contain a specific blueprint for every single situation Seth encountered, he did find that it gave him sound principles on which to base his decision making.

Many people, like Seth, have found that God's Word lights the path of recovery, where previously darkness and confusion prevailed. Are you allowing God's Word to lead you in his direction, or are you still stumbling around in the dark?

Lord, thank you that you provide a clear resource when choices seem uncertain.

> *"Both riches and honor come from You,*
> *And You reign over all.*
> *In Your hand is power and might,*
> *In Your hand it is to make great*
> *And to give strength to all."*
> —1 CHRON. 29:12

I remember the first road race I participated in. I had trained relentlessly, bought better shoes, and watched my diet. I was really psyched up for this.

The race started and I was running well. My first mile was probably the best mile I ever ran. Soon, though, I began to feel awful. I felt the strength leaving my legs, and I didn't seem to have the mental endurance to keep going. Where was my strength going to come from to finish this race? I couldn't embarrass myself in front of so many people. Somehow I found the inner resources to complete the race.

I learned a very important concept, though, about running any race we are in (life, recovery, a project). If we look within us, we find that before long we have run out of resources. But if we look to God to give us the strength to complete our journey, we find an inexhaustible supply of strength and power.

Father, help me to look to you for the strength to complete my journey toward recovery.

*Come to Me, all you who labor and are heavy
laden, and I will give you rest.* —MATT. 11:28

Backpacking in the mountains can be a wonderful
experience. You may have a hard time understanding
this pastime unless you have had a sunrise breakfast
overlooking glorious snowcapped peaks or have seen
mountain goats playing in the wild. But those who
have will talk endlessly about the experience.

On the other hand, sometimes it can be exhausting
carrying all the necessary supplies on your back, and
rest is a welcome diversion. For those carrying emotional backpacks full of past hurts, the journey through
the mountains of life also is exhausting. The load is
heavy and the trip often seems as if it will never end,
and an emotional backpack is not easily taken off.

God has an extensive knowledge of such burdens. In
fact, once he became man and carried ours for awhile.
Not only does he understand, he has offered to give
rest to those who come to him. Are you ready for some
relaxation? Let God help you with that heavy backpack you have carried around for so long. The trip will
seem much easier once you have rested.

Lord, I need a break. Please help me with this load.

> *Lament and mourn and weep! Let your laughter be turned to mourning and your joy to gloom. Humble yourselves in the sight of the Lord, and He will lift you up.*
> —JAMES 4:9–10

The first step to making the right choices is to realize the destructiveness of past incorrect choices. Most of us want to skip this step. That's not to say we don't want to get better; we just want to get better without experiencing the pain of looking at our past. God tells us this isn't possible. In fact, if we want to get better we must realize that our choices have been *so* bad that we will "lament, mourn, and weep" over them.

How do we get to that point? We must be willing to take stock of how our choices have adversely affected us and others. The alcoholic must realize how his drinking is affecting himself as well as his family members. This isn't easy. Our initial response is to say, "I may have affected me, but not others; and if I did, not that much." One alcoholic early in his recovery stated in anger, "My drinking only affected me, not my family!" The following week he was drinking. What motivation will we have to make the hard choices in the future, when we minimize the impact of the old choices on our past?

Lord, give me the courage to take stock of past choices and see their effects clearly.

But recall the former days in which, after you were illuminated, you endured a great struggle with sufferings.
                                                    —HEB. 10:32

In any recovery program and subsequent maintenance it is important to take time out to remember. If you were to go into any household, I'm sure you would see many things in that house that have sentimental value. Why? Because they are connected with the past, and they help people to remember those times that were special.

The writer of Hebrews wanted his audience to recall their struggles of earlier days during the time of their persecution. His purpose was not to create more misery. Rather, he wanted to remind them of the road they had already come down and the progress they had made. He also wanted to help them keep their focus on the goal before them.

Throughout maintenance it will be important for you to "recall the former days." During these times you will be encouraged by the progress you have made, and you will gain a broader perspective of the work God has brought about in you through your recovery. We need to remember what we have been through to gain encouragement from the past, and hope for the future!

Father, help me to take time to remember what you have done through my recovery.

> ". . . *visiting the iniquity of the fathers upon the*
> *children and the children's children to the third and*
> *fourth generation."*
> —EX. 34:7

Mrs. Hartley brought her son to our clinic for counseling. She was extremely concerned about his new friends, who were apparently inducing her son to use marijuana and alcohol. Upon further exploration, it became apparent that not only had she come from a dysfunctional and abusive family, but also she was a single parent using alcohol to fill the intense emptiness of her life

Her son was the person identified for treatment, but he definitely was not the problem. Rather he was part of a system that had been dysfunctional for years. You see, patterns of dysfunction are repeated across generations, something the Bible recognized long ago. Mrs. Hartley had passed on dysfunction to her children, much like it had been passed on to her.

We have a heavenly family that can help us break these patterns. If we fail to observe closely, we live our lives as we were taught. With the help of our heavenly family, we can break the chains of our dysfunctional past.

God, help me to be aware enough of my dysfunctional patterns to
prevent me from passing them on to the next generation.

So then each of us shall give account of himself to God.
—ROM. 14:12

Boundaries help each of us to distinguish between what we are and are not responsible for in life. In the verse above, God clearly tells us that each of us is responsible for his or her own choices, thoughts, and actions.

When boundaries are unclear, we frequently take on the responsibilities of others by attempting to alleviate the consequences of their behavior. We can also go to the opposite extreme and reject responsibility for our own actions. Boundaries are again unclear when we view ourselves as victims, unable to make active decisions regarding our behavior.

Establishing healthy boundaries means accepting responsibility for myself and allowing others to accept responsibility for themselves. It means remembering that God will ask me to account for what I have said and done—not what my spouse, boss, friend, or child has said and done. Establishing healthy boundaries also means that significant others in my life will not be held responsible for my actions.

When I think about the day God will ask me to account for my actions, I am motivated to concentrate on my own actions rather than the actions of those around me.

Dear God, give me the ability to distinguish my responsibilities from the responsibilities of others.

> *Your glorying is not good. Do you not know that a little leaven leavens the whole lump?*
> —1 COR. 5:6

I'm sure that most of you have been around someone who has just gotten a new puppy. Many adults are often overheard saying, "If they could only *stay* a puppy!" That also describes the challenges of the maintenance process, except that you can keep the issues small if you so choose. It is only by neglect that these inevitably grow into monstrous problems later.

Think back for a minute on the course of events that have led up to your seeking help. You became aware that something was definitely wrong and something had to be done. After getting up the courage you sought someone out to help you to recover from poor decision making. What was the process of recovery? Was it taking all your problems all together and attempting to tackle them all at once? No, it was taking one at a time, and slowly but surely trudging through them.

The process of maintenance is exactly the same but on a long-term basis. It requires keeping up with the little issues and irritations. In so doing, they are more likely to stay that way.

Father, help me to stay up-to-date on the details of my recovery and maintenance.

The violence of the wicked will destroy them,
Because they refuse to do justice.
—PROV. 21:7

Although Ernest would not describe himself as a violent man, his family did. Each time he experienced frustration he would fly off the handle, throwing things, yelling, even physically lashing out at times. Ernest believed that respect meant fear, and his way of keeping the family together was to instill his form of respect in those around him. He had other ways of explaining his behavior so that he never had to admit that he was wrong.

"My father," he reminisced, "was horrible compared to me," and he was right. His father was an alcoholic who would beat his children without cause when drunk. To use this as justification for his own rageaholism, however, was denial. Admitting that he had a problem meant that he would be like his father, and this was difficult for Ernest. He was extremely bitter about his childhood.

Ernest's children and wife confronted him with this early in treatment. He saw no other way of dealing with situations, even though he had alienated his family much like his father had done to him. While Ernest had good reasons to be angry, his rage had become an uncontrollable compulsion which had harmed those around him. Anger is fine as a feeling, but when it becomes abusive behavior, it is time to change.

Lord, help me to stop rationalizing my compulsive behaviors that injure others.

> *"Therefore do not worry about tomorrow, for*
> *tomorrow will worry about its own things.*
> *Sufficient for the day is its own trouble."*
> —MATT. 6:34

Making the right choices requires energy. In the verse above, Jesus tells us to focus that energy on the present. He knows how frequently we humans tend to drain our energy by worrying and obsessing about the unknowns in our future. He also knows that the only choices we have the power to act on are those that we make today. We are unable to travel forward in time or to anticipate the future. Today is what counts. It sounds simple, but it isn't for most of us. We often spend so much time worrying about the outcome of tomorrow that today is lost.

Cynthia admitted herself for inpatient hospitalization after experiencing her third abusive relationship with a man. In her first week of treatment, Cynthia focused on her poor choices and inappropriate boundaries with men. However, by the second week, all Cynthia worried about was what her life would be like after her discharge from the hospital. "What will I do when I leave? Will I make it? What if I fail again?" Much of Cynthia's time in treatment was wasted due to her inability to focus on the present. She lost a valuable opportunity to increase her understanding of herself and her actions.

Do you waste opportunities to grow emotionally and spiritually by worrying about the future?

Dear God, please help me to focus on the moment at hand.

For it was so, when Solomon was old, that his wives turned his heart after other gods; and his heart was not loyal to the LORD his God, as was the heart of his father David. —1 KINGS 11:4

Are there people in your life who make it harder for you to keep the focus on the changes you have already made? Solomon had such people in his life, and it resulted in the watering down of his devotion to God. It is important to identify such people in your life so that you can develop strategies for dealing with them.

These are the people who don't respect your boundaries and efforts you expend to set limits. In their presence you seem to be most frustrated. Sometimes you think that it would be a good idea to just quit seeing them at all because of the amount of frustration you experience.

These people, though, can also be seen as critical barometers of your recovery. If you can hold your limits with them, you can probably hold your limits with anyone! That is one way to overcome this obstacle—to see it as a learning opportunity. This type of perspective takes you out of the helpless role and into a position of learning and growth.

Father, help me to continue to learn and grow and not get hooked by other distractions.

> *Put on the whole armor of God.*
> —EPH. 6:11

There is a mistaken belief system that people get what they deserve. To some degree this belief makes life easier to understand by explaining why bad things happen to seemingly good people and vice versa: they must have done something to deserve it.

Unfortunately many people don't get what they deserve, so they grow up with bitterness and tremendous feelings of helplessness at the traumatic events that occur in their lives. Gail had been sexually abused as a child. For years she had sought to explain it by blaming herself first, and later, men in general. She continually found herself in abusive and dysfunctional relationships until she finally withdrew into a depressed shell.

As long as Gail resorted to a pattern of isolation and overgeneralized blame, her defenses were ineffectual. This protective pattern became part of the problem and contributed to her dysfunctional beliefs about relationships. The only males willing to stick around long enough to be part of her life were those who saw her strategy for what it was and took advantage of her neediness. She needed a new suit of armor, one that could adequately protect her from further hurt while simultaneously aiding her to hold her own in future relationships.

———

Is your "armor" adequate protection?

Do not be deceived, God is not mocked; for
whatever a man sows, that he will also reap.
—GAL. 6:7

Jim was an intelligent and talented young man. Unfortunately, however, Jim found himself going from one job to another without success. Jim couldn't make sense of his experiences. He'd always thought of himself as a brilliant individual with enormous potential, and yet his life experiences seemed to indicate otherwise. Jim concluded that he was the victim of unfair circumstances. There was little he could do but hope for a better break.

Jim's conclusion about his position was based on very selective observations. Although he focused carefully on the actions of others, he never stopped to examine the consequences of his own behaviors. Therefore, he neglected to note that he lost several jobs due to numerous absences and his failure to follow through on tasks. He perceived others as unfriendly, but he failed to acknowledge the numerous angry outbursts he made during discussions. An objective observer would note that Jim's current life situation was a direct result of his previous actions.

Are you like Jim? Do you view yourself as a victim of others? If so, it's time to examine the part you have played in your own circumstances. This experience is often painful, but it can also be extremely freeing. A victim has no hope, but a responsible person can learn to make new choices.

Dear God, give me the courage to examine the consequences of my actions.

What has happened to all your joy?
—GAL. 4:15 (NIV)

I just don't have the joy I used to have," a young man told me in the hospital. "There was a time when treatment was hard, but there was a certain amount of satisfaction and sense of accomplishment I felt even in spite of the difficulty. Where has my joy gone?" Does this sound familiar?

In spite of the tough parts of treatment, there *is* a certain amount of joy in seeing change occur. The problem is that this condition cannot last for too long. We can incorporate just so much change into our understanding of ourselves. Besides that, too much change too quickly is not healthy. It doesn't allow us to consolidate the gains *we have made.*

It is important to keep your expectations realistic surrounding your recovery. Remember your progress in assessing problems accurately, responding appropriately, and resolving feelings. That is indeed something to be joyful about. Remind yourself that this is a process you are involved in. As long as you focus on the changes you are making, you are on the right track. Behaviors and attitudes change slowly. We are often not aware of the change until it has already occurred, and then we look back and are amazed at what has happened.

Find joy in the process of recovery and maintaining the gains already accomplished.

"I will not execute the fierceness of My anger;
I will not again destroy Ephraim.
For I am God, and not man,
The Holy One in your midst;
And I will not come with terror."

—HOS. 11:9

Don's parents punished him severely when he did wrong. In his adult years he could see that the punishment they had given did not fit the things he did. Despite his maturity, however, he had difficulty recognizing that he did not deserve intense punishment when he made mistakes.

While Don believed in a loving God, he also experienced God as similar to his parents. He thought that God also punished severely when he made mistakes. Don placed a tremendous amount of emphasis on right and wrong—especially the wrong. Each time he erred he expected a backlash of punishment.

Don obviously had difficulty trusting in such a God. The higher power to whom he wished to entrust his future was, in his mind, just like his parents. Don's mistake was believing God to be like us, human. God forgives us when we fail, and he is far more gracious than even the most understanding parent.

God, help me to recognize you as you are rather than as other humans who have hurt me in the past.

He who speaks truth declares righteousness,
But a false witness, deceit. —PROV. 12:17

Many of us think we are honest people. However, we may not be taking into account the many times we deny our feelings. When we deny our feelings we are actually being dishonest with ourselves. Some of us may have been raised to deny our feelings "for the sake of others." When we do this, we deprive ourselves of the ability to be sensitive to our own needs. To make healthy choices we must be honest with ourselves about our feelings.

Margaret discovered this principle of honesty the hard way. She went through life with an inner hatred toward men, which she denied even existed. The hatred developed from being sexually abused by her father as a child. Margaret was well aware that the abuse occurred, but she insisted she had no feelings about it. Even when challenged on this lack of emotion by other friends with similar backgrounds, Margaret continued to deny any feelings of anger or resentment. Later in life, she suffered through three marriages and then vowed not to marry again. She blamed the broken marriages on her husbands, stating they were unreasonable and insensitive to her needs.

Obviously, Margaret's ability to make healthy choices was adversely affected by the denial of her emotions. Do you have feelings which you are denying? Are you willing to be honest with yourself in all areas of your life, including your emotions?

Lord, give me the courage to be honest about my feelings.

You ran well. Who hindered you from obeying the truth?
                                        —GAL. 5:7

The image of a runner is quite frequent in the Bible, and it is appropriate to the things we face in life. There are many kinds of people in this particular race. There are those who look like they are in a sprint, going full tilt all the time. On the other hand, there are those who look like they are out for a casual stroll on a Sunday afternoon.

What kind of person are you? What would people see if they observed your attempts to maintain the change you have already accomplished? Would they see someone who looks like they are in a sprint or a marathon? It is important to keep in mind that the process of growth is slow, and the way is filled with obstacles at times. If you are in a sprint, then obstacles will be devastating because you are pushing so hard. On the other hand, if you are in a marathon, obstacles are expected and prepared for. In addition, you have more time to deal with them because you don't intend to finish the race any time soon. Maintaining this perspective helps us view problems simply as things to solve.

Remember that you are in a long race towards growth, not a sprint.

> *Beloved do not think it strange concerning the fiery trial which is to try you, as though some strange thing happened to you; but rejoice to the extent that you partake of Christ's sufferings.*
> —1 PETER 4:12–13

Look at my life," Lori said to me. "I've never been happy. This has been going on as long as I can remember!" Her parents had been so wrapped up in their own problems when Lori was growing up that they had little time for her. They expected her to "carry her own weight" even when it was too heavy for her.

In order to fulfill family expectations that she fail, Lori had involved herself in some disastrous relationships with men, several of which were abusive to her. After she finally found a stable man, she began experiencing physical problems, several times entering the emergency room for treatment.

You see, as a child Lori had known her parents were uninterested in her life, and so she had developed a pattern of getting their attention by having crisis situations. When life finally settled down and relationships appeared to be improving, the physical crises began. The turning point in Lori's therapy was when she began to see pain, both physical and emotional, as a badge of honor, a way to participate in the sufferings of Christ. She then stopped viewing God as a malevolent, punishing father.

God, help me to see suffering not as something to be avoided at all costs or something strange, help me to rejoice instead.

*"The Pharisee stood and prayed thus with himself,
'God, I thank You that I am not like other men—
extortioners, unjust, adulterers, or even as this tax
collector.'"*
—LUKE 18:11

Fred came to therapy because he was ordered by the court to address his inappropriate discipline of his children. During sessions, Fred was confronted for making verbal threats to get his point across. Fred was aggressive with the counselor, as well as with his family. When his actions were discussed, Fred denied that he was being verbally abusive. Fred insisted that the counselor was exaggerating the extent of his anger. He stated, "My anger is no worse than my father's. In fact, I'm mild compared to him and others that I know."

Fred did not see his expression of anger as verbally abusive, nor at other times, physically abusive. Fred maintained his denial by *comparing* his actions to the actions of others. As long as he could compare himself to someone who was louder and more intimidating, Fred did not have to admit he had a problem.

Unfortunately, we may use this same defense to justify our poor choices in life. It's always possible to find someone with more destructive behaviors than ourselves. The key to making healthier choices is to stop comparing ourselves to others and start comparing ourselves to what God wants us to be.

*Lord, do my words and actions measure up to the person you created
me to be?*

Who is wise and understanding among you? Let him show by good conduct that his works are done in the meekness of wisdom. —JAMES 3:13

What is one of the most frequently heard criticisms of the church? Isn't it the one where the person says that she doesn't want to affiliate with a church because it is filled with hypocrites? The answer of course is that churches are indeed filled with hypocrites, but that is why they are there! Aren't we all hypocritical in one way or another? The minute we level that accusation at someone else is the moment that it can be leveled at us as well. Probably one of the hardest things for us to do is to live in a way that is consistent with what we believe to be true.

Living in a way that is consistent with what you have learned is also the challenge of recovery as well. You must always be on the alert for the time when you are not "walking the talk." That is what consistency is all about. We exhibit the wisdom and understanding we have developed by putting it into action. Without action, there is no evidence of change. Change only remains to be an empty concept that you enjoy talking about, but never follow through on.

It is important to "walk the talk."

Do not be envious of evil men.
—PROV. 24:1

The first steps of change are difficult ones. You must make a decision to leave behind old patterns and friends that contribute to a dysfunctional lifestyle. Sometimes the past can be like broken-in shoes, more comfortable than a newer, stiffer pair. There may be a sense of nostalgia, even a longing for the certainty of old ways, regardless of the pain caused.

This longing is dangerous! You may watch others practice an irresponsible lifestyle and become jealous of how much easier they seem to have it. The struggles you have begun to experience on the way to health initially may not seem to outweigh the potential gains of continuing the change process.

Don't give up. It is the beginning that is the hardest. With time, even new shoes become more comfortable. New patterns will, too. Keep in mind that the people you envy because of the apparent ease they seem to exhibit are just as miserable inside as you once were.

What unhappiness led you to begin the change process? Is the grass really greener on the other side?

> *Let no one say when he is tempted, "I am tempted*
> *by God"; for God cannot be tempted by evil, nor*
> *does He Himself tempt anyone.* —JAMES 1:13

Bill was a blamer. No matter what was going wrong in his life, the answer to the problem was found in someone else's wrongdoing. He accused others of not understanding him or not being compassionate enough with him. He made statements such as "It's your fault that I lost my job!" Bill based his life on the false assumption that his behavior was caused by the behavior of others. In other words, Bill believed that others did have the power to control his life. Of course, this wasn't true.

In Bill's case, he did lose his job because of his own laziness and lack of attendance. Like Bill, we all have problems in our lives. For some of us, the easiest way out is to point our finger at someone else for causing the problem. In reality, our part of the problem is usually the greatest part—and sometimes the only part.

The ultimate act of blaming is blaming God for what has happened in our lives and for the choices we have made. Bill stopped attending church because he blamed God. As a result, Bill didn't have to look at his part in the problem nor take responsibility for his actions and choices. We can learn more about our choices and boundaries if we stop blaming others and focus on our responsibilities only.

God, help me to focus on my responsibilities only.

He who sows iniquity will reap sorrow.
—PROV. 22:8

Life is somewhat like farming: the behaviors in which we engage are like seeds resulting in a harvest of habits. A farmer who plants corn certainly expects corn to sprout, not wheat. When we engage in behaviors that are counterproductive to healthy living, we can expect dysfunctional habits.

Parents bringing children and teens for therapy sometimes are surprised that we ask them to be involved in the process. They expect that somehow we will get their children to change and be model citizens while ignoring their involvement in the process leading to problems. Children, however, react to the environment in which they are raised. If that environment has planted problem seeds then problems will grow.

On many occasions parents have become angry when the focus of therapy emphasized problems in the cultivation of healthy children. It is much easier to look at the problem crop while neglecting the mistakes that caused the problem. When children are raised within a dysfunctional family it is natural that behavioral difficulties will arise. As parents, we must look at ourselves rather than just blaming our children for their inadequacies.

God, help me to see the impact of my own inadequacies on those dependent on me.

> *For you did not receive the spirit of bondage again*
> *to fear, but you received the Spirit of adoption.*
> —ROM. 8:15

Fear is a harsh taskmaster. It drives you to act in ways that are not ultimately in your best interests. When you are afraid, you find it difficult to engage in new activities and behaviors that free you from your dysfunctional past.

In therapy I often use images of bondage and slavery to describe the intense hold that the past has on clients. Imagine chains holding you back from experiencing the freedom you so greatly desire. Sometimes it is helpful to personify your fear, seeing it as a person forbidding you to move on, keeping you from growing into a strong, assertive individual that no longer engages in patterns that are uncomfortable. Perhaps you are locked in a dungeon or forced to do things you know are not conducive to change, and always present is the slavedriver fear.

God, however, is not only willing to free you from your slavery to fear, he is willing to adopt you into his family. Certainly when God is your parent he will not allow others to enslave you and keep you from becoming the whole person he intended when you were born.

Are you willing to give up slavery to fear for adoption by God as a child?

And the eye cannot say to the hand, "I have no need of you."
                                                —1 COR. 12:21

To make positive choices we must understand God's plan for us as relational people. In the verse above, the apostle Paul is talking about the body of Christ. As people, we need strong relationships with others who share our faith. Although each of us has unique and diverse abilities, none of us can successfully operate as an isolated entity, independent of all others. Only God is self-sufficient. Only God can be complete in himself. Therefore, God directs us, as his people, to recognize our need to establish healthy, interdependent relationships.

A young man reached a point where he was able to list the consequences of the poor choices he had made in his life with regard to his use of food. However, he rejected the recommendation that he join a support group to aid in his recovery. He was convinced that he could change his behavior on his own, and he really didn't want to take the risk of being vulnerable with others. Of course, he never did seem to be able to stay on the path of recovery. He was continually slipping back into old patterns, unaware of these recurring patterns until he was once again dealing with their consequences. His desire to change was real, but he resisted God's plan for his growth by insisting he could do it without the help and support of others.

Lord, help me to remember that you designed me to grow through interdependent relationships.

> *Do not be overly righteous,*
> *Nor be overly wise:*
> *Why should you destroy yourself? . . .*
> *It is good that you grasp this,*
> *And also not remove your hand from the other;*
> *For he who fears God will escape them all.*
> —ECCL. 7:16–18

Some of us may have memories of watching circus performers on the tightrope. We watched in rapt attention, waiting to see if the performer would get all the way across the rope without falling into the net.

A walk on a tightrope describes our lives sometimes. Often we find ourselves in balance, but sometimes we feel like we are about to fall off the tightrope. It is important for us to formulate our strategy for maintaining balance in our relationships with others. How will we judge when our boundaries are getting walked on? And what will we do when we feel that someone is not respecting our boundaries? If we can begin to answer these questions, then we stand a better chance of achieving a balance. Otherwise we will always be compensating for a previous incident, teetering on our own tightrope, and never becoming steady.

Dear Lord, help me to find balance in my life by developing principles to live by in my relationships with others.

Be of one mind, having compassion for one another; love as brothers, be tenderhearted, be courteous.
— 1 PETER 3:8

At twenty-six Karen was baffled about relationships. She had never experienced one that felt good to her. Furthermore, she had just begun to realize that she was continually repeating the problems of her childhood family in her adult life. With this in mind, Karen asked a very important question: "What is a good relationship?"

This wasn't a simple question to answer. Frankly, it was much easier to point out to her all the characteristics of bad relationships and what to avoid. As we began to discuss this issue, it became increasingly apparent that Karen had had no good relationships in her life for comparison.

The five ideals of good relationships outlined in this verse were helpful to her: harmony, compassion, brotherly love, tenderness, and courtesy. All were things she had lacked throughout most of her life but greatly desired. It was important for Karen to understand that relationships could be worthwhile, especially when they began to emulate positive ideals, so that she knew what to look for as she began the process of change.

God, help me to find relationships that fit your higher standard instead of those that are detrimental to my recovery.

> *Two are better than one,*
> *Because they have a good reward for their labor.*
> —ECCL. 4:9

Making consistent choices that benefit us in a healthy way is hard work and often elusive. One reason for this difficulty may be found by examining our own family background. We may have been raised in a family that taught us to only rely on ourselves, not others. An example of this kind of teaching can be found in the statement, "If you want to get something done right, do it yourself."

We may have also been told not to talk about our problems or our family's problems. In fact, we may have been severely punished if we let out a family secret. The message given is clear: "Don't get help from others. Deal with a problem by yourself." Some families package this same message in different wrapping. They say it with more appealing words such as "You can do it . . . . Be your own person . . . . Be strong, not weak." Our American culture often gives us similar messages.

Because of family and cultural influences, it may feel uncomfortable, unnatural, and even threatening for us to begin to reach out and talk about our problems with other people. But as we do, our ability to make consistently healthy choices will increase. As the passage emphasizes, we benefit by including others when we need help.

Lord, give me the courage to reach out and ask for help when I need it.

Demas has forsaken me, having loved this present world, and has departed for Thessalonica— Crescens for Galatia, Titus for Dalmatia.
—2 TIM. 4:10

I have had numerous clients report to me that the worst thing that could possibly happen to them would be to have someone abandon them. Often their history of codependency reveals a long string of abandonments that made them even more determined to do what they had to to keep people close enough to take care of them no matter what the cost was to them emotionally.

The feeling of abandonment is one that is not uncommon to anyone. The above quotation reveals that even Paul, the great apostle of the faith, no doubt felt very abandoned at this point in his ministry. Where were his friends when he needed them? How could they abandon him now of all times? Sound familiar?

Probably one of the most discouraging incidents that happens to people who are in the maintenance phase of recovery is to discover that someone with whom they have gone through recovery has given up on the process. It is important during these times to allow yourself to feel the loss and the accompanying feelings. Hang on to what you know to be true, and look to others around you to help you keep the focus in the midst of confusion.

Father, help me to let others fail and not fail myself on my path to recovery.

> *And let us consider one another . . . not forsaking*
> *the assembling of ourselves together, as is the*
> *manner of some, but exhorting one another.*
> —HEB. 10:24–25

When you are unhappy and depressed you tend to isolate yourself. It is uncomfortable to be around others, seeing them having fun while you feel miserable. Isolation further contributes to depressed feelings because you have no outside help, no one to push you to see things in a more positive light.

As you struggle with destructive patterns in your life, you may find your energy is depleted. It takes much work to walk through the change process. Codependent individuals tend to see themselves as self-sufficient and independent, the strong one in the relationship. Therefore, when their energy level is diminished, they have difficulty letting others know, fearing that others will see them as weak.

It is at this point that you need a solid group of supportive people in your life. Unless others understand and are able to care and prod you to continue, you may feel like quitting. Before you begin to change codependent patterns in your life, find others who will understand and encourage you to continue.

Why do you fear letting others know of your struggle? Can you give this fear to God and allow others to help you in the struggle?

*For the law of the Spirit of life in Christ Jesus has
made me free from the law of sin and death.*
—ROM. 8:2

We often feel as if a battle is raging within us when it comes to making right choices. The choice that seems most godly often seems most unfamiliar, difficult, painful or even unfair. What's more, the choice we've identified as never wanting to make again seems to be the alternative we choose most consistently. Examples of this confusion with choices include the mother who promises herself she'll never curse at her son again, and the husband who shamefully realizes he's been unfaithful one more time. How can each person be making true choices when the choice results in the same destructive action taken over and over again? The cycle becomes endless. Resolutions to make new choices never seem to be strong enough.

Many people today want to tell us that the answer lies in improved willpower. "Just try harder. If you really wanted to change, you would." But the cycle of destructive behavior continues, while frustration and discouragement increase. To break any cycle a completely new action must be taken. A simple modification of an old approach will not be successful. God tells us that Jesus' death and resurrection were a radical alternative to the old and worn cycle of sin and death. What's more, he promises that the breaking of this cycle can be experienced in our own lives when we make the decision to depend on his power rather than our own.

Lord, when I depend on you I have the freedom to make right choices.

> *This hope we have as an anchor of the soul, both*
> *sure and steadfast.* —HEB. 6:19

I am always fascinated by the word pictures used by the writers of Scripture. They, like Christ, were acutely aware that we needed some kind of imagery to help us understand certain concepts and principles in Scripture. An anchor was a very understandable word picture used in Scripture.

Sailboats, particularly those which are used for long-distance trips, often have what they call a storm anchor. This anchor is used to slow the drift of the boat during stormy times. It wasn't meant to keep the boat in one place. It was meant to keep the boat in safe waters during the storm and to keep it from running aground.

Like a storm anchor, hope keeps us in safe waters so that we won't run aground emotionally. This hope is founded on the fact that our recovery will be complete and transforming. It is not an empty hope like that of a dying man who knows he will soon meet his maker with no assurance of salvation. No, this hope is one that is founded on God's continued faithfulness during our recovery. Hope is what first motivated you to attempt to change and kept you going through the harder phases of treatment. It also motivates us to continue to push for growth and further development of stable, healthy behaviors and attitudes.

Father, help me to grab on to the hope that only you can give.

"And you would be secure, because there is hope;
Yes, you would dig about you, and take your rest
in safety."
—JOB 11:18

Lane had not slept well in weeks. There were so many things to worry about, and every time she tried to sleep all of them would creep back. She was aware that many of them were quite trivial, but that gave her little comfort. Over-the-counter medications provided only fitful sleep, and the next day brought more anxiety.

For years she had rationalized this worry, making excuses to the others in her life affected by her obsessive focus on gloom and doom. If she did not pay attention to all the details, she feared her family would fall apart. Even when she did, it was overwhelming, and actually her family was falling apart largely because of her intense anxiety.

While there were some good reasons for her concern, many of the things she worried about simply were beyond her control. The more she tried to control, the more chaotic things felt to her. Lane needed to see the security of giving control to God. Then she would rest in the security of knowing that God would take care of her and her family. Hope was available to her, but only by resisting her compulsive need to worry about all the small details.

God, grant me the courage to give up my need to be in control and the worry that follows.

*"Watch and pray, lest you enter into temptation.
The spirit indeed is willing, but the flesh is weak."*
—MATT. 26:41

Janice was going to visit her daughter and son-in-law for the first time since she had begun the recovery process from her compulsive spending. She felt anxious about the visit because she knew that on previous occasions, she had greatly overspent her budget in an effort to keep her family happy with her. Over a number of years, this overspending finally led to foreclosure on her home, and separation from her husband. She now had a strong desire to gain victory over her spending habits.

Therefore, for this visit, Janice carefully prepared in advance. She asked her support group to pray for her. She also did a great deal of talking to God herself. She asked him to give her the strength to trust him for her happiness, instead of depending on her money. Janice also prayed during her visit. She prayed as she started each day, as well as during tempting situations. At the end of her visit, she thanked God as she kissed her daughter good-bye. Janice bought nothing during her trip other than necessary items.

Obviously, the foundation of Janice's ability to make new choices about her spending rested heavily upon prayer. In the past, Janice had relied on her own strength to maintain self-control. This time, through prayer, she relied on a much more powerful source of strength: God.

Our greatest resource for avoiding and resisting temptation is prayer.

*Therefore, whether you eat or drink, or whatever
you do, do all to the glory of God.*
—1 COR. 10:31

Most people are familiar with Nike's® commercials in which they have a well-known athlete working out. They always end the commercial with "Just do it!" It would be nice if we could be so easily motivated by such a simple phrase. We must have a reason for what we do, particularly things that require effort and endurance.

What is the motivation for recovery? Why are you putting yourself through such anguish to change your behavior? I'm sure that question has occurred to you more than once! Paul proposes a very good reason for making changes in our behavior—bringing glory to God. We gain identity and purpose from aligning ourselves with the Almighty. Not only do we make changes for us, but more importantly we make changes so that everyone can see what God can do in a person's life. That doesn't mean that we make the changes and God gets the credit. All begins and ends with God. If anything has changed it is because God has provided the power to make it happen.

So why do we persevere? To bring glory to God. Why do we bother to change? To bring glory to God! Who makes recovery possible? I think you know the answer!

Father, thank you for the power to complete my recovery.

For we do not know what we should pray for as
we ought, but the Spirit Himself makes intercession
for us with groanings which cannot be uttered.
—ROM. 8:26

Grasping the concept of a merciful, forgiving higher power is hard enough. But then there is the question of what to ask God. When you are new to the process of surrendering compulsive patterns this can seem complex. How do you talk with a God you have just met?

Frankly it is easier to do than you may think. Since God knows you from the inside out, he knows what you need at the same time you are struggling to put it into words. When you begin to look to God for help through prayer, something new begins to happen. Things will begin to come to mind, possibly things about which you have not thought in a long time.

Try it. Rather than worrying about how to pray, just do it. Begin by asking God to take control of your thoughts and to bring to mind things about which you need to ask for assistance. The words will come.

God, I need your aid in knowing how to ask for your help. Bring to mind things for which I need your intervention.

And another also said, "Lord, I will follow You, but let me first go and bid them farewell who are at my house."
—LUKE 9:61

Patricia, twenty-eight, is in therapy to address personal issues stemming from childhood verbal and physical abuse. Her parents are strict and insensitive and often take out their anger on her.

Part of Patricia's therapy is to accept that the childhood abuse actually did occur. The second phase of her treatment involves her recognition that her parents continue to be verbally abusive each time she visits them. For example, on her last visit, they told Patricia that no one would ever want to marry her because she was too dumb and ugly. Although Patricia acknowledged this statement was wrong, she denied that it hurt her by saying, "they always say stuff like that to me."

Patricia failed to make progress when she reached the second phase of treatment. For Patricia, to acknowledge the present abuse of her parents meant to begin to distance herself from them. She was unwilling to take this step because she still hoped they would someday love her and be the parents she never had.

Some of us have families like Patricia's. If we allow them to, abusive family relationships can choke our ability to make healthy choices and establish appropriate boundaries. We need to acknowledge our pain and the reality of our current family situation. We also need to let go of the fantasy that we can change abusive behaviors by tolerating them.

Sometimes, growing starts with letting go.

> *Thus says the LORD:*
> *"Cursed is the man who trusts in man,*
> *And makes flesh his strength,*
> *Whose heart departs from the LORD."*
> —JER. 17:5

It's incredible to me how slow we are to realize people's limitations. I often muse on the reasons we get into relationships, in spite of the inherent problems involved in them.

For one thing, I can't deny the fact that we need each other! As much as we would like to deny this basic reality, we still come back to people because people are all we have to depend on. Or are they? God made us to be social beings, and as hard as we try we cannot purge ourselves of this desire.

A second reason why we often turn to people is because the other alternative (God) is too frightening. After all, you can't hide anything from God, right? People, on the other hand, are often pretty gullible and easily fooled. You might be more prone to stick with people because they are a whole lot better than dealing with someone who knows everything about you.

Yet God accepts us in spite of the knowledge he has of us. We often don't know what to do with such love and acceptance. One of the keys to further recovery is working to accept ourselves as God accepts us without growing complacent.

It is important to accept those parts of yourself that are unacceptable in order to change them.

He knows those who trust in Him.
—NAH. 1:7

A child is born and instinctively trusts those caring for her. She cannot choose to trust only safe people; the child is totally dependent on the ones around her. As the child grows she learns that sometimes this trust can be abused. If she is hurt enough, eventually she has difficulty trusting.

Many individuals have had abusive childhoods. Their innate sense of trust has been repeatedly betrayed, and as a result they cannot commit to safe, trusting relationships. Because their parents hurt them, they fear that others who say they care will also create chaos and pain in their lives, and so they shun potentially safe, positive relationships.

Sometimes this fear becomes an inability to trust even God. The individual believes that even a relationship with a caring and nurturing higher power will become abusive and painful. Fortunately God has promised to care for those who begin to trust him. Although difficult at times, this trust can result in an incredibly rewarding experience of safety and security.

God, you understand my inability to trust. As I begin to invest in a relationship with you, show me clearly that you care.

> *"As the Father loved Me, I also have loved you;*
> *abide in My love."*
> —JOHN 15:9

Dependency often interferes with our ability to make healthy choices and set healthy boundaries. Dependency is based on the belief that our happiness and well-being can only be maintained by continuing a specific relationship. When we are dependent, we experience intense fear when a relationship seems to be unstable. Unfortunately, in an effort to keep the other person happy, we often respond in a desperate manner, compromising our own choices, opinions, wants, and goals. We justify these sacrifices by defining them as love and devotion. We ignore the fact that we are losing our integrity and self-respect.

Phil's relationship with his unfaithful wife provides a sad example of the destructive nature of dependency. A few months ago, Phil's wife announced she was involved with another man and was unsure about her commitment to the marriage. Phil felt devastated, and begged her to stay. He told her he would do anything he could to keep the marriage together. Phil began to ignore the anger he felt toward his wife. If she appeared unhappy, he canceled his own personal commitments.

Sadly, Phil confused extreme dependency with love. He failed to understand that true love enhances individuals rather than diminishes them. He looked for his security in his marriage, rather than in his relationship with God.

Do you rely on God for your security?

I have fought the good fight, I have finished the race, I have kept the faith.   —2 TIM. 4:7

Will you say at the end of your life what Paul said at the end of his? I'm not sure I will be so assured! However, it does highlight an important point about the process of recovery: The finish is almost as important as the race itself. If you have ever watched a footrace, the finish is important. It can often make the difference between winning and losing for the runner.

Why is the finish so important? Have you ever run a race against someone, and just as you were reaching the finish line, you let up on the speed in order to slow down? The finish is important because that is the time that we are most likely to let down on our concentration and pursuit of our goal. It is even worse if we think that we have the race won.

The maintenance phase of treatment is critical because it is the finishing process. Don't let up on the speed toward growth in this area of your development. The temptation is great, but it is critical to run to the end so that you, like Paul, can say, "I have fought the good fight, I have finished the race."

Father, help me to finish the race of my recovery.

> *Do you not know that those who run in a race all*
> *run, but one receives the prize? Run in such a way*
> *that you may obtain it.* —1 COR. 9:24

You have embarked on a journey with a goal. Like a race, the road to recovery is run with a prize at the end, healthy living. Many who start will not complete the course. Often the journey is considered too difficult and the prize too distant.

Joy entered therapy with her goal firmly in mind. She knew that life could not continue as it had. Desperately unhappy, she came to the first few sessions seeking rapid relief from patterns that had been in existence for many years. At first, this was sufficient motivation to change. Soon it became apparent to her that it was a much more tedious process than she had originally envisioned and she dropped out.

Joy lost sight of the prize, focusing instead on the short term and the difficulty she had with the new choices and boundaries required for lasting health. What Joy failed to realize was that a commitment to health is for the long run, and that at times she would have to bypass immediate symptom relief in order to assure herself a finish in the course upon which she had started.

———————

Are you focusing on long-term health or short-term relief? If you plan to finish the race, keep the prize in sight even though the race becomes difficult.

For I know that in me (that is, in my flesh) nothing good dwells; for to will is present with me, but how to perform what is good I do not find.
—ROM. 7:18

An intense struggle continually battles within those working in a recovery program involving addictions. A conflict exists between repeating old choices, no matter how harmful they have been, and making new choices. The old choices allow for familiarity and therefore security. On the other hand, making new choices requires risk-taking and vulnerability. Making new choices presents a frightening task for most of us. Therefore, a decision to return to our old choices often seems more appealing.

How do we break this pull back toward our old choices? The verse above indicates our first responsibility. We need to realize that "nothing good dwells in me" because of our sinful nature. The alcoholic must realize he will always want to drink. The food addict must admit that he will always desire to eat more than he should.

Unfortunately, many people often compromise their recovery program by saying, "I can have just one." When he returns to his former destructive choices, the alcoholic finds himself a slave to his alcohol once again.

Are you experiencing a struggle within yourself between old and new choices? Do you set out to make the right choices, but fail to do so? Are you acknowledging the powerful control your addiction has on you?

Lord, help me to acknowledge my sinful nature.

> *"But you, be strong and do not let your hands be
> weak, for your work shall be rewarded!"*
> —2 CHRON. 15:7

A crippling emotion while on the road to recovery is
disappointment. Whether directed at yourself or
toward someone else, disappointment simply means
that you have come face to face with the limitations of
yourself and people. In working with people who have
struggled free from many codependent behaviors, I often find them reestablishing new expectations of their
behavior in light of the changes they have made. This
wouldn't be so bad if these expectations were more
realistic than their previous ones. What happens,
though, is that they fall back into the old perfectionistic, rigid expectations they had in the past. They say,
"Well, I'm really on my way now, the rest should be
easy!" Or, "Hey, this is coming along pretty well, I
should be done soon."

It is a natural thing to formulate expectations about
future events; this is how God helps us adapt to novel
situations. It is important, though, that they reflect the
limitations of reality. A realistic person will say, "I am
really grateful that changing my behavior is going so
well. I'm determined to stick with it as long as it takes!"

---

*Develop realistic expectations about the important changes in your
life to prevent disappointment.*

"God is my strength and power,
And He makes my way perfect."
—2 SAM. 22:33

We all know that suffering is hard. But suffering is also sometimes needed as a precursor to growth. A good athlete recognizes this and struggles daily, pushing himself harder, often experiencing physical pain, to become stronger and better.

Ralph was a bodybuilder who had pushed himself to develop strong muscles. Unfortunately, he had been enabled repeatedly by his family to not take responsibility for his aggressive behaviors as an adolescent. It was only after some legal problems, when his parents could no longer bear for him the consequences of his actions that he sought treatment.

His emotional muscles underdeveloped, Ralph reacted aggressively to confrontation from his peers in group therapy. He responded angrily, as if he were entitled to different treatment than others. His family had not prepared him adequately for adulthood; now Ralph needed to make his sense of responsibility as strong as his biceps.

God, help me to trust when you are giving my emotions a workout so that I can develop a strong sense of responsibility.

> *If we confess our sins, He is faithful and just to*
> *forgive us our sins and to cleanse us from all*
> *unrighteousness.*
> 1 JOHN 1:9

Guilt often produces very painful feelings. Nobody likes to feel guilty, but we all experience this emotion at various times. Although guilt is generally unavoidable, many of us do try to ignore its presence in our lives. As guilt feelings go unrecognized, many of us get caught up in a cycle in which we alternately punish and comfort ourselves with compulsive behaviors.

Rachel is a middle-aged woman who knows this cycle well. She punishes herself by accepting consistent abuse from her husband, and then she prides herself in her self-sacrificing behavior. Recently, however, Rachel has embarked on a change process. She is beginning to identify the intense guilt she has carried within herself for years. Although it is painful, she is beginning to acknowledge some of the specific thoughts and actions that are sources of her guilt. This process takes courage, and Rachel's courage is growing as she experiences God's forgiveness in her life. Forgiveness is a new gift for Rachel.

Forgiveness can be a new gift for you, too. If you're like Rachel, you're probably getting pretty tired of the race to avoid dealing with guilt. If so, confession before God is a good place to start.

Lord, thank you that your forgiveness can free me from my guilt.

Have I therefore become your enemy because I tell you the truth?
—GAL. 4:16

Sometimes we need a "good enemy." Usually we are quick to surround ourselves with people who are more than willing to tell us what we want to hear. It is comfortable and reassuring to know that someone agrees with us, and it is easy to transform this into acceptance.

But, this isn't what we *need*. We need someone who will look us squarely in the eye and care enough about us to say, "You are starting to drift, and you need to reevaluate what your priorities are." Actually, this person is far from being an enemy; rather he is a precious and an incredibly loving friend who is willing to risk your rejection to say what you *need* to hear.

The Galatians are a useful example to examine. They did not like what Paul had to say to them. Suddenly they turned on him because he was confronting them with the truth—that they needed to make vital adjustments in their faith. Are you like the Galatians? Or do you have someone who is caring enough to tell you the truth even if it does hurt? Be prepared. Friends like this come in many shapes and sizes, and they may have an insight into your behavior that is useful and vital to your continued recovery.

Father, help me to listen to "good enemies" who give me valuable feedback.

> *Little children, let no one deceive you. He who*
> *practices righteousness is righteous, just as He is*
> *righteous.*
> —1 JOHN 3:7

Evie was an extremely sensitive adolescent. She had come from a rigid and perfectionistic family and would immediately feel hurt by input that had even a remotely negative flavor. She based most of her shaky self-esteem on how she believed others saw her. She was extremely dependent on her peers for the little worth she felt, and any criticism from them would ruin her week.

This made Evie very vulnerable. First, she was apt to follow the beliefs of her friends even when they ran counter to her own. This led to some uncharacteristic behaviors that created difficulties for her. Secondly, she was so eager for approval and acceptance that she fell apart when criticized, rather than bettering herself because of it. Evie had become a follower, and she was unable to stand up for herself.

Frankly, input from others can be helpful. An outside viewpoint enhances growth, especially when it relates to something we have overlooked in ourselves. On the other hand, basing our personal sense of value and worth on the opinion of others leaves us very vulnerable to peer pressure. The result can be engaging in behaviors that we know are not in our best interests.

If you don't know where you stand, you will fall for anything.

No temptation has overtaken you except such as is common to man.   —1 COR. 10:13

Grandiosity is a common word heard at many support group meetings. It is generally used when talking with the newcomer who brags about his greatness. It is interesting, though, to hear the newcomer be corrected for being grandiose when he is identifying himself as the *worst* person, or having problems *worse* than anyone else. By identifying himself as the most troubled, he places himself in the position of being different, unique, and sometimes even special as compared to others. The end result is that the newcomer is saying he is the greatest person at the meeting.

Tom, a newcomer to Cocaine Anonymous, was such a person. He attended a meeting because he felt his cocaine usage was getting out of control. At his first meeting Tom shared his difficulties with others. A regular attender with ten years of abstinence listened to Tom's troubles. As Tom concluded his cocaine stories he said, "You see, I'm probably the worst addict ever." At that point, the regular attender stood up and confronted Tom in anger, "You will not remain drug-free until you realize you are no different from anyone else here."

Do you set yourself apart from others by saying your problems are worse than anyone else's? The only way to begin to make changes in your life is to admit that your problems are common to everyone.

Lord, remind me that my problems are not unique.

You will keep him in perfect peace,
Whose mind is stayed on You,
Because he trusts in You.
—ISA. 26:3

There will be many things that could potentially rob you of your peace during maintenance. Some of these things will be new, and some will be shadows of the past. Whether new or old, you will still need to be ready for them.

Peace and trust go hand in hand. As the Scripture passage indicates, when we trust in God we have a peace that we never had before. The best way to understand this is to think like a child. When you were a child you felt secure as long as one or both of your parents were around. You trusted them so much that you had a peace that was safe and secure.

When you are faced with situations that threaten to rob you of peace, keep your mind focused on God's faithfulness and complete trustworthiness. He gave you the power to undertake treatment; he can also be trusted to restore your peace in the face of chaos. Remember that peace can exist in the midst of confusion when our minds are focused. As we begin to experience the calming effect of focusing on God's faithfulness, we can then experience more of the peace he intended us to have.

Father, help me to keep my mind steadfast on you.

And let the peace of God rule in your hearts, to which also you were called in one body; and be thankful.
—COL. 3:15

Listening to a talk radio station one day, I heard a man rambling about how he had tried to be a peaceful person but had given up after realizing that others would only take advantage of him. He described himself as a pastor's son who was tired of being a "good boy." At one point in his life he had heard of God's peace but had later begun to believe that this was a myth.

It occurred to me that this man did not understand the concept of powerlessness. Rather than relying on God and being thankful, he had taken matters into his own hands repeatedly and had discovered the futility of his own ability to live peacefully. His difficulty with relationships stemmed from not allowing God to be in control. His failure resulted in anger at God.

Peaceful living in a chaotic world requires superhuman intervention. When we fail, rather than blaming God, we need to look at ourselves. When we succeed, we need to be thankful, giving credit where it is due. Blaming God only distances us from the serenity we so desperately need.

Grant me your peace, and thanks in advance.

I will praise You, for I am fearfully and wonderfully made;
Marvelous are Your works,
And that my soul knows very well.
—PS. 139:14

We are able to set clear boundaries in relationships with others when we have a sense that we are the whole people God created us to be. When we are unsure of who we are or when we see ourselves as defective or incomplete, we tend to look to others to fill up our missing parts. Although we need relationships with others, these relationships can become unhealthy when we lose our own identity.

Sarah found herself in a struggle to establish healthy boundaries with her husband, Pete. Sarah had become increasingly dependent on Pete for her self-esteem and her happiness in general. When Pete threatened to leave Sarah, she told him she would die without him.

Finally, Sarah sought professional help. She learned that God had created her to be a whole human being, complete with her own thoughts, feelings, interests and opinions. Gradually, she began to tolerate differences of mood and opinion with her husband. As she allowed God to help her define herself, she experienced less of a drive to control Pete. In fact, over time, her marriage relationship was strengthened.

Are you like Sarah used to be, dependent on others to define who you are? Perhaps it's time for you to clarify your personal boundaries.

Lord, thank you that in you I can have a sense of wholeness.

"I, even I, am He who comforts you.
Who are you that you should be afraid
Of a man who will die,
And of the son of a man who will be made like
grass?" —ISA. 51:12

How can you not accept your feelings, you ask? Oh, it's really easy. You see, if you don't accept the feelings you really don't like, they won't exist for you and you won't have to worry about them.

"If I admit that I have these feelings, I really would feel awful about myself!" A young woman sat across from me in my office and was quite angry at my suggestion that she accept the feelings she had toward her mother. She had spent a good deal of her childhood making sure her mom was happy. She didn't want to deal with negative feelings toward her mother. If she did, she would feel overwhelmingly guilty.

Accepting uncomfortable feelings is a powerful way to overcome being bound by others' wishes and desires. If you can begin to accept the existence of these feelings, you can also begin to talk about them honestly in a way that will strengthen your relationships. It will also enable you to come honestly to your heavenly Father for the comfort he can provide.

Father, help me to accept uncomfortable feelings and find joy and comfort in my relationship with you.

My God, My God, why have You forsaken Me?
Why are You so far from helping Me,
And from the words of My groaning?
—PS. 22:1

This passage by David shows that he sometimes felt very distant from God. In the anguish of dealing with codependent relationships, you may wonder where God has gone.

Married to a workaholic, Mary often wondered where God was. Because her husband worked in Christian ministry, she regularly excused the fact that he did not spend as much time with her and the children as she thought necessary. She tried understanding, turning the other cheek, constantly explaining to the children why father was not home. Through it all she became bitter and angry, keeping the feelings inside until she felt she would explode.

While Mary recognized a problem, she failed to confront it directly. In her frustration she would use passive-aggressive means to express her feelings, even at times becoming angry with God for taking her husband. Mary needs to know that God can tolerate these feelings; in fact he wants to hear them directly. After telling God, she will feel free to express them directly to her husband and begin standing up for herself and her needs.

———

Tell God about your feelings, especially if you feel him to be distant.
He can tolerate your anguish.

But with me it is a very small thing that I should be judged by you or by a human court. In fact, I do not even judge myself. For I know nothing against myself, yet I am not justified by this; but He who judges me is the Lord.   —1 COR. 4:3–4

Gretchen was raised in a family with rigid, authoritarian parents. One of her strongest memories is of her parents' need to uphold a good reputation. Gretchen's father raged, her mother was passive, and Gretchen was expected to pretend everything was fine.

Now Gretchen is older and out of her parents' home. She is married and has three children. One of her greatest difficulties in life lies in the area of decision-making. When examining the problem, Gretchen identified a strong fear of being judged by others if she made the wrong decision. Her concern about the opinions of others paralyzed her from making any decisions.

The lesson learned in Gretchen's case is clear. We cannot make healthy choices in life when we are concerned about keeping other people happy. We may wonder what they will think or whether they will approve. The verse above emphasizes that the only one who has the right and ability to judge us is God. Do you make decisions based on how others may judge you? Is having a good reputation a primary goal in your life?

God, help me not to base my decisions on the judgments of others.

> *"Blessed are those who mourn,*
> *For they shall be comforted."*
> —MATT. 5:4

I *can't take that chance!!"* a woman across the coffee table in my office exclaimed. This was in response to my suggestion that she allow her friend to know her struggles. It just wasn't worth the risk to expose herself so completely with no possible way of escape. At the same time she complained that she felt isolated from people. See the dilemma? She had inadvertently put herself in the position of feeling even more helpless than before she started to change.

Trying to live life with no risk is living life in denial. We deny our needs because they put us too much at risk. I am not suggesting you indiscriminately share your deepest hurts and pain with just anyone. On the other hand, the solution to this dilemma is to take calculated risks with those who have earned your trust. In so doing we strengthen healthier behaviors. Of course, this doesn't assure success. You will probably still experience some disappointment with people, but in the process you will also be exposed to those who are worthy of your trust. You will also feel the love and comfort they can offer you in a healthy, safe environment.

———————

Father, help me to risk being cared for by others.

He who trusts in his own heart is a fool,
But whoever walks wisely will be delivered.
—PROV. 28:26

Maria learned a lesson when she was young: You cannot trust anyone but yourself. Streetwise from an early age, she had grown to distrust even her closest allies, believing that given a chance, even friends would betray her. There was a strong aura of independence about her, but also tremendous isolation. Although she was quite depressed and wanted guidance, she was afraid to be vulnerable enough to accept feedback from others.

Change came slowly for her. She had erected strong defenses to protect herself emotionally. Allowing herself to be open to criticism from caring people was something foreign to her. Each time a statement pricked her protective isolation, she would become angry and defensive. Maria had been self-reliant for so long that she did not know how to be cared for.

Letting her guard down felt frightening to her because she fully believed that her tough exterior was what kept her safe, even though it also kept her lonely and unhappy. Maria needed to learn to trust others, while simultaneously giving up her mistaken notions that isolation provided safety.

Has your independence provided you the safety you desire? Begin to trust God to provide others in your life to help you break compulsive patterns of self-reliance.

> *But indeed I count all things loss for the excellence*
> *of the knowledge of Christ Jesus my Lord.*
> —PHIL. 3:8

One of the biggest differences between the American culture and the Spanish culture is found in the choice of greetings. Americans ask, "How are you *doing?*" while the Spanish ask, "How are *you?*" The emphasis in the Spanish culture is on the person's well-being, whereas the American culture emphasizes the achievements of the individual. Unfortunately for some of us, achievements can become our main focus in life. As a result, we soon choose to focus our values on what we achieve and begin to base even our moods on what we have accomplished. For example, when asked "How are you doing?" we may respond, "Not that well, because I didn't get much done today."

In the process of focusing on our achievements, we forget what really counts in life. God is the most important resource we have to help us with our choices. However, many of us choose to rely on money, status, careers, friends, and even our families as the source of security and value in our lives. A local church leader made the following point in reference to keeping our focus on God: "The main thing is to keep the main thing (God) the main thing." From the verse above, we learn our achievements are considered as a loss, compared to our knowledge of the greatness of God. Is God real enough to you to place him above your achievements? Is God the main thing in your life, or are you finding value in what you do?

Lord, keep my focus on you.

Brethren, . . . one thing I do, forgetting those things which are behind and reaching forward to those things which are ahead. —PHIL. 3:13

Goals are essential in sports as well as recovery. A coach used to tell me to keep my eyes on the basket when I was shooting the basketball. My shot would follow where my eyes were glued. Of course, it took an incredible amount of practice to make shooting the basketball easy. That is where you are in your recovery. You have spent hours practicing healthier behaviors, and you have gotten to the point where they come relatively easy in most situations. Your focus must now be on your goal.

A little boy once asked a tightrope walker how he managed to never fall off. The tightrope walker replied, "I always keep my eyes on the platform at the other end, and I never look down." He understood the importance of keeping his eyes on his goal and cutting down on the distractions.

In maintenance, concentration and keeping your eyes on the goal are essential. There will be many things to distract you, but as long as your goal is well in sight, failure is far away. Keep your eyes on your goal: healthier behavior, firm boundaries, and better decisions.

―――――――――

It is important to keep your eyes on your goal.

> *But Moses said to God, "Who am I that I should go to Pharaoh, and that I should bring the children of Israel out of Egypt?"*
>
> —EX. 3:11

Low self-esteem can be a dangerous thing. Ultimately Moses would go on to become a major historical figure, but in the beginning he made numerous excuses about himself and his limitations to avoid doing God's will. Had Moses not allowed God to work through him, the lives of many people would have been radically different.

It is easy to see the negative things about yourself. Everyone has defects. It may be that you feel too stupid, too ugly, too fat to be any good. When you derive your value from the opinions of others, it is difficult to accept and see positive qualities in yourself.

God does not look at the qualities you see in yourself. He looks deep inside and sees you as you really are. Because he made you to be someone special, he ignores all the defects upon which you focus and visualizes a finished product. Before you put yourself down, before you believe that you really are good for nothing, ask God to help you see the things he does.

Lord, I may have many qualities that I don't like but that is not all that I am. Show me the positive characteristics you have given me and help me believe they are real.

"Therefore whoever hears these sayings of Mine, and does them, I will liken him to a wise man who built his house on the rock." —MATT. 7:24

The power and impact of words often depends on the life of the person who is speaking them. If the words ring true to what we know of the speaker, we are much more likely to pay attention to them than if the words sound hypocritical. The statement quoted above was spoken by Jesus Christ. Since his life was consistently perfect, these words have authority. What about our words? Certainly our lives cannot be perfect, but we can check ourselves for consistency between our words and our actions.

Two people were both working on making new choices in the area of spending their money. Both were able to talk about the specific new actions that they must take. Both appeared to be on the road to recovery. Unfortunately, only one of the two was beginning to make new choices. The other talked about what she must do, but she did not match her words to her actions. Instead of trying out new behaviors, she was continually reverting to old destructive actions. Her apparent recovery was little more than an illusion. Soon this illusion was shattered when she again found herself in serious financial debt.

The contrast between true recovery and lip service became apparent to those observing both of the people mentioned above. There can be little question as to who was the wiser of the two.

Do your actions match the words you claim to believe?

> *Every purpose is established by counsel;*
> *By wise counsel wage war.*
> —PROV. 20:18

Have you ever planned to fail? That sounds ridiculous but it does happen, particularly among people who are struggling to define their boundaries more clearly.

A lady sat in my office one day, reporting her latest failure in her attempts to say no to important people in her life. The longer we discussed the situation, the more she realized that she had actually expected to fail. She had behaved in such a way that she virtually assured failure for herself. She said, "It was almost as if I planned to fail because I was already feeling bad and disappointed even before the situation arose." And when she felt bad, she behaved in such a way that others treated her badly. She hadn't spoken up when she needed to say no, and the person she was dealing with assumed that by her silence she was consenting to the course of action they embarked upon. Of course, she knew how to handle this. She had failed so many times before it had become comfortable and safe.

It is important to examine your behaviors to see if you are planning to fail also. Do you find yourself assuming that whatever you try won't work and making plans as to what you will do then? Do you behave in a way that assures failure? Do you continue to act passively when you need to practice more assertive behavior?

Father, help me to practice planning for success by being more assertive.

*He will be very gracious to you at the sound of
your cry.*   —ISA. 30:19

As psychotherapists we often hear peoples' cries for
help. Usually they take the form of self-injury, suicidal
gestures, dulling the pain with illicit medication, fits of
rage, or some other indirect way of letting others know
that life has become too difficult. In our society there is
an unfortunate belief that we should be strong and
overcome crises on our own and that allowing others
to help us would be a sign of weakness.

Much of the time people seek help only after a crisis
has reached epidemic proportions and there is no-
where to turn. Many times such crises could be averted
if we would ask for help before life's struggles become
disastrous.

God is not only willing to be available when circumstances become difficult, he is gracious and eager to be
there when we need assistance. God does not look for
us to be strong and self-sufficient. He recognizes that
we are fragile beings in need of a comforting, helpful
partner. We can never be too needy to rely on a caring
God's ever-present help.

*God, help me to understand that you care and are willing to help me
at my weakest moments.*

> *Being confident of this very thing, that He who has begun a good work in you will complete it until the day of Jesus Christ.*
> —PHIL. 1:6

A conscientious, motivated man made a commitment to himself and his family to make new choices in setting limits on time spent at his job. His desire for change was strong. His understanding of the limits he must set was fairly clear. However, each new situation was unique and therefore required an expenditure of emotional energy as well as careful thought. By the third week, this dedicated man was discouraged. He had made several positive choices, but he had also been slow to identify some specific pitfalls. His success record was mediocre.

Change is difficult! Making new choices on a consistent basis demands concentration and much energy. Often, the pace of change is uneven. On one day many positive decisions may be carried out, while on the following day, old patterns may appear unavoidable. The potential for discouragement is very real.

It is important to remember that growth is a process, and God generally brings about change within the human framework of time. When I feel my own strength failing, I try to remember that God has promised to be with me until I reach the destination he has prepared for me. While it is often natural to experience discouragement during the journey, defeat never need be on the road map unless I choose to put it there.

Dearest Father, I am grateful that you have promised to bring your work in me to completion.

He who walks with wise men will be wise,
But the companion of fools will be destroyed.
—PROV. 13:20

After every election in which there is a change in administration, the newly elected official begins to select people to advise him and help him with his job. Ideally, he will choose people who can do the best job and who will be independent enough to give him an alternative point of view. Obviously, this process has often broken down, and the elected official has been ineffective. Instead of choosing people who can think independently, the official makes the mistake of choosing people who will only agree with his views.

It is equally important if you are to succeed throughout the course of your maintenance to surround yourself with people who are wise and willing to give you feedback at the risk of offending you. The writer of Proverbs was certainly aware of that when he wrote the passage for today. You will grow wise if you walk with the wise. That may not always be comfortable, but don't expect it to be if you want these people to do what you have asked them to do. It may be an indication of how well these people *are* doing their jobs by how uncomfortable you are by their honesty!

Father, help me to find wise people who will help me grow wise too.

Little children, let no one deceive you.
—1 JOHN 3:7

Creating new boundaries for yourself is a major part of recovery. This means removing yourself from old relationships or not allowing others to negate the new changes you are seeking to establish. The first steps in this process are the most difficult.

Telling a significant person in your life that you no longer can continue engaging in the patterns of the past may have repercussions that are uncomfortable. Because the ways you have related have been established for quite some time, they will find it strange that you have become different. They may say, "You are so holy and righteous," or "What makes you so much better than me?"

It will be helpful to recognize that this may happen and prepare in advance. There is tremendous pressure as you begin the changing process to give up and just be the way you were. Given your desire to make others happy and have their approval, this can be the most difficult part of developing healthy behaviors. Your part is simply to do what you are learning is right and to not worry that others are not changing as quickly as you would like.

Help me to live as I have learned I should. Help me to draw boundaries around relationships that will further my health and sanity.

> *Not that we are sufficient of ourselves to think of*
> *anything as being from ourselves, but our*
> *sufficiency is from God.* —2 COR. 3:5

I feel so insecure! If only she would treat me more lovingly. I can't be happy unless she starts giving me more attention." Do words like these sound familiar? We hear them frequently, if not in song lyrics, then from ourselves or our loved ones. The belief underlying these statements goes something like this: I can't be happy unless I feel valuable as a person. I can't feel valuable unless someone special to me treats me as special. The problem with this belief is that it's not true. My value or adequacy does not depend on other people's actions towards me. If it did, then my value would constantly fluctuate depending on the various moods and responses of others.

The great news is that my value depends not on the opinions of others, nor on my own actions. It is based instead on the unchanging value and adequacy of God. What a relief! When I set my mind on God's truth, then I can step off the roller coaster and stop trying to win the approval of others. Getting off the roller coaster means stepping onto the solid foundation of who Christ is and what he has done for me. My boundaries become more firm when I am standing on solid ground.

Thank you, Lord, that my value comes from you.

Whereas you do not know what will happen tomorrow. For what is your life? It is even a vapor that appears for a little time and then vanishes away.
—JAMES 4:14

Have you ever heard anyone say they can't wait for a certain event? My daughter gets excited as Christmas approaches. She will often say, "Is it tomorrow yet?" Other than sounding comical, it is very accurate for her. She just can't wait, and she gets so excited that it almost ruins the fun of the day she is already in!

Does that sound familiar to you? One woman said to me, "I just can't wait to have this all behind me, and then I can get on with my life." It was almost as if she had placed her life in suspended animation waiting for recovery to occur. Once that was done, she could then go back to *really* living.

We don't know what will happen in the future, but sometimes we can act like we do. We make plans just as if we know what tomorrow will bring. It is important to take recovery and maintenance one day at a time. For some, the road is so hard it is better to bring it down to one hour at a time because that is what it takes to make it through. By making our goals for recovery more realistic we set ourselves for further success and growth.

Take your recovery one day at a time.

But now after you have known God, or rather are known by God, how is it that you turn again to the weak and beggarly elements to which you desire again to be in bondage? —GAL. 4:9

An ongoing threat to the maintenance of changed behavior is the threat of turning back to the old behavior. There are many reasons for this, but probably the most prominent one is that these old behaviors are comfortable.

It is hard to look at dysfunctional behaviors in such a positive light as this, but it is also important to understand that there was a reason for adopting them in the first place. If you can understand these reasons, you can also prevent yourself from turning back once you have begun to make more positive changes.

Once a person has adopted a dysfunctional pattern of behavior and has found that it works to get needs met, he soon becomes comfortable with this pattern of behavior—it's predictable and pretty effective. That is what makes it so difficult to change!

Once you turn back to old patterns, you become enslaved again. Never underestimate the power of those old, comfortable dysfunctional behaviors. Are you getting a little too comfortable?

Father, help me to not turn back to my old ways of living and relating to people.

> *In regard to these, they think it strange that you do not run with them in the same flood of dissipation, speaking evil of you.*   —1 PETER 4:4

Birds of a feather flock together." How true this is for people, as well as for birds! When we consistently make unhealthy choices and establish unhealthy boundaries, we generally attract friends who condone these behaviors. Our friends may encourage continued poor choices by making statements like the following: "Don't worry about it," "You worry too much," or "Don't listen to your therapist, he doesn't really understand your circumstances. You *need* to take care of your husband. If you don't, who will? Your therapist doesn't have to live with your husband, you do!"

As we begin to make changes, these same friends may vigorously oppose our change. Those in recovery support groups call this opposition "sabotage." When we change our actions, we make a statement that our old choices were wrong and/or unhealthy. Because of this statement, our friends and family often feel threatened or abandoned. They may even become abusive.

Unfortunately, many people have allowed the reactions of others to stop the change process. It is difficult to be the target of opposition, but the verse above tells us that this opposition is to be expected. Unfortunately, making healthy choices may mean losing friendships or family relationships that are not supportive of this change. Thankfully, God can provide us with new, more healthy relationships to take their place.

What kind of a common thread holds your friendships together?

Now may the Lord of peace Himself give you peace
always in every way. The Lord be with you all.
—2 THESS. 3:16

If you were to look at your behavior, would you say you are at peace? It seems that some of the hardest decisions faced by those struggling to establish new boundaries are involved in maintaining peace. They have for so long run their lives by attempting to maintain peace, it cost them their own emotional stability. They have attempted to get the outside circumstances to influence their internal feelings. In other words, they have manipulated the people and circumstances around them, hoping that they will experience peace when all is finally at rest.

It is a vain struggle. Only the Lord can deliver that kind of peace. It is easy, though, to fool ourselves into thinking that we can accomplish such a feat. The solution seems to lie where we would least like to look. When we stop trying to bring about this peace, we experience freedom to trust God to change others. It also helps to focus us further on that which we need to deal with that obscures our peace with ourselves and with God.

Father, help me to focus on the things that hinder my relationship with you.

> *Fools mock at sin,*
> *But among the upright there is favor.*
> —PROV. 14:9

Unfortunately, for some of us, making amends is perceived as giving in to another person. The media often teaches us that to apologize or ask for forgiveness is a sign of weakness. In addition, nobody wants to admit personal error.

Greg was a rageaholic. He had great difficulty admitting he was wrong. Whenever he did not get what he wanted, he would yell, curse, and sometimes use physical intimidation to get his point across. For him, admitting his actions were wrong was next to impossible. He felt threatened, vulnerable, and out of control when stating he was wrong. As a result, he chose not to say he was sorry unless he absolutely had to do so, and even then his apology lacked sincerity. Greg lost his marriage, friends, and job because no one could stand to be around him and his self-righteous attitude.

Choosing to make amends when we are in the wrong, rather than having to prove our point at any cost, is vital to our recovery. It is a violation of healthy boundaries to insist that others see every situation from our perspective. This attitude will also cause us to make destructive choices. Is it acceptable for you to be wrong at times, or do pride and control issues get in your way?

Wise men and women know when to say "I'm sorry."

> *"Therefore if you bring your gift to the altar, and
> there remember that your brother has something
> against you, leave your gift there before the altar,
> and go your way. First be reconciled to your
> brother, and then come and offer your gift."*
> —MATT. 5:23–24

There are many blocks to progress in therapy. One important block is unresolved conflicts from the past. Often we counsel with individuals who cannot understand why feelings of bitterness cannot be overcome. Every time an attempt is made to move forward, frustration results.

This is especially true in spiritual development. Bitterness keeps us distant from God and contributes to feelings of spiritual emptiness. It is very important to recognize the role of unresolved conflicts in relationships, especially those in the distant past, when searching for reasons behind impeded progress.

This needs to be a priority in recovery. Make an attempt to go back to the person or persons you have wronged and reconcile the relationship. Then see if your spiritual development begins to grow.

God, bring to mind people I have wronged. Give me the courage to discuss with them the true nature of these wrongs and to ask humbly for their forgiveness.

And for this reason He is the Mediator.
—HEB. 9:15

Often in families when there is a problem with people sheltering and rescuing each other from their feelings, there is also a person who acts as the mediator of family members' emotions. In the movie, *The Great Santini,* father and son are involved in a friendly game of basketball. Slowly but surely the son pulls ahead and wins the ball game. The father is irate, and almost hits his own son. Later, as the son watches his father practice basketball in the rain, the son is approached by his mother. She asks, "Do you know what your father is saying to you? He's saying that he loves you, and he's admitting that you are better than him in basketball." To that the son replies, "Then why doesn't he just say that to me?"

This often happens in families that have their boundaries mixed up. The wrong people are talking. Communication is mediated by someone else. The person who plays mediator is often the same person who feels the pain of the lack of communication for everyone else. We have to learn to let others be responsible for themselves. If we rescue them, we contribute to their lack of communication.

Father, please help me to let the other members of my family deal with each other directly.

Bear one another's burdens.
—GAL. 6:2

In codependent relationships, boundaries are a problem. Individuals fail to recognize where their responsibility ends and the other's begins. Individuals can be so wrapped up in the problems of their family that they totally neglect themselves. At first glance, this verse would seem to indicate that this is actually how one is to live his or her life.

One example is the husband of a prescription-drug addict who constantly takes up the slack of a difficult household allowing his wife time to "rest." Another would be the mother who believes her acting-out child is just "going through a phase" and so overlooks important signs of dysfunction.

These are examples of enabling, or bearing so much of the other's burden that he gets to continue with his unproductive behaviors. Eventually more and more is given until the enabler becomes resentful and angry, and then she becomes a burden to others.

Balance is the key. In order to aid in the process of bearing a burden, we must be certain that our own burdens are being carried adequately, while simultaneously helping the other to bear his or her own load.

God, help me to avoid being the pack mule for others, thus enabling them to further injure themselves.

> *But when they opposed him and blasphemed, he*
> *shook his garments and said to them, "Your blood*
> *be upon your own heads; I am clean. From now on*
> *I will go to the Gentiles."*
> —ACTS 18:6

Knowing when to let go and end a relationship is not always easy. Some of us sincerely believe that it is our personal duty to change others and get them to see things our way. We may even believe that God put us on this earth to help others and to guide them to the truth.

Connie was the kind of woman who believed she had the ability to change others. She knowingly married an alcoholic and chose to ignore the reality that his alcoholism would have a detrimental effect on their relationship. Although she had failed in several attempts to change other men she had dated, she still convinced herself that this relationship would be different.

In the verse above, Paul demonstrates healthy boundaries by leaving town. It was obvious to him that further efforts at evangelism would only produce continued abuse. He understood that if the Jewish people did not accept Christ as Savior, he was not responsible.

Connie could have benefited greatly by learning from Paul's example. If she had faced the reality that it was her boyfriend's responsibility to change, she could have ended the relationship before she committed herself to marriage with an alcoholic.

Are you hanging on to a relationship because you want to change someone? If so, establish healthy boundaries and let go.

For now we see in a mirror, dimly, but then face to face. Now I know in part, but then I shall know just as I also am known. —1 COR. 13:12

There are times that life and people are profoundly disappointing. It is a fact that we cannot escape, as hard as we may try. As a matter of fact, the issues you have been dealing with, and are now trying to maintain, were areas in which you tried to pretend that life wasn't as bad as many were saying.

It is critical to keep in mind the fallenness of the world in which we live. As Paul makes clear, what we see here on earth is dim compared to what we will see in heaven in God's presence. Like using one of those mirrors in the circus, there will always be distortion as long as we are in our fallen bodies and living on a fallen earth. We need to adjust our expectations of people and events to take into account the nature of reality. This may be surprisingly joyful or it may be profoundly disappointing. That is the nature of the reality we live in. If we don't adjust, we may be setting ourselves up for failure, and our maintenance will be sidetracked.

———————

Keep in mind the limitations of the world and the people you live with.

> *For whoever shall keep the whole law, and yet*
> *stumble in one point, he is guilty of all.*
> —JAMES 2:10

There are many good people, conscientious and moral individuals who are respected by others. There is nothing wrong with being an upstanding person. However, if one begins to rely on the positive things they have done rather than on one's higher power for a sense of well-being, then pride can occur. This leads to distance from God—after all, we don't need God if we think we are doing well on our own power.

The Roberts were indeed good people, but their daughter had become depressed. In the first family session it was suggested that perhaps they had contributed to her feelings of emptiness. In fact: their focus on the good things they had done led to their belief that they had a defective child. The more they clung to this belief, the worse the daughter perceived herself to be.

When this was suggested to them, they became irate, threatening to withdraw their daughter from treatment. They would not look at the possibility that they had done anything wrong. Their daughter became afraid to be honest, withdrew into her depressed shell, and continued to believe that she was simply a rotten person. The Roberts' belief in their own goodness kept them from seeing that they needed help as well as their child.

God, keep me open to my shortcomings and to my need for your assistance.

The Lord is my strength and my shield;
My heart trusted in Him, and I am helped.
—PS. 28:7

Stephanie was a very industrious and creative person. Over a number of years she devised numerous methods for keeping her eating under control. She critiqued several diet books and combined plans to come up with the perfect diet. When these diets failed, Stephanie tried other special methods. However, although many of her ideas appeared to be brilliant, Stephanie never seemed to be able to stick to any of them.

Have you ever poured all of your time and energy into an attempt to make a specific change in your life, only to discover that your terrific ideas and efforts weren't working? If so, you're certainly not alone. Many of us consume ourselves with trying to devise a foolproof plan for making change. Unfortunately, no plan can ever be foolproof. Here lies the problem. When we set our sights on carrying out the perfect plan for change, we do so with the assumption that we can conquer a difficult problem completely on our own. This assumption is incorrect.

The Bible confirms what we experience in real life. As human beings, we can never be self-sufficient. By ourselves we are often powerless to make the very choices that we say we desire for our lives. However, the Bible does tell us that God is willing and able to make up for the strength that we are lacking. Certainly his strength is much more powerful and consistent than our own.

Are you ready to acknowledge that your own strength is limited?

> *Is there no balm in Gilead,*
> *Is there no physician there?*
> *Why then is there no recovery*
> *For the health of the daughter of my people?*
> —JER. 8:22

Have you ever used a medicated salve as a balm for those aching muscles? What kind of balm do you have to keep you on the path of recovery? Maybe it is a support group. Maybe it is a devotional guide like this. Maybe it is another person to whom you are accountable for your behavior. These are all good balms to weary souls. We need this kind of nurturance.

One of the aspects of recovery and maintenance that is often overlooked is nurturing yourself. In other words, take care of yourself. This is critical to a good maintenance program. There will be times when you need to have "balms" that you can take advantage of so that you can refresh your soul. Develop a list of things that you can do to take care of yourself, and find refreshment. Don't allow yourself to go back to a routine that doesn't allow you to nurture yourself. Plan for times when you can step back and take a second look at how you are doing. That is one way that you can assure a steady pace for your recovery.

It is important to develop balms to help refresh you along the path to recovery.

Whoever has no rule over his own spirit
Is like a city broken down, without walls.
—PROV. 25:28

Deborah swore to herself she would never be used again. She had erected elaborate controlling defenses to protect her from ever being vulnerable. To avoid being seen as weak, she embarked on a course of reckless behavior designed to show others that she was tough and could handle any situation.

While she believed herself to be successful, those around her saw the incredibly self-destructive path she had chosen for what it really was. It was as if she had covered her own eyes and then was telling herself that others could not see her. Instead of adequately protecting herself, she had made herself more vulnerable. The only people who would befriend her were others who were similarly self-destructive and did not really care about her.

The results were catastrophic. After she got past her denial, she was horrified at what she had become. Instead of protecting herself, her lack of self-control had left her wide open to further abuses. Recklessness and irresponsibility had not given her the toughness she believed they would—they had had the opposite effect. She would need to develop a vulnerability to God who could provide the protection she so strongly desired.

Grant me self-control so that I can exchange my facade of strength for your true power.

> *But his wife looked back behind him, and she*
> *became a pillar of salt.*
> —GEN. 19:26

Fear of letting go of the past can be a major obstacle for someone attempting to establish healthy boundaries. We may try to hang on to our families, old friendships, or past behaviors, regardless of the damage and hurt they caused.

Joyce experienced great difficulty with letting go of her parents. As a child, she had been verbally and physically abused by both her mother and father. Now thirty-three years old, she continued to receive much verbal abuse from them. Joyce developed a growing awareness that her already negative self-esteem was being reinforced at every contact with them.

Even though Joyce received encouragement from her pastor, therapist, and friends to detach from her parents, she initially failed to do so. She kept saying, "I need to give them more time to change" and "I must be doing something wrong. Maybe if I'm more accepting of them they will be more accepting of me." These rationalizations and attempts to change her parents went on for another five years. After her father slapped her in the face during a rage, Joyce finally realized she could not make her parents change. She could not make her family healthy.

Due to her fear of letting go of the past, Joyce put her fragile self-worth through another five years of abuse. Is your growth process blocked because you are hanging on to something in your past?

Don't let the past keep you from experiencing the present.

Why do you spend money for what is not bread,
And your wages for what does not satisfy?
Listen diligently to Me, and eat what is good.
—ISA. 55:2

Do you ever invest your time and money in things that do not really satisfy? No banker would take the money given to her to invest and find accounts and stocks that don't make a profit.

Take a look at the investment of your time and emotional energy. Are you investing in relationships that satisfy and stand the test of time? Or are you taking what you can when you get it? I guess it's a matter of short-term versus long-term investments. Are we willing to go for the short run, just to get the temporary satisfaction right now, only to have to do it all over again?

These questions apply in our relationships with others. We can give up our rights to others, just to secure the short-term satisfaction of their pleasure and attention, but in the process we give away our own importance because we don't defend our boundaries. The most important relationship is with God, and finding our significance in him. This relationship will truly satisfy our deepest needs.

Lord, help me to listen to you and invest my energies in things that last.

> *Has God not chosen the poor of this world to be*
> *rich in faith and heirs of the kingdom which He*
> *promised to those who love Him?*
>
> —JAMES 2:5

Our society measures success much differently than does God. While we strive to collect outward evidence of riches, God looks at what is inside. It doesn't matter how successful you seem to be if your heart isn't in the right place.

Many stories from our experiences with hurting people illustrate this principle. We have worked with corporate vice presidents, television personalities, models, doctors, and other outwardly successful individuals, all of whom shared inner pain. To each of these individuals success was not enough to make life easier—sometimes it did the opposite. Each needed something more.

Do you believe that if you only had more, more money, status, or power, you would be happy? If so, you have chosen to view life through the eyes of the world. God has a different view—he looks inside to determine how rich life is for you. Our worldly status has little to do with happiness, because it never fills our need to be rich in God's eyes.

God, help me to desire the inheritance you have promised me, rather than pursuing the unfulfilling signs of outward success.

UNDERSTANDING WHO GOD IS – *April 14*

*Behold what manner of love the Father has
bestowed on us, that we should be called children
of God!*
                                    —1 JOHN 3:1

Jenny was a young woman who had been attending church for as long as she could remember. She was trying to make a major change of direction in her life because she had incurred a significant amount of pain in an abusive relationship. Several trusted friends had encouraged her to allow God to take over the control of her life, but Jenny really struggled with this advice. She was afraid to give God control of her life. What if he decided to do things that would hurt her?

Although Jenny had been exposed to teaching about God, her understanding of God's character was incorrect. Since she did not believe that he is a kind and loving God, she was very afraid to entrust her life to him. Jenny's struggle demonstrates that belief in God's existence is not always sufficient for true growth. Developing a correct understanding of God's character is an important part of the belief process.

Jenny talked about her misgivings with caring friends. Gradually her ideas about God began to change, and she eventually became willing to trust God with small aspects of her life. Jenny was learning that her understanding of God greatly affected her ability to depend on him.

Is your understanding of God helping or hindering your ability to trust him with your life? Make sure your understanding is based on the truth of who God is.

> *And not only that, but we also glory in tribulations,*
> *knowing that tribulation produces perseverance;*
> *and perseverance, character; and character, hope.*
> —ROM. 5:3–4

I have heard it said that the severest test of character is not so much the ability to keep a secret as it is, but, when the secret is finally out, to refrain from disclosing that you knew it all along. The development of character is also the goal of recovery and maintenance. Ralph Waldo Emerson once suggested that "people seem not to realize that their opinion of the world is also a confession of character." No doubt, you have seen quite a bit of change in your character through the process of recovery you have undergone. Has your opinion of the world also changed? That will be the litmus test of character change.

It is through the transformation of character that a person begins to be hopeful for the future. We see it every day in the hospital. Men, women, and children come to us filled with hate, bitterness, anger, and hopelessness. Through the testing of character and their perseverance through this process, they begin to experience hope once again. So ask yourself, *What am I after? Transformation of character or a quick fix?* If it is the former, then be prepared for the long haul.

Father help me to stay the course of character change.

Let every man be swift to hear, slow to speak, slow to wrath.
—JAMES 1:19

Anger is an important feeling. While there is nothing wrong with feeling angry, there is a difference between feeling something and acting it out. Feelings can become behavior, and behaviors can become habits or compulsions which are not conducive to healthy living.

When anger becomes aggressive behavior, listening is impossible. Instead, a contest of wills develops and both parties seek to win. Winning means controlling, a trait many codependent individuals must work to avoid.

The alternative is slowing down the angry impulses, listening carefully to what the other person is trying to say, and speaking only after you are certain that she is really understood. In your own life there probably have been times when you spoke too quickly without clearly understanding what a person was trying to say. If you answered out of anger you missed a chance to allow God to be in control of the situation.

Help me, Lord, to be quick to listen and slow to respond angrily so that I may experience the righteous life that you desire for me.

> *Do not say, "I will do to him just as he has done to me;*
> *I will render to the man according to his work."*
>   —PROV. 24:29

Each weekday I work on an inpatient adult psychiatric unit where I see various patterns of coping among the patients. Some cope by withdrawing, others cope by becoming compulsively busy, and still others respond by pretending that everything is running smoothly. One of the most destructive coping patterns I have observed is one that involves vengeful anger. This pattern is typified by the patient who paces in anger, vowing to get even with those who have offended her.

Betty was such a patient. The night prior to her admission, she had attempted suicide by taking an overdose of pills. First on the unit, she was quiet and withdrawn. Within one week of therapy, however, Betty began to storm around the unit in anger. She called her parents names and vowed to get them back for abusing her as a child. Although the surfacing of her anger was beneficial, Betty chose to express it in an unhealthy manner. By allowing her desire for revenge to consume her, Betty became focused on her parents and not on her own needs.

Seeking revenge is destructive. It causes us to lose our focus. We attempt to take into our own hands something that only God can do. Are you hanging on to a grudge? Are you wanting to pay someone back for what he has done to you?

Choose to let go, not get even.

"And yet for all this her treacherous sister Judah has not turned to Me with her whole heart, but in pretense," says the LORD.   —JER. 3:10

Pretending comes easily for adults. It is an effective means to look OK and not attract attention. That is what pretense is all about. It helps us to avoid and deny aspects of our lives that we would rather not face. We begin to believe that everything is indeed OK because we are doing all the right things that someone in recovery would do. Before long, the dysfunctional behavior is buried behind a wall of denial and pretense.

People who have built their lives on the pretense of having everything under control are carrying a tremendous burden. Not only do they have to contend with the conflict of internal issues, they also have to expend the emotional energy necessary to keep up the front of control and poise. Before too long, the facade comes tumbling down.

It is terribly easy to fall into the pretense of having everything figured out and under control. We can fool people awfully easily about how well we are doing when in fact we are not. The remedy? Honesty. Complete, brutal honesty, not only with yourself but with trusted others as well. Keep pushing yourself to be honest!

Father, help me to be honest with myself and others about my progress.

Every way of a man is right in his own eyes,
But the LORD weighs the hearts.

—PROV. 21:2

Xavier believed he was right. No matter what the situation, he always thought he was right, even when he was wrong. Raised by his grandparents, he found out as an early adolescent that his "sister" was really his mother who had run from the responsibility of raising him soon after he was born. Imagine his shock.

By the time he arrived at the clinic for help, he had difficulty trusting anyone. This made therapy arduous, since the interventions we tried with him were strongly resisted. After all, he had been hurt so many times before, he always felt a need to "look out for number one."

Coupled with his egocentricity was an aggressive and controlling power struggle with anyone who got in his way. Many relationships had suffered because of his powerful facade that really served to mask a deep sense of insecurity. Before any progress could be made, Xavier had to fully realize his need to control others and the destructive pride that made caring relationships difficult for him.

Fierce pride and need for control drives others away, and honest, caring relationships become almost impossible.

How do you try to control others? How is pride involved?

> *For I say, through the grace given to me, to everyone who is among you, not to think of himself more highly than he ought to think, but to think soberly, as God has dealt to each one a measure of faith.*
> —ROM. 12:3

A prominent businessman began exhibiting symptoms of alcoholism. One evening, he danced on a table during the cocktail hour at a conference. The next day, he was asked to seek professional help. He refused. He knew that no one would really challenge him because he was the chief executive officer. As expected, without receiving help, his behaviors became worse. Several more incidents occurred. When confronted by the board of directors about these episodes, the man maintained that he was too valuable for them to fire.

Within three months, this man found himself without a job. His six-figure salary was gone as well as his company car and his expense account. He was ruined financially. When he lost his job, his wife and children left him too. They asked him to seek help, but he refused, telling them arrogantly, "You need me! What could you do without me? Who would pay the bills?"

A serious roadblock to establishing healthy boundaries and choices is thinking too highly of ourselves. Pride keeps us from soberly looking at reality and evaluating our past actions and their consequences. If we are not willing to acknowledge a problem, we can't work toward its solution.

Are you honestly evaluating your behaviors?

> *And being found in appearance as a man, He*
> *humbled Himself and became obedient to the point*
> *of death, even the death of the cross.*
> —PHIL. 2:8

I have found in working with adolescents that probably the worst thing they could ever be accused of is being conceited. Teens get this value from parents and society. We are attracted to those who have great talent but who are humble. Having humility as our goal is certainly worthwhile. The only problem comes when we use the wrong strategies to get there.

Adolescents and adults alike seem to beat up on themselves in order to be perceived as humble. Now that you are in the maintenance phase of recovery, you may have already come through this stage and realized that self-abuse is not the path to humility. So how do you keep the balance?

We can use Christ as an example of this balance. He humbled himself from his high position as God's son to take on human flesh. Humility is not something we do in response to conceit in our lives. It is an inward change that convinces us that we are indeed precious in God's sight, and because of this conviction we desire to obey him. Then we find that the process of growing in humility will take place continuously.

Father, help me to grow in humility.

If anyone among you thinks he is religious, and does not bridle his tongue but deceives his own heart, this one's religion is useless.

—JAMES 1:26

A gossip is a person with a poor self-image who elevates himself by talking secretively about others. Codependents are especially prone to this as they experience low self-esteem stemming from their deep emptiness. It does little good for a gossip to work on spiritual issues if he continues to derive pleasure from talking behind people's backs.

Freeing yourself from codependent patterns requires that you be direct with others when things are not right. It does no good to gossip, because the problem does not get resolved. Furthermore, it sends a signal to others that you will not be honest in relationships, even to the persons with whom the gossip is being shared.

It is very important as you begin the recovery process that you look at the things you say. Chances are your anger has been expressed indirectly for years through passive-aggressive behaviors such as gossiping. While spirituality is very important to change, it is worthless if you are not controlling your words.

God, help me to be direct in my expression of my feelings. Bring to mind times I have failed to watch my words, and give me the strength to change these patterns.

> *"Blessed are the peacemakers,*
> *For they shall be called sons of God."*
> —MATT. 5:9

Making peace with another is often a valuable part of the healing process. God knows that we as humans need some way to rid ourselves of the burden of shame and guilt that grows from inappropriate actions. This burden can be lifted, in part, by making a sincere apology. Saying "I'm sorry" can repair a damaged relationship. Asking for forgiveness provides the opportunity for peace to be reestablished between people.

Susan learned the value of asking forgiveness while working a twelve-step recovery program for her codependency. Susan was plagued with guilt, shame, and remorse for teaching her children to be caretakers and to ignore their own needs. She realized, after understanding the destructiveness of her own codependency, that her children were afraid to feel their own feelings and to talk about their own needs. She had, in essence, taught them how to be codependent.

Until Susan reached the point of making amends, she was having difficulty forgiving herself for what she had done. As a result, her relationships with her children were strained and tense. When Susan asked her children for forgiveness, she felt as though a huge weight had been lifted from her back. Peace between her children and herself was reestablished. When we make sincere amends, this peace is possible for us as well.

Lord, give me the desire to be a peacemaker.

"But let your 'Yes' be 'Yes,' and your 'No,' 'No.' For
whatever is more than these is from the evil one."
—MATT. 5:37

Most of us remember Nancy Reagan and her battle against drugs. It is still ringing in our ears—*Just Say No!* At times we are confronted with the same problem in our relationships with others. We are confronted with multiple situations where we have to decide how and when to say no. We have to figure out where to draw the line. One mother said in despair, "I just don't know how to get along with my son!" She couldn't figure out when she was being taken advantage of and when she wasn't. She was so hooked into giving him what he wanted, she hadn't learned how to set limits when it was appropriate.

One has to learn how to take the risk of making another person angry (particularly one's own child) and to find out in the process that that person will eventually get over his or her anger. Needless to say, it is easier said than done. The key is knowing that we are secure and safe in our position before God. He loves us no matter what, and we don't have to jump hurdles in order to secure his love. This gives us a solid basis from which to confront the anger of those we love.

Dear Lord, help me risk saying no to those I love.

> *For where envy and self-seeking exist, confusion*
> *and every evil thing will be there.*
>
> —JAMES 3:16

Codependency is synonymous with emptiness, an internal void needing to be filled. There is a tendency to look at others around you and be jealous of their apparent happiness. At times, competition can result, especially when the internal neediness seems to be due to an inability to "keep up with the Joneses."

One such person was Martha. She believed that if only her family were as successful and wealthy as others in their church, then she would be truly happy. She had trouble concentrating on the message the pastor was delivering because this jealousy would constantly intrude into her consciousness.

Martha's husband and children sensed this and felt powerless to please her. They often perceived success as a moving target—when they achieved what they thought would make her happy, she would push for more. For them contentment was something unattainable, since there would always be others who had more. True happiness could only come from being satisfied with what already was there.

How has your discontentment made it hard for others to be satisfied with what God has already given?

My heart is severely pained within me,
And the terrors of death have fallen upon me.
Fearfulness and trembling have come upon me,
And horror has overwhelmed me.

—PS. 55:4–5

Admitting complete defeat is not our society's way of handling problems. Ironically, this is the essential ingredient to any recovery program for addictions. The first step of the twelve-step recovery program insists that we come to grips with our powerlessness to control our addiction. This same step also involves the acknowledgment that our lives have become unmanageable as a result of our addiction.

Understanding our powerlessness and unmanageability is not just knowing our problem, but feeling the pain it has caused. It's not just admitting we are out of control, it's accepting the destructiveness of our actions.

Do we really know the pain we have caused ourselves and others? Have we been open to the truth of our actions? Placing ourselves in the shoes of others is a good place to start. We need to ask the question, "How would I feel if someone did that to me?" Most important of all, we need to have an attitude of openness and a desire to feel the powerlessness in our hearts. Allowing ourselves to feel the true pain of our addiction is the first step toward recovery.

Lord, help me to experience your healing pain in the midst of my defeat.

> *He shall enter into peace;*
> *They shall rest in their beds,*
> *Each one walking in his uprightness.*
> —ISA. 57:2

It is easy to be "driven" in our society today. We often call it the rat race. We do everything fast, efficiently, and effectively, and the next job must be done the same way. We often carry this over into our treatment and recovery programs as well. There is no accommodation made for rest, no time for putting down the wearying load we carry and kicking back.

Jesus knew we needed rest from this race. He knew we needed a purpose for this race and we needed time to restore our emotional and physical resources. That is why he offered it to us in a relationship with him. It is often very hard to allow ourselves the luxury of rest because we are afraid that we will begin to lose ground. That all depends on how we rest!

If we allow ourselves to lose our edge, I suppose our fears are well-founded. On the other hand, we can rest and maintain the edge.

You can give yourself permission to relax the pressure you may be putting on yourself to do everything just right. You can also rest while thinking about the next area you need to work on. That kind of rest will be productive and restoring.

It is important to schedule time for rest from our labors of maintenance.

"The Lord will guide you continually,
And satisfy your soul in drought,
And strengthen your bones;
You shall be like a watered garden,
And like a spring of water, whose waters do not fail."
—ISA. 58:11

Although God has promised to meet all our needs if we ask, there are times when this is hard to believe. Life at times can feel like a barren desert where nothing grows, empty and lonely. A desert is sparsely populated, dry, and a difficult place to live.

On the other hand, there are oases in the middle of the desert. These places are lush and green and a welcome respite from the hot, dry sun and endless sand. In order to discover such beauty, you need to travel through inhospitable terrain, past the cactus and tumbleweed. Perhaps in the journey you might even see a mirage and become disheartened.

While life sometimes feels like an uncomfortable and isolated desert, God has promised that with his guidance you will find the things you need to make the trip worthwhile. If you give up when it becomes difficult you may miss out on the beauty and richness of the hidden oases nestled in the midst of the sunscorched land.

God, guide me in my journey. Push me when I feel like quitting. Don't let me miss the wonderful richness you intend for me.

> *For I acknowledge my transgressions,*
> *And my sin is ever before me.*
> —PS. 51:3

Bruce was willing to admit he had a sexual addiction, but the thought of taking a close look at it horrified him. It caused him a great deal of pain to remember his sexual acting-out experiences. In fact, he rationalized to himself that if he could only "put it behind him" he would be able to make healthier choices in the future. He convinced himself that his sexual addiction would no longer grip him as it did now.

Bruce tried his theory out. Two weeks after he finally admitted that he was a sexual addict, he found himself taking unnecessary risks. One of these risks was hanging around his old friends who were also sexual addicts. He thought blindly, "It won't hurt me; maybe I'll be a good influence on them." Bruce took the first step back into his addiction. He forgot the hold it had on him. Within days, Bruce admitted himself to a treatment program so he could learn a better way to deal with his addiction.

While in treatment, Bruce learned that the way to change past unhealthy choices is to do the opposite of what he had tried to do. His original theory was that he needed to put his addiction behind him. Now, he keeps the knowledge that he is an addict in the forefront of his thoughts, and he remembers the devastation his addiction caused.

God, help me not to forget the devastation that resulted from my poor choices.

> *"So they come to you as people do, they sit before you as My people, and they hear your words, but they do not do them; for with their mouth they show much love, but their hearts pursue their own gain."*
> —EZEK. 33:31

There comes a time for everyone in the recovery process, particularly during the maintenance phase, when they get just plain bored with the whole thing. A sure sign that you are beginning to get bored is when you continue to do the right things, but you don't have your heart in it. That was the case for the Hebrew people during the time of Ezekiel. They came, just as usual, but they weren't following through on their talk. They did right things, but their hearts were greedy.

"But," you say, "I'm not greedy!" Take a careful look. That is one element of our human experience we can never completely destroy. Greed drove the bad decisions of the past and your unwillingness to set limits on your own or others' behavior. It motivated you to act in such a way that people stayed close to you so that you didn't have to experience the pain of their absence.

Be aware of your greed for people and their presence. Take a careful evaluation, because evaluations are a continuing process all through maintenance.

Father, help me to be honest about my greed and apathy.

> *O LORD my God, I cried out to You,*
> *And You have healed me.*
> —PS. 30:2

Many people beginning the recovery process from codependency believe that all options must be exhausted before God will intervene. Perhaps you've felt that it is only as a last resort that you can call out to God for help. And so you experience many failures and feel an increasing sense of hopelessness and powerlessness.

The flaw in this belief is the codependent notion that on your own power you can change the situation. If this were true, there would be no need for a higher power and there would be no dysfunction in the first place. Admitting that you are powerless requires that you stop depending on yourself and your own power to effect change.

Furthermore, God does not reward those who are powerful and in control. Those individuals usually will not depend on him. Before anything else, ask God for help in those situations beyond your control. Depend on his strength rather than your own; you will find his solutions are far better than what you originally envisioned.

Are there times you attempt to do it on your own? How has this contributed to a sense of powerlessness? Ask God to give you his healing power.

But godliness with contentment is great gain.
—1 TIM. 6:6

Being content is a great asset for someone attempting to make healthy choices and establish healthy boundaries. Contentment allows us to let go of the things we cannot change, and at the same time, it allows us to identify things for which we are thankful. Being discontent, on the other hand, breeds resentment, jealousy, and an intense desire to control others.

Chuck was not a content person. Those who knew Chuck described him as a pessimist and complainer. Instead of counting his blessings, Chuck went around counting his mishaps and struggles. His discontentment was quite evident when he entered a rehab program for his alcoholism. According to Chuck, everyone and everything became sources for his problems. Instead of being grateful for his family's intervention, he became consumed with rage, and he told them it was their fault he was experiencing so much pain. Chuck soon lost his family due to his disgruntled attitude.

Discontentment influences us to focus inappropriately on others and their need to change instead of on ourselves. Because of Chuck's discontentment, he focused on his family's problems rather than on his own. The secret to contentment is to be grateful for what we do have and to focus on what we ourselves can change. What about you? Are you content, or are you like Chuck?

Lord, help me to be grateful for what you have given me.

*And we have seen and testify that the Father has
sent the Son as Savior of the world.*
　　　　　　　　　　　　—1 JOHN 4:14

I can't leave!" a woman stated firmly. "Why not?" I
asked. She said, "Because if I leave who will he turn on
next?" "So in other words," I said, "if you take care of
yourself and your feelings by removing yourself temporarily from the situation, then there will be no one to
protect the other important people in your life." "Well,
I guess so," she admitted.

This woman was convinced that if she didn't remain
in the situation and take this man's verbal abuse the
other people he would turn on would be helpless to
protect themselves. Someone had to take the abuse, so
she elected herself.

It is hard to assess situations we have routinely
played out for years and begin to think and act differently. In this woman's situation, it means (1) seeing the
situation as abusive, (2) realizing that she needs to protect her own boundaries, and (3) being responsible for
her own emotions and actions. We need to reevaluate
old behavior to see if we, too, are trying to save others
who are more than capable of protecting themselves.

*We need to begin to be responsible for our own emotions and help
others to do the same.*

Bless the LORD, . . .
Who forgives all your iniquities,
Who heals all your diseases,
Who redeems your life from destruction,
Who crowns you with lovingkindness
*   and tender mercies.*   —PS. 103:2–4

The young woman sat in my office in total despair. Nothing she did was right and she had caused her family tremendous grief. As she recited her long list of sins it became apparent that she believed she was so bad that nothing could save her short of suicide.

When asked what she would like to be different, she revealed that she would settle for a minor cessation of the unhappiness she experienced constantly. She could not envision being anything but the scapegoat for her family, the one who took responsibility for all the dysfunction they experienced. And so she was willing to continue in this role if only she could be a tiny bit happier.

This young woman failed to realize that not only could she be happier, but God was also willing to give her a crown of love and compassion. Too often we are willing to settle for less than God's best for us, less than total forgiveness and healing. Our experience of powerlessness leads us to believe that God could not possibly give us freedom from the bondage of our compulsive behaviors.

***

Are you failing to give God credit for his rich healing power? Don't quit short of God's ideal.

> *And the Lord was sorry . . . and He was grieved in His heart.*
> —GEN. 6:6

There is nothing fun about feeling emotional pain. Ted hated it. By the time he was twenty-five years old he had suffered numerous painful losses in his life. His father died when Ted was eight years old, and his mother died when Ted was fifteen years old. He was raised by his uncle, a verbally abusive alcoholic. Ted married at twenty but was divorced by the age of twenty-three. His wife had multiple affairs and was a drug addict. At twenty-five, he landed in a psychiatric hospital, overcome with suicidal thoughts.

Ted learned from his hospital experience that as a child of eight, he must have decided to avoid any emotional pain after his father's death. In essence, he attempted to numb the pain. Emotionally he chose to stop growing; as a result, his ability to identify his own needs was crippled.

Unfortunately, if we want to grow and mature emotionally, we have to experience emotional pain. Being emotionally mature helps us in the choices we make in life. We are then able to understand our own needs as we can identify and express our feelings. Ted learned the hard way. Many of his losses in life occurred because of his choice to numb the pain. As he identified his feelings and expressed them to others, Ted's depression lifted. What feelings of pain are in your heart?

Emotional pain can cause us to grow if we let it.

Sing, O heavens!
Be joyful, O earth!
And break out in singing, O mountains!
For the LORD has comforted His people,
And will have mercy on His afflicted.
—ISA. 49:13

Imagine for a moment that you have broken your arm. You are in incredible pain and agony. Your friends have rushed you to the emergency room. You go through the necessary admission procedures, and you are taken to a place to sit and wait. The doctor finally comes in and begins to examine your arm. The pain seems to be getting worse, and you wince. Before too long, you say, "Sorry, doc, this hurts too much: I think I'll just go home and let it heal by itself." Sounds ridiculous, doesn't it? Unfortunately, though, the only way to achieve healing in this case is to induce more pain.

The same condition exists in the process of overcoming the tendency not to draw firm boundaries. It is painful to say no to someone, but that is the way of healing. Until you can give yourself permission to hurt in order to heal, there isn't much that can be done to help. In other words, don't deny the pain. Be willing to feel it in order to respond in a way that is healthy. That kind of pain is the kind that leads to healing.

Allow yourself to hurt so that you might find healing.

> *Do not be wise in your own eyes;*
> *Fear the LORD and depart from evil.*
> —PROV. 3:7

Everyone would like to believe that they are stronger than the friends they have. So it was with Cal. He thought it was inconceivable that his good friends could influence him to do anything. In fact, he saw himself as the leader of the group.

In many ways Cal was a leader. Others did respect him and admired his apparent confidence. He had a way of carrying himself that appeared suave and cool, and he totally disregarded potential consequences of his risky behaviors. It was, however, the admiration from his peers that kept this outward demeanor in place. Cal could clearly see that many of the choices he had made were ultimately hurting him.

For a while Cal refused to see the influence of those around him on his behaviors. Because of this, change was impossible. Eventually Cal would need to acknowledge that his own belief in his strength was faulty and that he was influenced by pressure from friends. This would be a positive step toward making changes that would free him from dysfunctional patterns.

Are you humble enough to admit that others influence the choices you make?

The hand of the diligent will rule,
But the slothful will be put to forced labor.
—PROV. 12:24

Ryan was in his ninth year of recovery from alcoholism. He worked a good program. He attended two or three Alcoholics Anonymous meetings per week and contacted his sponsor at least weekly. He was also a sponsor for two alcoholics in early recovery. In this ninth year, however, the meetings became dull and boring for Ryan. He had heard everyone's story at least a dozen times, and he had taught the twelve steps so many times he could almost repeat his talks in his sleep. His zeal for working his own twelve-step program began to diminish. He wanted to spend more time with his family, especially now that his boys were playing sports in high school. Taking a drink was the farthest thing from Ryan's mind. Unfortunately, so was his sobriety.

Ryan soon cut back on his program to once-per-month meetings without sponsorship. Sadly, within a year and a half, Ryan drank again. He never regained his sobriety. He died while drinking and driving on the way to his son's football game.

We need to be diligent in the pursuit of our recovery programs. We need to caution ourselves against complacency. We cannot afford to lose our zeal for making the right choices in life.

God, please give me diligence so that I can avoid a return to slavery.

Without counsel, plans go awry,
But in the multitude of counselors they are established.
—PROV. 15:22

Often I have seen people enter into the process of changing their codependent behaviors. They are meticulous in the assessment of these behaviors and equally as motivated in their pursuit of changing areas of concern to them. The problem comes when they have reached the end of this process, and they begin to go back to the task of living daily with these new behaviors. The novelty of change has worn off.

If you feel this way, it's because you haven't planned for the maintenance phase of your behavior change. It is important to look to others to help you maintain appropriate perspective. They can give you specific feedback about how you interact with others. The way we behave in the presence of others is an important indicator of what our *real* motivations are. If you can see the importance of looking honestly at these interaction patterns you will also begin to see the importance of listening to objective observers. Does your plan include valued advisors who can help you maintain the focus for change?

———————

Father, help me to depend on trusted people to support me in the maintenance of change.

"And whenever you stand praying, if you have anything against anyone, forgive him, that your Father in heaven may also forgive you your trespasses."
—MARK 11:25

Nancy was reviewing her life. For the most part she was a deeply spiritual person. When she wronged someone she tried to make things right. When she was wronged she tried to forgive. But there were several individuals she absolutely could not do this with. She felt their wrongs were so terrible that forgiving them would be impossible. She also believed that doing so would make her vulnerable to further hurt at their hands.

To be completely honest, it was hard to disagree with her—she had indeed been deeply wronged. On the other hand, she needed to let go of the bitterness that so strongly controlled her life. Even in the absence of the individuals who had hurt her, their influence still strongly controlled her as long as she remained bitter and angry.

Forgiveness is a step toward letting go. Not doing so allows distance to grow between oneself and God. Nancy had confessed all her sins but one—that of not forgiving. Until this conflict was resolved she could not experience God's complete forgiveness.

Help me, God, to forgive even the most unforgivable individuals in my life.

> *In You, O LORD, I put my trust;*
> *Let me never be ashamed;*
> *Deliver me in Your righteousness.*
> —PS. 31:1

Many children raised in dysfunctional families feel ashamed of themselves. These children were never taught that their value is based on God's love for them. Instead, their parents emotionally abused them by blaming family problems on them. Their parents may have said, "You were trouble since the day you were born," or "I wish I aborted you when I had the chance." With these tragic statements in mind, many of us walk through life with feelings of low self-worth. Subsequently, this feeling of shame becomes an extremely destructive force in our lives.

Many choices are made and boundaries established based on our feelings of shame. Judy, a forty-five-year-old recovering codependent, allowed feelings of shame from her childhood to dictate her life. She married an alcoholic husband because she felt it was her duty to take care of others. Judy allowed herself to be a doormat, not only for her husband but for others as well.

Judy realized from the verse above that God wanted to deliver her from her shame. She no longer had to be a doormat for others, because the messages she had received from her parents were not God's truth. She could make healthier decisions in life because her worth was found in God.

Shame destroys lives. Our acceptance of God's love builds lives.

*By purity by knowledge, by longsuffering, by
kindness, by the Holy Spirit, by sincere love. . . .*
—2 COR. 6:6

Maintenance is a somewhat confusing phase because
it is a time both for keeping on and pressing ahead.
This dual focus can be very frustrating. It is a little like
having two equally important projects to work on with
the same deadline. It is certainly a monumental task!

Purity of character is one of those things which fall
into the category of pressing ahead. When someone
mentions purity, we may think of precious jewels without blemish and of unspeakable value. Remember that
they didn't get that way overnight.

For example, consider the diamond, a symbol of purity. But no diamond is without blemish. It has gone
through centuries of tremendous pressure by the
earth's surface to produce such beauty.

There are similarities between the production of purity in a diamond and the production of purity in the
human character. It takes time, tremendous energy,
and a lot of digging to produce such purity. It does not
come easily or painlessly.

*Purity requires the same process as a diamond—time, energy, and
digging.*

> *Therefore you are inexcusable, O man, whoever*
> *you are who judge, for in whatever you judge*
> *another you condemn yourself; for you who judge*
> *practice the same things.*
> —ROM. 2:1

It is easy for a codependent to see half the problems in a relationship. Quick to pass judgment on the other, he is quite slow to evaluate himself. In the first session there usually is a long recitation of injuries he has experienced, which then becomes a drawn-out fight between spouses.

Divorce is usually discussed early in the first few sessions. Both are so tired of the problems the other has caused that giving up seems the only solution. Sometimes this turns to anger at the therapist as the pattern of blaming is addressed. Neither wants to see that passing judgment has hurt the relationship. The reality is that *both* have hurt each other and *both* need to stop pointing out only the defects of their partner.

It takes two to create a relationship and just as many to keep problems going. Before you find the other guilty, assess your own involvement in the ongoing problems in the relationship.

God, you be the judge because I am far less competent to see the whole picture.

*Therefore we also, since we are surrounded by so
great a cloud of witnesses, let us lay aside every
weight, and the sin which so easily ensnares us,
and let us run with endurance the race that is set
before us.*
                                        —HEB. 12:1

Every recovering addict must be focused on the goal
of abstaining from the addictive agent. In addition,
every addict needs to identify related behaviors that
contribute to maintaining his addictive cycle.

Bernie did not understand his need to stop activities
that contributed to his cocaine addiction. Although he
wanted to live a life free of cocaine use, he conve-
niently ignored his gambling problem. Bernie continued to place bets at the race track even after he was
discharged from an intensive treatment program.
Within two weeks of leaving the treatment program,
Bernie was overwhelmed with gambling debts. This
pressure choked his recovery program, and soon Bernie was using cocaine again. His gambling entangled
him in a web of destruction.

We must make sure that nothing hinders our own
recovery program. We each need to examine the various activities in which we participate. If any of these
activities have been associated with our addictions, we
seriously need to consider whether they will help or
hinder our recovery.

---

*Lord, is something keeping me from running the race you have set
before me?*

Now no chastening seems to be joyful for the present, but grievous; nevertheless, afterward it yields the peaceable fruit of righteousness to those who have been trained by it.   —HEB. 12:11

The problems you face in attempting to maintain the changes you have made come in different shapes and sizes. This is true for those around you as well. You may sometimes be too quick to intervene on their behalf when they face trials and tribulations. It is much like the father who, attempting to help his son learn how to play basketball, never allows him to make a single shot! The boy cannot learn if his father does it for him.

Often when you are in the presence of someone who is experiencing pain in his life you may be too quick to save him. There are two reasons for this. First, you don't like to see anyone in pain. Second, when someone else feels pain, you feel pain; therefore you will do what you can to remove his pain so that you can take care of your own. As you can see, the first is other-motivated; the second is self-motivated. It is important to realize that difficulties in life are essential for us to grow and gain strength. If you interfere with others' difficulties, you may be interfering with their growth as well.

Father, help me to allow others to grow through the trials in their lives.

The light of the eyes rejoices the heart,
And a good report makes the bones healthy.
—PROV. 15:30

There are ways to choose happiness. Depressed individuals often do not make use of these, focusing instead on the misery around them. Often such people fail to see even the most obvious positive things, restating them mentally from a negative perspective. A smile is difficult for such hopeless individuals.

Change requires that they begin acting as if they were happy. If they waited until happy feelings arrived, change could not happen. This is because they cannot see clearly the good things happening in their lives. Rather than waiting for something that is never going to happen, they need to begin living as if happiness had already arrived.

Some of these actions are normal for the average person: smiling, complimenting others and accepting compliments, focusing mentally on positive occurrences, and allowing oneself the luxury of having a well-groomed outward appearance. Don't wait for happiness and joy to fall in your lap. Begin living the part and the feelings will come later.

What are some ways you could begin to live in recovery even though you may have just begun?

> *And Elijah came to all the people, and said, "How long will you falter between two opinions? If the LORD is God, follow Him; but if Baal, then follow him."*
> —1 KINGS 18:21

Indecisiveness is one of the most common characteristics in a codependent person. The codependent person is indecisive because he attempts to please others. Since he can't please everyone all the time, the codependent person wavers back and forth, trying to avoid making the wrong choices.

Indecisiveness resembles chameleon-like behavior. A chameleon is a reptile that changes its color based on the color of its environment. An indecisive individual seems to change his mind based on whom he is talking to at the moment. We may not like to be compared to chameleons, but if we change our choices based on whom we are with, this is an accurate comparison.

Obviously, the prophet Elijah noticed this indecisiveness in people during Old Testament times. Elijah's command to the people was to make a decision, and to stick to it. We need to follow this same directive.

The key to making decisions is to have confidence in ourselves and an understanding of our own needs and desires. This may be extremely difficult for some of us. We may have even convinced ourselves that our needs are not important. On the contrary, our needs and desires are important, not only to ourselves, but to God as well.

Dear God, help me to grow in my ability to be decisive, and to make decisions that please you.

"'Fear not, for I am with you;
Be not dismayed, for I am your God.
I will strengthen you,
Yes, I will help you.
I will uphold you with My righteous right hand.'"
                                        —ISA. 41:10

Many people make pretty demeaning comments about the need for a crutch. When we hear such comments, we secretly say to ourselves that we will never be caught dead with a crutch.

If we believe that it is wrong to have a crutch, we have bought into the more prevalent lies of our day. Is it so wrong for the crippled to have a crutch? Of course not! In some fashion or another we are all crippled with some handicap. It is foolish to think that we can limp along in life, bravely stoic, because we are too proud to take advantage of the crutch God offers us in his strength.

We need to be honest enough to admit that we need help through our struggles in life. It is not an admission of weakness to be that honest. Rather, it is an admission of the way things are—we need help sometimes. Sometimes we can get too confident and proud, and that gets in the way of taking advantage of the help that is freely offered to us in God.

Lord, help me to be humble enough to use your crutch of strength.

> *Then Peter came to Him and said, "Lord, how often shall my brother sin against me, and I forgive him? Up to seven times?" Jesus said to him, "I do not say to you, up to seven times, but up to seventy times seven."*
>
> —MATT. 18:21–22

Forgiveness is a process. As I discussed this concept with a young man he was surprised. For many years he had berated himself for being unable to forgive his father for things from his childhood. Despite tremendous sincerity he often felt that he had failed to fully forgive. He believed that he should forgive once and it should then be forgotten.

Unfortunately life's hurts do not magically disappear when one utters the words, "I forgive you." There are still the memories of the wrongs done that haunt and hurt. These are the times to again forgive. Each time bitterness crops up, another opportunity to forgive presents itself.

Take advantage of such opportunities. Practice the art of forgiving not only once, but as many times as necessary. Remember to not put yourself down just because the memories do not disappear.

Teach me the art of forgiving others repeatedly, seventy times seven or more.

". . . they should repent, turn to God, and do works befitting repentance." —ACTS 26:20

Gary entered therapy because he had an explosive, vicious temper. When he wanted to prove his point, he typically yelled loudly and hit the person with whom he was arguing. Although his aggressive anger was a significant problem, Gary had another problem as well. After his temper exploded, he demonstrated intense remorse for what he had done, and promised it would never happen again. His apologies seemed sincere because he usually wept, asked for forgiveness, and vowed to make it up to his victim. Sometimes, however, he returned to his destructive rages only hours after his last display of remorse. Obviously, his actions were not consistent with his words. He made no real effort to address his raging behavior until his wife threatened to leave him.

When Gary was in treatment, he continued his quick displays of remorse. As soon as he expressed his anger inappropriately, he stated, "I'm sorry." After a few of these episodes, his peers asked him to keep his apologies to himself unless he was willing to follow them up with action.

The questions to ask ourselves are, "Am I sincere when I make an apology? Am I using an apology to manipulate the situation?" Our apologies are sincere only when a change in action follows them.

Lord, let my actions demonstrate my sincerity.

> *"For which of you, intending to build a tower, does not sit down first and count the cost, whether he has enough to finish it."*
>
> —LUKE 14:28

It is very costly to change our behavior in positive directions. Some of you may be saying, "You make change sound as if it is something bad and to be avoided!" In some respects it is. I have found that people often underestimate the cost of maintaining healthy behaviors.

Think about it. They have spent a good portion of their lives keeping their emotions and actions in check in order to keep the important people around them close. To begin to change this pattern can make them feel very upset and vulnerable. In the past, healthy behavior was seen as behavior that would alienate the people we so desperately needed.

It is important to keep in mind that healthy behaviors and behavior patterns are important enough to pursue no matter what the cost. Sometimes the cost is failure (people being unhappy) or sometimes the cost is success (maintaining a healthy boundary). All the same, if it comes down to continued mental health or a relationship that is contributing to your codependency, isn't it time you begin to make a change?

Sometimes we may have to decide between continued health or more codependent behaviors.

*For the good that I will to do, I do not do; but the
evil I will not to do, that I practice.*
—ROM. 7:19

Control is elusive. It would be great if we all could be
thoroughly in control of our behavior—that way we
could immediately stop patterns we did not like. Unfortunately it is often the behaviors we wish to put an end
to that linger past their welcome. Thus it is with codependent patterns.

The most difficult dysfunctional behaviors serve a
purpose. They are in response to inner feelings such as
fear, worry, low self-esteem or mistrust. Because they
initially seem to fill the needs they were first called
upon to meet, they continue, often after they have become part of the problem creating the original need.
Eventually they seem to be out of one's ability to adequately control them. This is compulsive behavior.

Admitting your powerlessness to change these compulsive patterns is a first step to health. Trying continually on your own power usually results in frustration
and even hopelessness. But relax—this isn't all bad. In
fact, often frustration leads to a realization that without input from your higher power there cannot be lasting change. It is because of this powerlessness that we
turn to God, the true source of health.

*Have you discovered that you are powerless to stop compulsive pat-
terns by yourself? If not, you may not be fully using God's help.*

> *Be anxious for nothing, but in everything by prayer*
> *and supplication, with thanksgiving, let your*
> *requests be made known to God.* —PHIL. 4:6

Harold compulsively worried about every detail in his life. When he entered college, he obsessed about his assignments and grades. He also worried about staying in God's will. In an attempt to alleviate his anxiety, Harold discovered the art of making lists.

Harold made a list for each day's responsibilities. His lists began with two or three items but soon grew to two or three pages. Harold worried so much about forgetting an important duty or event that he wrote everything down. His lists soon contained minute details such as when he would get up in the morning, when he would brush his teeth, and what he would eat at every meal. It took Harold at least one hour each morning to make sure his lists included everything he needed to do. Instead of containing simple reminders of important responsibilities, his lists soon controlled him. They lost their value and became destructive. Harold's worrying ended up controlling his life.

Do you worry like Harold does? Do you allow life's problems and responsibilities to overwhelm you? Most of us worry about things over which we have no control. Harold thought he could control every detail in his life by keeping a list. His attempt at control failed miserably. In the verse above, God tells us to talk to him about our concerns and to leave them with him.

Worrying is a bad choice to make in life. You can make the choice not to worry.

And He said to them, "Come aside by yourselves to a deserted place and rest a while." For there were many coming and going, and they did not even have time to eat. —MARK 6:31

Do you have a quiet place where you can rest without intrusion? Many great men and women of the faith all seem to have in common a place they called their own where they met with God and found refreshment in his presence. Some people feel selfish if they take care of themselves. They feel that if they withdraw from others they are only thinking of themselves. Is that really true?

It is possible to think of others by taking care of yourself. You need to do something to keep your resources high enough so that you can help others and yourself over the long haul. That is certainly what Jesus had in mind for his disciples. They were busy in the ministry with him, and he recognized that they weren't even taking time to eat. Was it selfish of him to take them aside and allow them to rest? I don't think so. Instead he had a long-range view in sight. By taking time for rest and solitude they would be better prepared for the trials ahead.

Take a page out of Jesus' ministry. Set aside a place for peace and quiet rest. That will be taking care of yourself and others.

It is important to have a quiet place of rest.

> *And we know that all things work together for*
> *good to those who love God, to those who are the*
> *called according to His purpose.* —ROM. 8:28

At first this verse made Timothy angry. In his life there had been so many negative and hurtful situations that he could see no good at all. As a victim of childhood abuse and a chaotic home, Tim had little reason to assume that anything good could come of it.

Timothy felt angry at a God whom he perceived let abusive things happen to children. Such a God was not worthy of Timothy's time and energy. His anger was part of his grief process, mourning the loss of the parents who should have kept him safe and nurtured him. If God was part of that, Timothy wanted nothing to do with him.

Eventually Timothy came to realize that God was nothing like his parents. This came only after he grasped that his anger was acceptable to God, one who understands his anger and hurt. As Timothy began to surrender his bitter feelings, he also started to understand that God can bring good things out of even the most painful situations.

Protecting Father, at times there are situations in my life that seem far from good. Show me the good things you are able to bring about from these situations.

"Therefore do not fear them. For there is nothing covered that will not be revealed, and hidden that will not be known."
—MATT. 10:26

Secrets are a sign of unhealthy boundaries. When Cindy grew up in her family, she was taught to keep secret all that occurred. Unfortunately, Cindy's parents were abusive to the children. Her mother screamed, while her father slapped them and left bruises all over their bodies. The more the abuse occurred, the more insistent her parents became: "Don't tell a soul, or you'll get more." Finally, when Cindy was twelve, an observant school teacher noticed some of the bruises on Cindy's legs. Even though Cindy insisted she fell on the way to school, counseling was recommended for the whole family.

Cindy was afraid to reveal her family's secrets. In addition to being afraid of her parents' response, she did not want to be disloyal to them. Gradually, however, Cindy began to talk about her family life. Initially, she felt relief, and then she began to experience the painful reality of the abuse. As an adult, it became evident to Cindy that secrets had fueled the fire of her family's dysfunction.

As in Cindy's case, secrets are often used as a way to avoid reality. Secrets are used to manipulate people and to hide destructive behaviors. Cindy learned that secrets keep families and relationships from growing.

Lord, help me to end secrecy in my life.

> *And he did what was right in the sight of the LORD,*
> *but not with a loyal heart.* —2 CHRON. 25:2

Have you ever heard someone say that she feels like she is just "going through the motions"? It means that she is doing all the right behaviors but there is no heart motivation in her heart. In the process of change, everyone gets to the point where they feel that their heart just isn't in it anymore.

It is important to keep this in mind. It is expected that throughout the process people will feel that they simply can't keep going. However, their behavior indicates that they're doing pretty well. If you don't remind yourself that feeling burned out is normal, you will interpret your lack of motivation as losing ground and lose heart all together.

When you begin to feel that you are "just going through the motions" you need to go back to the basics. Review different portions of reading material you used to motivate yourself in the past. Write down your feelings and thoughts. You may be surprised at what you find yourself writing. Out of this you will get the focus back about what you are striving for. Make plans as to how you will focus more clearly on specific areas. Finally, act on your plans.

Father, help me to continue the wholehearted change I have begun and not just go through the motions.

*Do you not know that to whom you present
yourselves slaves to obey, you are that one's slaves
whom you obey, whether of sin to death, or of
obedience to righteousness?* —ROM. 6:16

The bad news is, "You're a slave!" The good news is
that you have a choice of masters. You see, we are either in bondage to sin or to a loving, caring God who
allows a tremendous amount of freedom. Anyone truly
ready to take on the recovery process must begin to
understand the nature of this slavery.

Because codependency consists of compulsive behaviors, a first step is recognizing that the behaviors
have become unmanageable. Usually there is denial
when we first get confronted with this fact. We don't
like to admit that our lives are beyond our control.

After we face the fact that the patterns have become
compulsive, we must surrender to another master,
God. Either way we do not control our lives. We can
only choose which master to serve; compulsions
which lead to unhappiness or God which leads to freedom.

*God, help me to recognize that I am not in control, even though I
sometimes believe I am. Take control of my compulsive behaviors
and grant me freedom from bondage.*

*Finally, brethren, whatever things are true,
whatever things are noble, whatever things are just,
whatever things are pure, whatever things are
lovely, whatever things are of good report, if there
is any virtue and if there is anything
praiseworthy—meditate on these things.*

—PHIL. 4:8

The definition of a relapse is not necessarily when the first drink or use of drugs begins. Rather, relapse occurs when our thoughts and attitudes return to the active phase of our addiction. Often, the return to old thought patterns can emerge months or even years before the first drink is taken. This is a valuable lesson for us. If we desire consistency in our recovery, we will need frequently to examine our thoughts and attitudes.

A young man in early recovery from alcohol and drug abuse attended an Alcoholics Anonymous meeting to gain support for his recovery. Much to his surprise, he found many people at the meeting talking as if they were in a bar or at a party. His comment after the meeting was, "They weren't using, but they might as well have been!" This young man was keenly aware that unhealthy choices will quickly return when unhealthy thinking continues. He chose to replace his old thoughts with new, healthier attitudes.

The verse above encourages us to reflect on the positive elements in life. When we concentrate on things that are admirable, excellent and pure, we are more likely to make positive choices.

Godly thoughts perpetuate godly actions.

Whatever the LORD pleases He does,
In heaven and in earth,
In the seas and in all deep places.
—PS. 135:6

Sometimes we lose sight of the fact that we have very little control over our world. It's no wonder. If we kept that firmly in sight, we might feel weak and helpless! We have an amazing capacity to fool ourselves into thinking that we can control everything in spite of the fact that we would deny we have such power.

Why do we get ourselves into such a position? One of the reasons we do it is so that we can avoid the realization that we really *don't* have much control. That is a very frightening thought. It follows that if I don't have control, I am helpless to protect myself or others I love. To a point that is true. In an ultimate sense, we are very helpless without God's protection and control over this world.

That doesn't mean, though, that we are totally helpless. We *can* choose to recognize the limits of our control and deal with only those things over which we have control—namely us. I *can* do something about how I think. I *can* do something about my dysfunctional behavior patterns. By limiting our focus, we can assure ourselves a more realistic view of the world and ourselves. Also, we can see how gracious God is in his divine control of the world.

Father, help me to recognize your control, and limit mine.

Weeping may endure for a night,
But joy comes in the morning.
—PS. 30:5

Grieving a loss is painful. When we experience the death of a loved one, or when we lose something very valuable to us, we become familiar with the pain of grieving. We are especially familiar with this pain when we grow up in chaotic families. In these families, emotional pain and hardship are the norm rather than the exception. At times, the pain may seem unending.

Because some of us are afraid the grieving will never end, we attempt to avoid it at all costs. We deny feelings like sadness, sorrow, and hurt because we fear that the pain will last an eternity. Although we think the pain will last forever, it won't—not if we actually face it, acknowledge it, and express it.

The fear of unending emotional pain is one reason alcoholics, addicts, and codependents have difficulty with grieving. An alcoholic once said, "I'd rather drink than face the pain of my losses. It would hurt too much; I'd never be able to get over it." He confused the intensity of his pain with the longevity of it. Many of us do the same. Ironically, if we do not acknowledge our pain, we fail to experience the growth that occurs from expressing it. If we are truly grieving our losses in life, the pain will be time-limited and emotional growth will result.

Lord, give me courage to face my losses and to grieve them.

> *Blessed is the man*
> *Who walks not in the counsel of the ungodly,*
> *Nor stands in the path of sinners,*
> *Nor sits in the seat of the scornful.*
>
> —PS. 1:1

Behaviors in your life requiring change often are held in place by others who are accustomed to seeing you the old way. Some people will be uncomfortable as you become different. Perhaps they will pressure you not to change or coerce you to engage in the old behaviors that you have determined to be destructive.

Billy had determined that he would make a new start. He fully believed that he would be strong enough to influence his friends to do the same. What a shock it was to him when they called him a wimp because he was swimming against the old current. The pressure was tremendous to conform to his old style and eventually Billy gave in.

There are times when you will have to decide whether or not a relationship impedes your progress toward health. While difficult, it may be wiser to develop new friendships, rather than succumb to the pressure to conform to previous standards. Billy's failure to do so, despite repeated warnings he ignored, resulted in relapse and a resumption of behaviors he knew weren't in the best interests of long-term growth.

God, grant me wisdom as I engage in relationships. Help me to find ones that further my growth rather than result in unhealthy behaviors.

> *Trouble and anguish have overtaken me,*
> *Yet Your commandments are my delights.*
> —PS. 119:143

I often advise people to allow themselves to feel hurt. When you have spent so much time pleasing others, you haven't allowed for your own feelings of hurt and pain. Also, you might feel guilty if you allow yourself to feel hurt.

It is important, though, to allow ourselves to feel the hurt we experience in our relationships. When we allow ourselves to feel the hurt, we can then begin to tell others honestly how we feel and experience the acceptance we so deeply desire.

The problem with going out of our way to not feel hurt is that we make it harder for ourselves to feel connected to important people in our lives, and we isolate ourselves further. This often leads to more hurt, but because we don't allow ourselves the privilege of feeling, we get deeper into the hole of isolation and denial. Do you see the progression?

It is important for us to allow ourselves to feel the hurt so that we can begin to communicate this to others and build healthy boundaries.

Let yourself feel the hurt in relationships so that you can begin to participate more fully in them.

"I am the bread of life. He who comes to Me shall never hunger."
— JOHN 6:35

Love hunger is an inner emptiness resulting from too little childhood love and nurturance. The result is a strong desire to fill this void with things that do not work, such as food. Eating disorders begin when the food does not fill the emptiness and we eat larger amounts. The emptiness becomes more intense when the "cure" does not work, and we eat even more.

Isadore had been in this cycle with painful results. As a model she needed not to gain weight, so she would purge herself of the food after bingeing excessively. At first, this was the only problem she could clearly see in her life, but it soon became apparent to her that she was a perfectionist. She had created much of the emptiness by setting standards so high that she could never reach them. The more she berated herself for not being perfect, the more emptiness she experienced in her life, and the more food she used to fill it.

Her relentless pursuit of perfection had failed to make her feel successful, so the hunger she felt was spiritual and emotional. She needed to start filling herself with the bread of life, one that would not leave her empty and hungry.

God, give me the spiritual food needed to fill my emptiness and free me from the pursuit of fillers that leave me longing for more.

> *But the end of all things is at hand; therefore be serious and watchful in your prayers.*
> —1 PETER 4:7

Tanya is a recovering bulimic who has worked the twelve-step program of Overeaters Anonymous for two years. Recently she realized she was experiencing great difficulty when she tried to pray to God. Tanya and her sponsor from O.A. were bewildered by Tanya's roadblock in her prayer life. The most puzzling aspect was Tanya's consistent attendance at her support group meetings and her obvious discipline in her eating habits. What was the reason for this obstacle?

Tanya soon discovered that the problem was not with her eating disorder; at least not directly. You see, Tanya met another bulimic at her support group, and they began to go out for walks together after the meetings. The problem was that this friend was a married man. Although Tanya knew it was not wise to spend time alone with a married man, she rationalized it. "It's only a walk; and besides, we can help each other."

Tanya put a wall between herself and God by choosing to develop a relationship with a married man. When Tanya recognized this barrier, she ended the relationship and asked for forgiveness. Her prayer life returned with fervor and meaning once again.

Do you struggle with keeping a clear mind? Is there something blocking your prayer life?

Lord, keep my communication with you open by giving me a clear mind founded on self-control.

"Whoever drinks of the water that I shall give him will never thirst. But the water that I shall give him will become in him a fountain of water springing up into everlasting life."
—JOHN 4:14

Our longings for acceptance and recognition run deep. If you examine your motives closely, you might find that a lot of what you do is motivated by that thirst for acceptance. Yet, this thirst will never be completely satisfied because of the nature of people.

It is important to realize that the thirst we all have within us is one that will never be completely satisfied except by God himself. Only he is the spring of living water that satisfies completely. We must grapple with the disappointment inherent in human relationships. People are fallible and sometimes very disappointing. They will often let us down, just like we sometimes let them down. They will disappoint us not by any design on their part, but just because they make mistakes.

If we can keep this in mind, we can then accept the limitations and resist the temptation of setting up unrealistic expectations. We will also be free to begin to accept what people have to offer rather than constantly looking for more.

Father, help me to live with the thirst of acceptance and accept what people have to offer me now.

> *I will both lie down in peace, and sleep;*
> *For You alone, O Lord, make me dwell in safety.*
> —PS. 4:8

As you begin working to change the patterns of codependency you will need to confront the past. Perhaps there are painful memories, fears, regrets, or simply things you have avoided confronting for a long time. As you begin to focus on these things, you may also experience difficulty sleeping.

Bedtime is when the cares of the day are put aside, so that you can rest and emerge refreshed to face another day. This is not easy when difficult recollections intrude on your consciousness. This is especially true when these memories cause you to feel unsafe or insecure. Quite possibly the worry will keep you awake.

If you find this to be true, it will be helpful to envision the God of safety with his invisible protective armor surrounding you as you lie in bed. David, the psalmist, was able to rely on God for the deep sense of security preceding a good night's sleep. Rather than dwelling on the pain and fear at bedtime, try allowing yourself to experience God's invincible protection and dwell in safety.

_____

As I try to sleep, allow your safety and peace to overcome my fears, worries, and insecurities.

*He took with Him Peter and the two sons of
Zebedee, and He began to be sorrowful and deeply
distressed. Then He said to them, "My soul is
exceedingly sorrowful, even to death. Stay here and
watch with Me."* —MATT. 26:37–38

It is painful to go through life alone, with no one to
provide a listening ear. Some of us were raised in families that were characterized by this type of pain.
Others may have been raised in families with some
level of communication, but we still experience an
emotional vacuum in current relationships. Regardless
of the specific details of our childhood experiences,
many of us rarely express our true feelings to others.

One of the most significant actions a therapist can
take is to give an individual permission to express her
feelings. She can then learn to express those feelings
to a support group, friends, or family and ask for help
when needed. Sharing emotions is essential to emotional healing.

Unfortunately, if we do not choose to reach out to
others, our suppressed emotions may turn into resentment and bitterness. Expressing our feelings to others
is often uncomfortable and sometimes frightening.
Christ demonstrated, however, that it was necessary in
his life to talk about his sorrow and to ask for comfort.
If this expression of feeling was necessary for Jesus, it
is even more necessary for us.

*Lord, help me to follow your example and reach out to others for
help when I need it.*

> *He answered and said to them, "When it is evening you say, 'It will be fair weather, for the sky is red.'"*
> —MATT. 16:2

In this particular passage, Jesus was referring to a saying of the day that attempted to predict weather. We still have a remnant of it today: "Red sky in the morning, sailors take warning; red sky at night, sailors delight." Over the generations, families hand down myths about how to love people as well. One of these myths goes like this: "We should get quite upset over other people's problems to show that we care about them."

This myth breaks down boundaries between people rather than keeping them intact. It conveys the thought that when you feel, I will feel the same thing, and that is the best way to show you that I love you. This way of thinking makes decision-making and setting limits virtually impossible. Do you see how counterproductive it is to hold this belief? You need to respect others' boundaries and your own enough to let them have their own feelings without having their feelings be confused by yours as well. The most loving thing you can do for others is to identify with their plight and listen, but don't feel the same. This gives them permission to feel without fearing that you will fall apart too.

_____

It is important to feel with *others instead of feeling* for *them.*

For all have sinned and fall short of the glory of God.
—ROM. 3:23

There is a tendency among codependents to try and prove their worth. The empty feelings from which they are running often find temporary relief in the newest accomplishment. Some turn to doing good, as if they could please their higher power with their good works.

Charles wanted to be a good father. He had a reputation as a solid Christian man who was involved in his church, and he did many good things for others. In family sessions, he seemed baffled with his children who resented him. They recited a long list of complaints that had a single theme: their father was pushing them to be the kind of person he was; yet they could see his inconsistencies and felt he was a hypocrite. Sometimes his standards were so high that they felt pleasing him was impossible, and so they had stopped trying.

Charles had tried so hard to earn the approval of God and his peers that he had neglected to see how far away he had pushed his family. Basically Charles had forgotten that there was no way his good behavior would earn him freedom from sin. All have sinned and it is only by God's grace, not by good works, that God's strength, power, and forgiveness is granted.

Have you been trying to earn God's approval through good works?

> *"Therefore bear fruits worthy of repentance."*
> —MATT. 3:8

Tony was involved in a vicious sexual addiction. He had numerous affairs during his marriage, and his wife knew about all of them. During each affair, his wife confronted him and demanded that the affair stop. Each time, Tony was quick to promise, "It will never happen again." His wife, convinced he was sincere, trusted him to maintain his fidelity. No major changes were required of him, except to stop seeing his girlfriends. Tragically, within months of ending one relationship, Tony was beginning another one.

Finally, Tony's wife threatened to leave him unless he got help. Tony agreed to enter a treatment program. While there, he complied with treatment and vowed to change his behaviors. However, after Tony returned home from the hospital, the staff found letters addressed to Tony from his girlfriend. His wife received a phone bill listing calls to his girlfriend's home from the hospital. Once again, Tony's actions did not match up with his words. Within two weeks of completing treatment, Tony resumed his affairs. His wife ended the marriage.

The key to making healthy choices on a consistent basis is to put our words into action. If we desire change and are truly repentant, our actions will clearly demonstrate our intentions.

Lord, remind me that my actions need to demonstrate the level of my repentance.

For if when we were enemies we were reconciled to God through the death of His Son, much more, having been reconciled, we shall be saved by His life. —ROM. 5:10

You don't like it that I am concerned about you in spite of the fact that I know so much about you." I was talking with a hopeless adolescent. He felt that everyone had abandoned him, with good reason. He had done so much wrong; he was completely unlovable. He hated talking to me because I still cared about him even when I knew him so intimately. My very presence contradicted what he believed about himself.

This adolescent is a lot like many other people who desperately hang on to the belief that they are unacceptable and unlovable. Even after treatment the belief often returns, particularly during times when we feel the most threatened. It's almost as if we say to ourselves, "Well, there is proof once more that I am unlovable, I guess it's true." Then, we take it the rest of the way down to where we feel completely deflated and depressed.

Remember that God reconciled himself to us in spite of our behavior toward him. So, like the adolescent, our personal fable of unacceptability has a glaring hole in it. If we believe God accepts us, then we can withstand the tendency to wallow in our self-pity.

Father, help me to accept your intense love and acceptance of me.

> *How much better it is to get wisdom than gold!*
> *And to get understanding is to be chosen rather*
> *than silver.*
> —PROV. 16:16

Wisdom and understanding can be chosen. Unfortunately, many individuals who see themselves as powerless victims in an abusive society do not understand this. I have heard people express disappointment that they were not "blessed" with these virtues and because of it could not better themselves. This is a mistake!

Sean believed himself to be stupid. Throughout school he had been an average or below-average student. Parents and teachers assumed that this was a genetic quirk. He had bought this view and credited poor choices he made to this lack of intelligence. In a sense Sean had given up. He believed he was to make poor choices resulting in a life of unhappiness.

There was a certain amount of complacency involved as well. Sean could minimize his personal responsibility for bad decisions by calling himself stupid. Sean's view, however, was wrong. It is possible to choose wisdom and understanding even though one may not have been born a genius. Sean eventually reached a turning point: he accepted himself as someone who could change and grow.

God, help me to choose wisdom and understanding instead of seeing myself as an inferior and helpless victim of my genes.

> *"Yet they did not obey or incline their ear, but*
> *walked in the counsels and in the imagination of*
> *their evil heart, and went backward and not*
> *forward."*
> —JER. 7:24

When we hear the word *stubborn,* we may initially picture an older person who is stuck in his ways. This stereotyped image of stubbornness misses the broad scope of stubbornness. If we examine ourselves honestly, we will soon realize that our own stubbornness has been with us throughout our lives. As two-year-olds, we had temper tantrums. As teenagers, we stayed out past curfew to prove to our parents we were in charge.

As adults, we may insist that our way is the only way. Or, we may insist that change is impossible because we've been doing a particular behavior for years. For example, a woman once said, "I've been having promiscuous relationships for ten years. How do you expect me to change now?" Unfortunately, we can use stubbornness to avoid changing unhealthy choices and boundaries.

When we are stubborn, it is a clear indicator that we are struggling with the principle of trusting in God. Stubbornness demonstrates our desire to be in total control. We do not consider God's input for our lives. Therefore, being stubborn defeats our ability to learn to trust and to allow God to work in our lives. Stubbornness will only cause us to go backwards in our recovery.

_____

Choose not to be stubborn today.

> *"For whoever desires to save his life will lose it, and
> whoever loses his life for My sake will find it."*
>   —MATT. 16:25

A paradox is a solution that seems to be the opposite of the way we think it should be. There is much about change that is paradoxical. Often healthy behaviors feel like they are hurting us, and dysfunctional behaviors are the ones that feel the most comfortable. That is what makes change so difficult.

This is particularly true in the area of setting new boundaries. Change always feels awkward and uncomfortable, enough so that we even think we may be doing the wrong thing. We have spent long years convincing ourselves that other people's happiness and contentment are more important than our own. That thinking is now a barrier to healthier living.

There is nothing wrong with adopting a perspective where we attempt to put others' interests ahead of our own; as a matter of fact, it is biblical. The extreme of this is what you should try to overcome. This means that you will probably be sensitive to others' feelings simply by force of habit. It will be important to focus on being honest about your own feelings, even if you feel you are doing something wrong.

Help me to overcome the discomfort of healthy behavior, Lord.

*All things are lawful for me, but all things are not
helpful; all things are lawful for me, but all things
do not edify.*   —1 COR. 10:23

The New Testament often teaches about freedom. In
our work with people with addictions we often run
across individuals who have interpreted this freedom
much too liberally. One such individual was Ken, a
twenty-five-year-old ex-serviceman struggling with an
addiction to alcohol.

In the Navy Ken had been lauded for his ability to
drink others under the table and to have a new girl in
every port-of-call. Despite having liver surgery from a
problem caused by excessive drinking, he continued to
imbibe, believing that his freedom in Christ allowed
him to do so. He would start with a glass of wine at
dinner, and eventually he would order an entire bottle.

While our God is a God of freedom, our freedom is
not to be taken lightly. When a behavior becomes excessive, we need to set limits on it. Ken needed to
make choices that were beneficial and constructive in
the long run.

*What behaviors in your life need limits? How can your choices be
more beneficial and constructive in the long run?*

> *But let your "Yes" be "Yes," and your "No," "No,"*
> *lest you fall into judgment.* —JAMES 5:12

One of the best ways to avoid responsibility is to remain vague and non-committal. Jack learned this early on in his marriage. As his gambling addiction progressed to the point that he spent six to ten hours per day betting, he needed to make excuses for his absence from home and work. When his wife asked him for help around the house, his response would be, "If I get time, I'll do it," or "Tomorrow, dear." Jack made the same empty statements to his children. They were never sure if he was going to attend school functions until he actually showed up.

Jack also gave vague answers to his employer to avoid being responsible for his lack of performance. He often told his employer he was doing the best he could, knowing full well he was not even trying. In time, Jack's words were not trusted by anyone. His wife caught him at the racetrack when he was supposed to be at home with the children. His employer found him absent from work on a regular basis, and his children stopped asking him to go to the park. The significant people in his life knew he resisted being straight with them in order to avoid responsibility.

If we are to grow from our choices, we need to ensure that our "yes" means yes, and our "no," no. We need to avoid using vague words as a means to elude commitment and accountability.

Lord, help me to say what I intend to do, and to do what I have said.

Sow for yourselves righteousness;
Reap in mercy;
Break up your fallow ground,
For it is time to seek the LORD,
Till He comes and rains righteousness on you.
—HOS. 10:12

Imagine for a minute that you are a gardener. You have spent time choosing your seeds; you have also spent time preparing the soil for these seeds. You look forward to the day of planting, and you enjoy getting dirty during this process. Now, you wait . . . and wait . . . and wait. You inspect your garden and strain to see the first shoots of your precious plants. But, wait . . . they're weeds! You are disappointed and downcast.

Isn't this what happens after we begin to deal with our codependent behaviors? Once we begin to make changes it is like we have sown new seeds. We have carefully torn up the old weeds of dysfunctional behaviors, and we await the new sprouts of healthier behaviors. But, alas, what meets our eyes? More weeds. We seem to think that once we have torn up all those old weeds, they will never reappear. We must be careful to keep our garden of healthy behaviors carefully weeded. We must also not assume that if we have made changes once, that is all it takes.

Be careful to continue to be vigilant for the old weeds of codependent behaviors.

> *Always be ready to give a defense to everyone who*
> *asks you a reason for the hope that is in you.*
> —1 PETER 3:15

Georgette was about to be discharged from the hospital. She had worked hard and was quite different from the day she checked in. Numerous destructive patterns had been addressed and changed, and she was feeling strong and ready to face the world. But there was one nagging question: "What do I tell others about the new me?"

Good question. Just because you become different doesn't mean the others in your life have changed as well. Others are accustomed to the dysfunctional you, not the healthy, new person that is developing. Frankly, others are expecting things will be easier, but often changing requires confrontation. You must stand up for what you know and continue behaviors which are healthy but difficult for significant others.

There will come a time when you need to give reasons for the new ways you are behaving. If you are not prepared for this, others may challenge the changes you have undergone and you may falter. Be ready to give an explanation to others. Stand up for what you believe so that you don't fall.

Spend some time writing down reasons for the changes you are beginning to implement in your life. Be prepared to share this with others.

I have restrained my feet from every evil way,
That I may keep Your word.
—PS. 119:101

If I had a dime for every time a person with an addiction told me recovery was a lot of work, I'd be independently wealthy. The fact is, making healthy choices *is* a lot of hard work! Much of the work involves preparing ahead of time in order to avoid tempting situations.

Alberta should have prepared for her first visit home. Alberta, in early recovery from codependency, struggles greatly with a drive to take care of others. She feels responsible for others and does not take care of her own needs. When others are not happy, Alberta blames herself.

These codependent traits are particularly strong in Alberta's relationships with other family members. During her first year in recovery, she did not plan ahead. She did not prepare a support network for her visit home. She did not pray or try to anticipate potential pitfalls.

Within the first day of her visit, her sister immediately started in on Alberta for not doing enough for the family and for making her parents angry in the past few months. By the time she left, Alberta had begun thinking and acting codependently. Alberta could have saved herself a lot of pain by planning ahead.

Planning ahead is a choice we can make.

That you may become blameless and harmless,
children of God without fault in the midst of a
crooked and perverse generation, among whom
you shine as lights in the world. —PHIL. 2:15

Probably the most difficult adjustment in recovery is coping with the changes that you have made and others have failed to make. You sometimes feel that you stick out "like a sore thumb" because you are so different from those around you. Your perspective probably has changed regarding interacting with others and making better decisions. You may even find yourself not seeing eye-to-eye with people you once agreed with. After all, seeing you protecting your boundaries can be quite alienating to someone who has been used to running roughshod over you.

Remember that this is to be expected. You have begun to make both subtle and dramatic changes, and in a sense, you have left others behind. This will inevitably change your relationship with them. You may need to help them understand the changes so that they can begin to relate to you in a different way. Don't expect them to take the changes easily. Change is harder for some than others, and you may find both types of people in your world of relationships. Be patient. The work you do in helping others to adjust to your change is worth the effort.

———

Dear God, help others around me to accept the changes I have made.

*But Jonah arose to flee . . . from the presence of
the Lord.*
—JONAH 1:3

We all know the story of Jonah and the big fish. At
first Jonah knew clearly what he needed to do, but instead of following through with this, he ran in the opposite direction and suffered some pretty strange
consequences. Like Jonah's story, the recovery process
can be quite a struggle. At times some people will
avoid doing what they know to be right, even though it
is an integral part of enduring change.

Initially Sheila was quite motivated to change; she
had endured enough and wanted relief. She didn't
know that the process wasn't going to be simple. When
Sheila began to experience some hardship in her recovery she quit for awhile, feeling that it was easier to
continue in her codependent patterns than to take the
next steps of treatment.

Running away from recovery was not the best solution for Sheila. At the time, though, it appeared easier
than working to change. She had hoped for some quick
fix that would immediately make things better, some
kind of magic cure that would make all the pain disappear. And so, like Jonah, she ran from what she knew
she needed to do to ensure lasting change.

---

*God, help me to last through the whole process of change. Remind
me that the final results are worth temporary setbacks and disappointment.*

> *Why are you cast down, O my soul?*
> *And why are you disquieted within me?*
> *Hope in God;*
> *For I shall yet praise Him,*
> *The help of my countenance and my God.*
> —PS. 42:11

Depression results, in part, from a biochemical imbalance that produces apathy. Usually, however, at least one emotional stressor is experienced prior to the onset of depression. When we choose to ignore these stressors or our emotional responses to the stressors, depression can result.

For example, Tracy began to believe life had no real meaning for her any more. Prior to her depression, she discovered her husband was having an affair. When she eventually confronted him, he denied that it was true. To avoid conflict and the potential loss of her marriage, she questioned her own motives and dropped the subject. Of course, over time she came across other evidence. The reality of her loss was inevitable, but Tracy refused to deal with it and the resulting emotional pain.

Again, depression results when we do not deal with our feelings. The verse above seems to be describing what it is like to be depressed. God wants us to feel good about ourselves and to desire the truth regardless of the outcome. Therefore, we need to be honest with ourselves about our losses and choose to deal with them, instead of running from them.

Lord, give me the strength to deal with my losses.

*Do you not know that those who run in a race all
run, but one receives the prize? Run in such a way
that you may obtain it.* —1 COR. 9:24

I remember reading about a woman who had trained
to run in a race. She arrived for her race, lined up, and
away she went! Soon she began to think that the race
for which she had signed up should have been over by
now. So, she asked someone along the route. To her
surprise, she had arrived at the race an hour too early
and had gotten into the marathon! She decided to stop,
but no one would let her off the route. So, she kept
running and running—probably farther at one time
than she had in her life.

This story is repeated over and over again for many
people who have undertaken the job of changing their
old ways of thinking and dealing with people. Somewhere along the way a little clock goes off in their
heads, and they think, "Time is up—this job should be
completed." Discouragement, disappointment, and fa-
tigue set in. They want to bail out.

It is important to commit yourself to doing the job *as
long as it takes to get the job done*. Remember that you
have embarked on the long process of living and
choosing in new ways.

Father, help me persevere in the race I have embarked on to the end.

> *Obey those who rule over you, and be submissive,*
> *for they watch out for your souls, as those who*
> *must give account. Let them do so with joy and not*
> *with grief, for that would be unprofitable for you.*
> —HEB. 13:17

Nadine felt tremendous bitterness for authority figures. Allowing others to be in charge was almost impossible, and keeping a job was difficult. Each time someone in authority would question a decision or offer constructive criticism, Nadine felt the old, angry feelings from her childhood begin to crop up.

While she knew intellectually that not all authority was abusive, this was not so easy emotionally. Her family had been unable to maintain a consistent set of rules, and consequences were given randomly. For example, she had stayed out several hours late one night with no consequence, but was grounded for a month for being five minutes late the next. With this background it wasn't hard to understand her resentment.

Not all authority is bad, however. Many individuals in charge got there because of their competence and solid ability to lead. Nevertheless, many people from dysfunctional backgrounds experience trouble with authority. Part of the recovery process is recognizing that this difficulty is something upon which to work.

Do you have problems with those in authority? Begin to look at why this is so, while asking God for help to deal with bitter feelings.

And He said, "Who told you that you were naked?
Have you eaten from the tree of which I
commanded you that you should not eat?"
Then the man said, "The woman whom You gave
to be with me, she gave me of the tree, and I ate."
—GEN. 3:11–12

Life is filled with tragedies. When they occur, the first one to be blamed is often God. For example, when someone is killed in a natural disaster, the first question is, "Why did God allow this to happen?" Although this question is understandable when we experience losses that are out of our control, it can become an escape when our own unhealthy choices become involved.

Shelly blamed God for her broken marriages. She was married three times and divorced twice. Her present marriage was only months away from ending in the same manner as the rest. In all three marriages, Shelly married abusive, alcoholic men. After her first divorce, a close friend encouraged Shelly to seek professional help. Shelly refused, explaining that the marriage ended because of bad luck. As the second and third marriages crumbled, so did Shelly's attitude toward God. By blaming God, Shelly did not have to take responsibility for her own choices.

When we blame God, we avoid responsibility just as Shelly did. We do not want to look at what we do wrong or make necessary changes. A blaming attitude toward God can be a major obstacle in our recovery. If we truly want to make healthy choices, we need to assume responsibility for our actions.

The greatest tragedies are those we could have chosen to avoid.

> *"The thief does not come except to steal, and to
> kill, and to destroy. I have come that they may have
> life, and that they may have it more abundantly."*
> —JOHN 10:10

Are there thieves in your life? A thief is one who takes something that is not his. Many things in our relationships with others can rob us of our joy and the abundance of a relationship with Jesus Christ.

One thief is a perfectionistic expectation of yourself. This thief robs you by setting up unrealistically high hurdles for you to jump. You believe that if you jump the hurdles then you are finally good enough to deserve others' attention and care. What hurdles are there in your life? Pleasing a spouse who can never be pleased? Doing a job "good enough" that your boss will reward you? Doing nice things for someone simply so they will notice you?

Only Christ can truly satisfy our deepest longings for significance. He is no counterfeit; his abundance is true abundance.

Watch out for the thieves in your life, and strengthen your relationship with one who can provide you with lasting abundance.

For those who are such do not serve our Lord Jesus Christ, but their own belly, and by smooth words and flattering speech deceive the hearts of the simple.
                                        —ROM. 16:18

Laurie knew that she was attracted to alcoholic men—something about them appealed to her. She was demure and quiet, very unsure of herself. They were strong-willed and brash, adding spice to her mundane life.

She had an intense need for approval in her life, possibly stemming from her childhood. Her father was an alcoholic and was verbally abusive to her, making her feel small and insignificant. She needed to feel cared for and appreciated. Usually her relationships began when the man was complimentary and charming. They ended with anguish when she saw that the man cared only for himself and not for her.

For Laurie to remove herself from this destructive pattern she would first need to believe good things about herself. Her need for affirmation could only be met by acknowledging her own worth, rather than letting herself be manipulated by flattery and smooth talk. As long as she relied on others to fill this need she would be vulnerable to deception and the destructive relationships would continue.

Help me to see the value you have given me. Let me rely on you to fill my need for affirmation.

> *Thus also faith by itself, if it does not have works, is dead.*
> —JAMES 2:17

How often have you heard the excuse after someone makes a mistake, "Well, at least his intentions were good." You may have used that phrase yourself, perhaps when cleaning up after a child attempting to help you. You may have added, "I know you didn't mean to do it," and subsequently, no punishment for the behavior was enforced.

At times, our mistakes are simply accidents, and consequences are not necessary. However, we often fall into the trap of negating personal responsibility for actions by focusing on good intentions only. Kris did this with her husband who was alcoholic and chronically unemployed. When confronted by her pastor about her husband's lack of personal responsibility for himself and his family, Kris replied quickly, "Well, he has tried to get a job, you know. His intentions are good; he is just having bad luck right now." Kris maintained that her husband was not at fault because his intentions were good.

Many of us have good intentions. Unfortunately, good intentions do not replace the action that needs to be present in our recovery programs. The camouflage of good intentions can hinder us from making a close and accurate examination of the choices we make in life.

Like faith, intentions are good only when followed by action.

But may the God of all grace, who called us to His eternal glory by Christ Jesus, after you have suffered a while, perfect, establish, strengthen, and settle you. —1 PETER 5:10

I stumbled across the finish line in the rain and looked at my coach with pain all over my face. We had just finished a grueling training session for our upcoming basketball season. I thought to myself, *Why are you putting yourself through such pain?* As we had run around the football field, our coach had hollered, "No pain, No gain!" Those words still haunt me today. To anyone who has been an athlete, those words will evoke many memories.

It is interesting, though, how true these words are. In attempting to make the kind of changes we have been talking about in this devotional, you are no doubt experiencing some kind of pain. This may be actual physical pain or emotional pain. In some ways, pain is an important barometer of whether or not you are really being honest with yourself about your dysfunctional behaviors. It is not an indication that something is necessarily wrong. As with sports, the harder you push in your self-examination both during the treatment phase and maintenance, the more stable the change will be.

Father, help me to persevere in the changes I am pursuing in spite of the pain.

> *"Go and wash in the Jordan seven times, and your flesh shall be restored to you, and you shall be clean."*
> —2 KINGS 5:10

Naaman was a valiant soldier; in fact, he was highly regarded as the commander of an entire army. So it was very difficult for him when he contracted a contagious and life-threatening disease. He received a message from the prophet Elisha that washing himself seven times in the Jordan River would result in complete remission of his physical affliction.

Naaman became angry. He expected a few well-chosen words and a quick wave of the hand, and magically the illness would disappear. Besides, the Jordan River was dirty and less convenient than other rivers. He was a proud man and did not wish to succumb to treatment beneath his dignity, and only after much urging did he comply. To his surprise, this strange treatment worked and he was fully healed.

Throughout the recovery process there will be times that the treatment seems worse than the cure. It is possible that you may have to try new behaviors that you would rather avoid. Like Naaman, you may be initially resistive and avoid trying. God works in mysterious ways. Don't quit before trying; you may come away healed.

God, nothing you direct me to do should be beneath my dignity. Help me to comply as I accept your healing process, as mysterious as it may be.

Peter, seeing him, said to Jesus, "But Lord, what about this man?" Jesus said to him, "If I will that he remain till I come, what is that to you? You follow Me."
—JOHN 21:21–22

Many of us experience life by always watching the other guy. Is he doing his job? Is he contributing his fair share? We become so preoccupied with making sure that he is doing his part, we often forget about our own responsibilities. By focusing on the other person's responsibilities, we develop unhealthy boundaries. For example, in the verse above, Peter seemed quite anxious about another disciple's future. Peter was quickly corrected and then instructed to focus on himself and his responsibilities.

Keeping our eyes on ourselves is difficult to do, especially if we were raised in a family which taught us to be responsible for our younger siblings' or our parents' behaviors. Alcoholic and other dysfunctional families teach poor boundaries well. A great deal of damage is caused to our own welfare when we focus on the responsibilities of others.

Whose actions are you keeping track of these days? Are they those of your spouse, your parents, or even your children? Are you truly taking care of your own needs and responsibilities? Remember, you can only be responsible for the choices *you* make in life.

Establishing healthy boundaries means keeping our focus on our own responsibilities.

> *Do not fret because of evildoers,*
> *Nor be envious of the workers of iniquity.*
> —PS. 37:1

I have had many clients who love to ask the "why" question. Like, "Why do I have to worry so much?" Or, "Why don't other people have the same kind of trouble that I have?" Even though you may not envy the ones who do wrong, often instead you envy the ones who don't have the same problems you do. In this process, you condemn yourself because you are not like everyone else.

We seem to be so intent on condemning ourselves! We often ask such questions to confirm our suspicions that we really are indeed a fraud. It is important to find a means to motivate yourself toward further growth and development, not less. Such labeling will be counterproductive to the commitment you have made to change. It is also a very subtle attempt to wiggle free of the responsibility to change completely. Growth and change are uncomfortable. Our nature is to find whatever means we can find to feel better. One of those ways is to label and condemn our efforts. Then, we can quit because obviously our best efforts amount to nothing.

Be on your guard for the tendency to compare and condemn.

They saw these men on whose bodies the fire had no power; the hair of their head was not singed nor were their garments affected, and the smell of fire was not on them.
—DAN. 3:27

Talk about trial by fire! Because of an enduring belief in God's rescuing power, three men risked being thrown into a large oven. Around them was tremendous pressure to conform to standards in which they did not believe, and so they refused at the risk of death. In the end, God did deliver them and thoroughly proved his ability to keep those who rely on him safe from harm.

Like these three young men, there will be times when your resolve is tested. During such trying periods, it is natural to wonder whether or not the difficulty will be too great for you to handle. It probably is. Fortunately there is a higher power available for assistance during crises.

God does deliver. As he did for the three men facing death by fire, he can do for you during your trials. You may feel tremendous pressure to resort to old patterns and to give up relying on God's ability to restore you to health and safety. Just remember that through faith and trust you will discover that no fiery trial is too difficult for God.

Deliver me, O God, from the fiery trials I will face. I am grateful for the safety you already have granted.

July 4 – YOUR INDEPENDENCE

*Now the Lord is the Spirit; and where the Spirit of
the Lord is, there is liberty.*　　—2 COR. 3:17

Over two centuries ago some upstart colonists got it
in their heads that they were being mistreated by the
British empire. They were audacious enough to assert
their independence and begin what has become an ex-
periment in democracy. Their Declaration of Independence embodies the right of individuals to control
matters that have an impact on them. Each year we
commemorate this historic event. We set time aside to
remember the sacrifices that have been made for that
freedom.

You have made a declaration of independence of
your own. It asserts that you will no longer be solely
responsible for the happiness of others. You will be
committed to maintaining firm boundaries and making better decisions that reflect a concern for others as
well as yourself. It also states that you will live free
from the constraints of saving others from themselves,
and that you give them the right to be responsible for
themselves. It is important that you, too, set time aside
to remember this commitment. See how far you have
come, celebrate, and plan for future growth. Remember that freedom is rooted in God's grace, and as the
verse suggests there is true freedom where his spirit
resides.

Father, thank you for my freedom!

*And if anyone thinks that he knows anything, he
knows nothing yet as he ought to know.*
—1 COR. 8:2

One of the most annoying kinds of people to be
around is a person who thinks he knows more than
others. A conversation with this type of person is usually one-sided. You listen while he rambles about his
opinionated ideas. We too can be this way at times.
This arrogant attitude can damage our ability to make
healthy choices.

Charlene could be called a know-it-all. Although she
had already been divorced three times, she talked con-
fidently about what it would take for her to have a
healthy relationship in the future. She made comments
like, "I'll know better next time. I know exactly what
kind of man I should marry."

When a close friend suggested that Charlene go for
counseling before marrying a fourth time, Charlene
acted insulted and stomped away. Charlene thought
she was fully knowledgeable and assumed she would
not learn anything new. Her attitude caused her to reject input from others that would have helped her
make healthier choices in her relationships.

Allowing ourselves to receive input from others is
essential for personal growth. Being open to the ideas
of others allows us to have more options to choose
from when making decisions. Are you the kind of person that might be described as a know-it-all? Is there
an area in your life in which you have difficulty accepting input from others?

Being a know-it-all means not growing at all.

> *He shall not die for the iniquity of his father;*
> *He shall surely live!* —EZEK. 18:17

Blaming is easy, especially if you were raised in a severely dysfunctional family. When you have been wronged repeatedly and have internalized an intense bitterness, it is very difficult to let go. Taking responsibility means painfully searching one's heart and owning your own guilt.

Early in treatment, Ken could only focus on the way his parents had neglected him. Ken recognized that by leading a chaotic life he had created problems for himself in the long run. Nevertheless, our conversations usually came back to the way he was neglected and hurt as a child. For Ken to succeed in treatment, he had to move out of this blaming cycle and begin to take responsibility for himself. In essence he had to grow up and finally leave the family.

While certainly it takes less work to focus on the source of the problems, in the long run it impedes true change. True growth and freedom require recognizing our personal culpability for the wrongs we have done. We must remove ourselves from a cycle of blame and self-victimization.

God, help me to grow as a person who owns responsibility for my actions, instead of giving responsibility to others in my past.

*Then Zacchaeus stood and said to the Lord, "Look,
Lord, I give half of my goods to the poor; and if I
have taken anything from anyone by false
accusation, I restore fourfold."*   —LUKE 19:8

Terri, a twenty-six-year-old mother of two children,
was working a twelve-step recovery program for her
codependency. She was in the process of working on
step nine, which required that she make amends to
those she had harmed with her controlling behaviors.
Before this step Terri had encountered few problems in
her recovery, but this was a difficult and emotionally
challenging step for her.

As she considered making amends to her husband,
she began to question whether her actions had been
harmful to their relationship. All she could identify
were the behaviors he did that angered her. Certainly,
her husband needed to take responsibility for his
contributions to their marital conflict, but so did Terri.
Unfortunately, however, Terri no longer wanted to acknowledge responsibility for her behavior. Within
days, Terri relapsed into her old controlling behaviors.

Terri was unable to maintain her recovery when she
failed to make amends to her husband. Her experience
is not uncommon. To flippantly say we are sorry is
easy. However, to conduct sincere amends and to follow through with action, as Zacchaeus did, demands
responsibility.

Dear God, please help me to recognize my need to make amends.

> *My brethren, count it all joy when you fall into*
> *various trials, knowing that the testing of your faith*
> *produces patience.* —JAMES 1:2–3

A young boy went walking in the woods one day and happened upon a butterfly struggling to get out of its cocoon. The boy decided that he would be helpful, so he pulled the butterfly out of the cocoon. But the butterfly looked pretty unstable, and its wings looked awfully crooked. First the boy blew on it so that it would dry off. Then he straightened the wings out so that they looked better. Before too long, the boy decided that he had done all he could do to help the butterfly. He stood back to see his masterpiece fly away. Instead, the butterfly died.

In the process of changing, we often assume that once we have made the initial changes, the way should be smooth and without struggle. That would certainly be nice, but it doesn't describe the necessary elements of change. Through struggles and difficulties we grow and learn more. Much like the butterfly, we need the struggles involved in growing and changing to face the trials and difficulties in the road ahead.

Don't assume when problems strike that you are doing something wrong. You may be doing everything right!

> *"Repent therefore and be converted, that your sins may be blotted out, so that times of refreshing may come from the presence of the Lord."*
> —ACTS 3:19

Rob's guilt was apparent from the first time he entered the room. Wringing his hands, he discussed things he had done for which he constantly blamed himself. On his wrinkled forehead there was a sheen from perspiration as he talked. Obviously the guilt he carried was difficult, and he appeared exhausted.

One of the first questions I asked was whether he had sought God's forgiveness for the things he had done. He had not. He believed that he needed to feel good about himself before God would find him acceptable and consider forgiving him. Rob was looking for relief.

He needed to put first things first. The refreshment he sought was available from God, as a result of repenting the wrongs he had done. However, Rob had not taken this avenue because he feared God would not even consider his troubles worthwhile as long as he was so rotten. Rob needed to know that God's forgiveness and subsequent refreshment are available to people like him. All that is required is the asking.

God, I humbly repent of my wrongs. Please grant me relief from the burden of self-blame and guilt.

> *But truly I am full of power by the Spirit of the LORD,*
> *And of justice and might.*
> —MIC. 3:8

When an apology is made for harmful words or actions, a relationship often grows stronger. In addition, the individual doing the apologizing is also strengthened in character. Given these benefits, why don't we practice making apologies more often? At least part of the answer to this question lies in the fact that although apologies provide opportunities for growth, they can also be frightening. When we make an apology, we risk the chance of being rejected. Pride may be another factor. It is often difficult to admit we are wrong in any way, because this means we are imperfect.

Kathy experienced this difficulty herself. She had just been confronted by an observing friend for being controlling in her relationship with her husband. She knew her friend was right, but she was afraid to apologize to her husband because of her fear of rejection.

Fortunately, Kathy remembered the above verse. She realized that God would provide her with the resources she needed to make her amends. If she had listened only to her fear of rejection, she would have kept herself drowning in the guilt caused by her actions. She also would have lost the opportunity for personal growth and relationship building with her husband.

Lord, when I make amends, help me to see that you want to replace my fear with your power.

> O LORD, *though our iniquities testify against us,*
> *Do it for Your name's sake;*
> *For our backslidings are many,*
> *We have sinned against You.*   —JER. 14:7

Losing ground is a hard topic to explore with codependents who are trying to maintain changes in their behavior. For much of their lives they have felt that they were losing ground and backsliding. It is very difficult for them to identify when they really are losing ground, because this condition has been so much a part of their lives for so long.

If I comment that it seems that they are beginning to lose ground, they will often react with denial first. It is just too discouraging to admit a problem. The next reactions are often blame, guilt, and shame. Again, they respond in some old ways to what is perceived as failure.

Finally, they may show disappointment—a more healthy reaction. This is healthy because it is an admission of a problem but with a motivation to do better. It is important to keep in mind that losing ground is a statement of performance, not a statement of your worth. If you are backsliding, you need to admit that something has gone wrong. Then find out what went wrong and make adjustments so that you can return to progress and growth.

Father, help me to admit when I have lost ground and make the adjustments to keep going.

> *For not he who commends himself is approved, but*
> *whom the Lord commends.*   —2 COR. 10:18

Everyone likes approval; it is natural to seek the acknowledgement of others. For some people this becomes a compulsion. They look to others to affirm themselves. Often they brag about what good they have done because they have a powerful sense that they do not measure up. They claim they are better than others to counter the low self-esteem they feel.

Unfortunately this method backfires. Most people feel uncomfortable in the presence of someone who boasts and puts others down. Rather than feeling better the individual may ultimately feel even worse as others react to their self-aggrandizement.

Rather than acting on low self-esteem by elevating oneself or putting others down, look to God for approval. Frankly, God accepts us as we are, warts and all, and he offers his approval despite our shortcomings. Allow yourself to feel good, not at the expense of others, but because you are valuable. Your value lies in the fact that God made you in his image.

God, thanks for your approval. Help me to stop looking to others for something you already have given.

For each one shall bear his own load.
—GAL. 6:5

Initially, we may react to this verse and say, "Of course I carry my own load. I responsibly complete all my work on the job, and I'm a responsible marriage partner and parent!" Although this may be true, we need to ask ourselves if we act responsibly on an emotional level. It is much easier to be responsible for the completion of specific tasks than it is to be responsible for our own needs and emotions. In fact, we may neglect to carry our own emotional load and try to carry someone else's load instead.

This confusion regarding personal responsibility was experienced by Lydia. Lydia grew up in a family where she was taught that it was her responsibility to make others happy. She carried this faulty thinking into her marriage. She blames herself because her husband drinks heavily. She reasons that if he were happy, he would not have to drink. Lydia is not concerned about how her husband's drinking is affecting her, even though she receives much verbal abuse when he's intoxicated. Lydia is consumed by her attempts to act in ways that will please him. She hopes her actions will stop his drinking.

Needless to say, Lydia's efforts are futile. Although her husband is acting irresponsibly, so is she. If she would identify and express her needs and emotions, she could confront her husband instead of taking the blame for his actions.

Lord, help me to be responsible with my emotions and needs.

> *"I am the vine, you are the branches. He who abides in Me, and I in him, bears much fruit; for without Me you can do nothing."*
>
> —JOHN 15:5

It is easy to forget. People have long been searching for ways to increase their memory. The Jews knew the importance of remembering as well. They cultivated a rich oral tradition of their history, and were quite committed to keeping it alive through the generations.

The same is true of recovery and the maintenance process. We must never forget who is the root of our power for recovery. Jesus made it very clear that without him we can do *nothing*. That is pretty unmistakable.

The word picture is very vivid. Without him as the vine from which we gain our strength, we will die and all of our endeavors will die as well. Don't let appearances fool you. It may look like the process is going on without his help, but that's not true. It is Jesus who gives us the power to overcome our wills so we can continue down the path of recovery. Staying connected to the vine will be the difference between bearing the fruit of a life in balance and withering to dysfunction.

Father, help me to remember the vine that gives me strength to be fruitful.

*Whose end is destruction, whose god is their belly,
and whose glory is in their shame. . . .*
—PHIL. 3:19

A seventeen-year-old bulimic came to a startling revelation during the course of her treatment: she had been trying to fill her empty heart by filling her stomach. Her childhood had been spent trying to earn her parents' elusive love, resulting in frustration and deep longing. She learned what many codependents eventually learn, that physical appetites can never fill the deep longing for love and approval.

Another insight came later after she attempted to reconcile this longing with her parents. They were unwilling, and perhaps unable, to meet her dependency needs. When both these avenues of relief were discouraged, she was left with a deep longing and no apparent answer to the problem of how to have her needs met. As long as she focused only on earthly things the emptiness continued.

Many with such unmet dependency needs focus only on objects immediately available to them like food, sex, alcohol, control, or money. Because they are trying to fill their empty hearts with material things, the emptiness continues. There is one true source of love that can fully satisfy the heart, a limitless source. God is love.

Loving God, fill my emptiness.

> *But the fruit of the Spirit is love, joy, peace, longsuffering, kindness, goodness, faithfulness, gentleness, self-control. Against such there is no law.*
> —GAL. 5:22–23

When something is going wrong in our lives, we generally feel anxious, upset, and perhaps even panicky. It seems that the more anxious we get, the more we want to control the situation at hand. The more control we attempt to gain, the greater the chance that our boundaries and choices will become inappropriate. When we try to control what we can't, we are unable to experience the "fruit of the Spirit."

Dave wanted to be a man with whom God would be pleased. He believed that if he could consistently demonstrate the fruits of the Spirit, his relationship with God would be enhanced. However, Dave felt insecure and out of control because he was a compulsive overeater. He attempted to overcompensate for his feelings by trying to control the environment around him. In business meetings at work and in elders' meetings at church, Dave was the one who always wanted to be in charge. Everything had to run across his desk before it could be approved or implemented. This control, of course, caused others to resent Dave. The fruits of the Spirit were not evident in his life.

Do control issues keep you from being gentle, patient, kind, self-controlled, or joyful? These characteristics will develop when you give God control of your life.

What kind of fruit is being produced in your life?

While He was still talking to the multitudes, behold,
His mother and brothers stood outside, seeking to
speak with Him. —MATT. 12:46

We have all seen the commercial extolling the importance of knowing when to say when. It refers to the value of knowing one's limits and the importance of stopping before these limits are reached. The same is true in our relationships with those we love. After learning how to make these new choices about limits, we are then confronted with the challenge of knowing when to say when.

Once we have begun to define our relationships in new ways, we often think that all should go well, just like the old fairy tale ending: "and they lived happily ever after." With that expectation we will inevitably fail, because we have so narrowly defined success. What happens if we don't live "happily ever after"? Does that mean that we have failed in our attempts to change? Definitely not! It simply indicates that the means by which we have chosen to change didn't work, that's all. It also means that you must adjust the plan to see more change. Remember, failure is an event, not a person.

Dear Father, help me to judge myself realistically and see my worth through your eyes. This will help me risk setting limits with those I love.

For do I now persuade men, or God? Or do I seek to please men? For if I still pleased men, I would not be a servant of Christ. —GAL. 1:10

Codependent individuals often try to make others happy at the expense of their own happiness. They expend so much energy toward this goal that they become miserable. This results in everyone else becoming miserable also, and so the attempt to make others happy backfires.

Vicky was embroiled in this pattern. She was bitter that no one appreciated her efforts. Repeatedly she had gone out of her way, only to find her efforts had resulted in continuing unhappiness for everyone involved. Certainly things had not turned out as she had planned. Trying so desperately to get satisfaction from continually caring for others had resulted in a failure to take care of her own needs.

Vicky had failed to recognize that true happiness is not based on whether or not everyone else is happy. She was powerless to create happiness in others since it was their choice to be happy or not. For Vicky to move forward in her recovery, she needed to stop investing all her energy in others and start caring for her own needs. From there she would have a better perspective from which to understand what others really needed from her.

God, free me from my need to please others. Let me please you instead by taking better care of myself.

*Confess your trespasses to one another, and pray
for one another, that you may be healed.*
—JAMES 5:16

Sitting in the last pew at church is Amy, a humble and
self-sacrificing Christian woman. Everyone in the
church views her as caring and giving. Amy developed
these qualities as she grew up in a home with an alcoholic mother. Since she was the oldest child in her family, Amy learned how to look after other people's
needs. She assumed the responsibilities of keeping
house, because her intoxicated mother was unable to
cook and clean.

Now, as an adult, Amy continues to take care of
others. She is the first to volunteer for every commit-
tee opening. She is usually the one in charge of major
church productions such as holiday programs and
church dinners. She never turns anyone away.

From all appearances, Amy should be a happy, ful-
filled individual. Unfortunately, she often feels lonely
and isolated from others. She is willing to listen to the
struggles of others but does not ask for help when she
is struggling herself.

The verse above clearly emphasizes the reciprocal
process of giving and receiving. Confessing our sins
and struggles with others is just as important as hearing confession. Spiritual and emotional isolation can
result when we only participate in half of this process.
Are you emotionally isolating yourself from others by
keeping your own needs and struggles hidden?

Lord, give me courage to open up to others.

The mouth of the righteous speaks wisdom,
And his tongue talks of justice.
—PS. 37:30

Some will remember the shuttle diplomacy of Henry Kissinger, or the tireless journeys President Carter engaged in to achieve an accord between Egypt and Israel. They hoped that by their influence and persuasiveness the two combative nations would begin to see the common ground that lay between them rather than the differences.

Often this same process can be seen on a smaller scale within human relationships. Usually there is one who feels the intense pull to play diplomat. They are always in the business of smoothing ruffled feathers, diffusing tension, and trying to make everyone happy. Of course, they inevitably fail because sooner or later someone gets angry. Then these fledgling diplomats feel that *they* are the failure.

This is where the boundary issue enters in. It is not a problem to attempt to be an agent of reconciliation between people. It is a problem when we do what we can, the process fails, and we blame ourselves for the outcome.

Lord, give me strength to allow people to fail in their attempt to reconcile with each other.

Therefore let those who suffer according to the will of God commit their souls to Him in doing good, as to a faithful Creator. —1 PETER 4:19

When the pain of living becomes difficult, individuals naturally seek a way to alleviate it. Some people use alcohol and drugs to numb the pain, often so thoroughly that they are unable to mature fully.

Chris was one such person. From an early age he ran from crises, turning to marijuana and booze and traveling through life in an foggy haze. Although chronologically much older, he presented himself in a childlike fashion, with an underdeveloped conscience. While he temporarily avoided any psychological pain, he also had neglected his moral development viewing right and wrong in terms of his personal pleasure. In fact, it was pointed out by a consulting psychologist that he could benefit better from jail as a result of his actions than treatment.

Chris had failed to understand that often pain is part of living, a necessary facet of mature growth. By completely avoiding pain, growth could not occur. Despite the difficulties we encounter, recognizing that a higher power is faithful to aid in hard times will greatly aid in the process of mature development.

God, help me make it through the hard times, recognizing your faithfulness and continuing to do what is right despite my personal discomfort.

> *Let us know,*
> *Let us pursue the knowledge of the LORD.*
> *His going forth is established as the morning;*
> *He will come to us like the rain,*
> *Like the latter and former rain to the earth.*
> —HOS. 6:3

Dale was in the tenth month of his recovery from drug addiction. He was about to embark on the eleventh step of his twelve-step recovery program. This was not going to be an easy step for Dale. Although he was raised as a Catholic he had rarely attended church, because his parents were actively alcoholic and did not pursue an understanding of God. Dale prayed as a child, hoping God would stop his parents from drinking. Since his parents divorced and his father died of alcoholism, Dale concluded God did not exist, and that if he did, God wasn't interested in the personal lives of those who sought him. In addition, Dale did not think he was important enough for God to pay attention to him.

Over the next six months, Dale learned through his sponsor, his church, and his personal meditation on the Bible that God was indeed interested in Dale and desired to reveal his will to Dale. He soon learned that God is bigger than his family, and bigger than his own ambivalence toward acknowledging God's desire to work in his life.

Do you acknowledge God's desire to work in your life? Do you realize that with his help, making healthy choices is possible?

When we acknowledge God, we can begin to get to know him.

For innumerable evils have surrounded me;
My iniquities have overtaken me, so that I
  am not able to look up;
They are more than the hairs of my head;
Therefore my heart fails me.

—PS. 40:12

One day I arrived home to be met by my sobbing daughter running to my arms. She had seen a movie, and she had been scared by the scenes of animals fighting. She was overwhelmed by the ferocity of the animals and the reality of the animal kingdom.

Sometimes the clients to whom I talk also feel quite overwhelmed by surprising things in their world. They, like my daughter, have been hit hard by shocking events they witnessed. Their response was to withdraw and isolate themselves because this was part of the pattern they had developed to protect themselves. Is protection the thing to do when you are feeling overwhelmed?

It is wise to talk to someone who can comfort and encourage us during the times that we feel overcome by feelings we can't explain. There is an indescribable feeling of safety and peace in sharing our fears and insecurities. It is worth the risk to open up and talk for the reassurance we can feel after it is all over.

Father, help me to risk vulnerability by talking to someone when I am overwhelmed.

> *"I say to you, if you have faith as a mustard seed, you will say to this mountain, 'Move from here to there,' and it will move; and nothing will be impossible for you."*
>
> —MATT. 17:20

Often in therapy I will use a certain metaphor. I will ask the question "How do you eat an elephant?" Answer: "One bite at a time." Initially problems seem insurmountable, especially when you have watched them grow out of control for a long time. Taken together they appear as an impossible feast!

Bill was like that. To fill a deep longing for love, an emptiness that was even larger than he first imagined, he had turned to illicit drugs. For many years these substances masked his yearning, until they no longer served the purpose for which they were intended and his young life began to unravel. Faced with the original problems leading to substance abuse, and the problems of years of neglect, his underlying depression shocked him.

Since he was a very proud young man, taking small steps toward recovery was initially discouraging. Bill wanted to eat the whole elephant in only one sitting. It would have been easy to quit but then Bill would have incurred even more consequences, leading to a much bigger elephant.

God, help me to see that with only mustard seed faith, even eating an elephant is possible.

"But take heed to yourselves, lest your hearts be weighed down with carousing, drunkenness, and cares of this life, and that Day come on you unexpectedly."
　　　　　　　　　　　　　—LUKE 21:34

Some of our choices help us, and some hurt us. The key to making more of the helpful kind depends on our willingness to be cautious. This became evident to me one day when I was talking to a recovering alcoholic. I asked him to reveal his secret for staying sober thirty years. I will never forget his response. He looked directly at me and said, "I wake up every morning and remind myself that I could make one bad choice today and that would cancel out every day of my recovery. Then," he said smiling, "I plan my day to make sure that bad choice won't be made."

It was obvious to me that this old-timer in recovery knew the secret of making healthy choices in life. Much of his success was based on his understanding that he would never be immune to possible relapse. As a result of this awareness, he made deliberate decisions to stay sober. He knew that the day he became complacent would be the day of his relapse. He avoided relapse by keeping his recovery program at the forefront of his mind. He planned his day carefully to avoid being engulfed by the day's anxieties. He also started each day by praying for help and guidance.

Lord, help me to be careful each day of my recovery.

> *"This Book of the Law shall not depart from your mouth, but you shall meditate in it day and night, that you may observe to do according to all that is written in it. For then you will make your way prosperous, and then you will have good success."*
> —JOSH. 1:8

What is your definition of success? Is it when other people like and approve of you? Is it when you are satisfied that you have accomplished what you set out to do? For some people who have struggled with protecting their boundaries success is often a pipe dream.

The key to this problem lies in our definition of success. Often we have a floating definition of success. Success is defined only by the people around us, and therefore the people we are with will determine whether or not we will feel we have succeeded.

It is important to define success by some benchmark that is unchanging: *I have succeeded in my relationships with others when I am able to say no without feeling guilty.* This is a goal that is both attainable and measurable. There is no need to set ourselves up to fail. Rather we need to set ourselves up to succeed, and by so doing we will help ourselves instead of depending on others to help us feel successful.

Set yourself up to succeed in relationships.

"With God all things are possible."
—MARK 10:27

Recently a thirty-five-year-old woman came into our offices. She was crippled by self-doubt. Her job was a dead-end ritual that brought no satisfaction. Friends did not seem to reciprocate her affection. Every time a male cared enough about her to ask for a second date, she became disinterested and distanced herself from him. Everyday decisions had become monumental to her, and things she previously found pleasurable no longer had any joy.

As we reviewed her past and the harsh criticism and rejection by her family, she began to cry. Her parents never approved of anything she did. She internalized this perfectionism. She expected so much from herself that she was never able to reach her goal of being perfect. She applied this goal to every area of her life, only to find she always fell short. It seemed impossible.

As a result, she quit trying. "After all," she reasoned, "if it can't be done, why bother?" This is another example of how God gets too little credit and how our past gets in the way of seeing clearly the present. The truth is, nothing is impossible with God; there is hope enough to try another time.

God of possibilities, help me to see the hope you offer.

> *"For everyone practicing evil hates the light and does not come to the light, lest his deeds should be exposed."*
>
> —JOHN 3:20

Looking at our shortcomings is humiliating, embarrassing, and painful. It is probably the most difficult step in recovery as we learn to make new choices and establish healthy boundaries. In the twelve-step program of Alcoholics Anonymous, the process is described as taking a moral inventory, and it is discussed in step four. This step involves looking at past choices and understanding the true nature of our character.

For those of us with unhealthy boundaries, worrying about what others think serves as a determining factor for the choices we will make. Therefore, the most common problem with this step is worrying about what others might think of us as we expose our character defects and our unhealthy choices. It is important, however, not to allow the fear of exposure to impede our ability to work through this crucial step.

Take some time today and examine the unhealthy choices you have made in your life. Write them down so that you'll remember them. Also, examine yourself and ask what parts of your character inhibit making healthy choices, such as arrogance, grandiosity, need for control, need for approval, or perhaps selfishness. Exposure of unhealthy choices and character defects begins the healing process.

Lord, give me courage to examine myself honestly.

> *All things are lawful for me, but all things are not
> helpful. All things are lawful for me, but I will not
> be brought under the power of any.*
> —1 COR. 6:12

There are many things that you will face during maintenance that you will have to make new choices about. An example of this would be any situation where you were asked to do something for someone else, and you wanted to say no (and you had every right to) but didn't. When a situation like this comes up again, you are now faced with a decision.

The quandry you are confronted with is just like the one Paul is talking about here. You have more choices now that you have freed yourself from the compulsion of keeping everyone happy. Not all of these are beneficial for you or anyone else. Just because you are free to do them doesn't necessarily mean that they are good for you.

You need to make the distinction between what you need and what you desire. There are many times that these come into conflict. You must determine what you *need* and act upon this. What will further your growth, and keep your goals for maintenance on track? What can you do in this situation which will be beneficial to keeping the boundaries intact? Remember, anything is possible, but not everything is beneficial.

Father, help me to be sensitive to the difference between my needs and desires.

Also do not take to heart everything people say,
Lest you hear your servant cursing you.
—ECCL. 7:21

When a person has experienced a mistrustful relationship sometimes she becomes hypersensitive and she may even actively look for hurtful words or meanings in the things others say. As you know, if she looks hard enough she can find anything, especially when looking for evidence of betrayed trust.

One such injustice seeker was Amelia. Her father had constantly talked about women as if they were lesser beings, and as she matured she began to believe this about herself. When she married she brought this baggage from her past, but failing to recognize this in herself, she regularly read things into conversations with her husband. She would become angry and lash out at him for his insensitivity, slowly driving him away.

It is important to know that past emotional injury colors the way we view the world. After exploring her childhood, Amelia was able to see this. She radically changed the way she related to her husband, a man very different from her father.

Does your own hypersensitivity impair the way you hear what others are saying to you? How can you listen differently?

Neither filthiness, nor foolish talking, nor coarse jesting, which are not fitting, but rather giving of thanks.
—EPH. 5:4

Brian attended his first meeting of Gambler's Anonymous when he was twenty-one years old. His life was ravaged because of his compulsive spending and betting. He had lost just about everything but his life, and even that was threatened because he owed loan sharks a great deal of money.

He went to the twelve-step meeting to find hope, serenity, and new meaning to life. When he arrived at the old church building, he saw many people assembled in several different rooms. Brian listened intently as the others talked about their addictions. As he listened, he noticed something disturbing.

Some of the members were describing their stories in a boastful, dramatic fashion. Several told jokes, exaggerated what happened, and swore frequently as they described their experiences. Then there were others who seemed sincere, grateful to be there, and saddened by their addictive behaviors. Over time, Brian noticed that those who had seemed to enjoy telling "war stories" were no longer attending. Those who seemed grateful to be there attended without absence.

Boasting, foolish talk, and coarse joking have no place in recovery. They keep us stuck in old thought patterns rather than helping us to start new ones. When tempted to use this type of speech, challenge yourself to be thankful instead.

Help me, Lord, to be grateful instead of boastful.

Consider what I say, and may the Lord give you understanding in all things. —2 TIM. 2:7

A female client was sitting across from me with an incredible look of frustration and pain. She felt that no matter what she did, she would never have the time she needed to reflect on issues she felt were critical to her maintenance. Does that sound familiar to you? We live in a society filled with distractions. Sometimes I wonder if that expresses how much we as a society would like to avoid the feelings with which we are uncomfortable.

Reflection requires a commitment on our part to avoid the distractions surrounding us. It means planning times for reflection and contemplation. At times it may feel very selfish, but remember the purpose of such reflection—to grow in your emotional health and to grow spiritually.

Reflect on what God has promised, on what he has done in your recovery, or on new insights with which he has blessed you. Paul makes it clear that there is a definite pay-off for such reflection. We will be rewarded with more insight, and with more insight we will grow both emotionally and spiritually.

Father, help me to set time aside to reflect on your word and your promises.

"And do not fear those who kill the body but cannot kill the soul. But rather fear Him who is able to destroy both. . . ."
—MATT. 10:28

Venus had spent most of her life in abusive situations. She was adept at recognizing abuse when she saw it, but she continued to fall into the same situations to which she had become accustomed. Despite a strong desire to change, and periods of health sometimes for years, she couldn't free herself from these patterns.

The problem was that Venus had difficulty recognizing when others were enabling old patterns to recur. Desperate for love, she would attach herself to well-meaning people who would fight her battles for her. These people had great intentions—they saw a hurting individual and wished to alleviate her pain. Venus would then become complacent and fail to recognize danger signs until it was too late.

Venus needed to develop a healthy fear of those who enabled her to quit growing. The love she needed was not the kind that removed the pain. Instead she needed caring friends who would help her face the pain.

God, help me to develop a strong ability to discern real caring from enabling behavior that permits me to continue unhealthy patterns.

> *Discretion will preserve you;*
> *Understanding will keep you.*
> —PROV. 2:11

We are not destined to continue making unhealthy choices in life, although we may draw this conclusion after observing others. For instance, we may know an alcoholic who continues to relapse after every treatment program he attends. We may be friends with someone who has been divorced three times. We may have a close friend who seemed very sincere in her recovery but still relapsed as if treatment never occurred.

Is relapse inevitable? Of course not! A way to prevent relapse is to avoid situations which might tempt us to make unhealthy choices. An alcoholic should not frequent the local bar to have a club soda just because he likes the company there. The drug addict needs to leave his drug-using friends. The person with an eating addiction needs to stay away from situations where she is isolated from others and has easy access to food.

The importance of avoiding high-risk situations seems obvious, but our tendency is to gravitate back to unhealthy choices. We usually deceive ourselves with the belief that we are strong enough to resist temptations. We forget our powerlessness over unhealthy choices made in the past. To counter our potential for relapse, we must carefully evaluate our daily activities and friendships as to whether they promote or hinder our recovery.

Lord, help me to use discretion by avoiding high-risk situations.

Sever yourselves from such a man,
Whose breath is in his nostrils;
For of what account is he?
—ISA. 2:22

It is important to realize the limitations of the people in whom we trust. We often view people as if they were perfect and would never betray us. If we say to ourselves, "Boy, I will never trust anyone ever again!" it means that we have not seasoned our trust with a solid realization that people are just as fallible as we are.

On the other hand, we may say, "Well, it sure hurts that Joe let me down, but it isn't the end of the world. I'm sure he will do better next time." This statement has within it both a sense of hurt and a sense of forgiveness. It communicates clearly that this problem will not happen every time.

Always be aware that people are just like you. They will make mistakes and will often let you down. The solution to this problem is not to avoid relationships with them. Rather, understand that you will be let down, but that it doesn't spell doom for the future of that relationship. Also remember that God will never let you down and that he is worth taking into account rather than man.

Dear God, help me to look to you for comfort in the midst of disappointments in my relationships.

> *For He does not afflict willingly,*
> *Nor grieve the children of men.*
> —LAM. 3:33

Helena believed God was responsible for the problems in her marriage. For years she had been the victim of her husband's verbal tirades. She was extremely angry and felt she had had enough. However, she would not divorce him, believing that this was right in God's eyes. Nevertheless, she felt God had not kept his end of the bargain as well as she had.

Helena's anger had become directed at God because he had not altered the marriage in a way that would make her happy to reward her for her faithfulness. Over the years she had begun to believe that God was somehow responsible for the abusive behavior of her husband, that it was a sort of punishment for some unknown wrong she had once done.

The result was that Helena had stopped trusting God to intervene in the situation and had resorted to feelings of bitterness. She saw the abuse as coming from both her husband and from God. Unfortunately this forced her to rely only on herself, but she was incapable of altering the situation on her own.

Are you blaming God for things others have done? How does this keep you from trusting God to work in your dysfunctional relationships?

God, I want to believe that you help, not hurt. Help me to see this in my situation.

And the LORD God said to the woman, "What is this you have done?" And the woman said, "The serpent deceived me, and I ate."   —GEN. 3:13

A man was talking to his pastor about a recent affair and said, "The devil made me do it!" He cried and told his pastor that he loved his wife too much to hurt her. He then promptly concluded that the affair was the devil's fault, not his.

This story may sound ludicrous, but it is true. In fact, many of us do exactly what the unfaithful husband did. We blame others for our problems. We may even blame God for life's unfairness and hardships. In doing so, we make other people, including God, responsible for our actions, and deny our own responsibility for the choices we make. As a result, we fail to learn from our mistakes and often end up repeating them.

As we try to make healthy choices, we need to start with the realization that no one is responsible for our actions except us. We cannot blame others for our drinking, drug use, angry outbursts, unkind speech, compulsive behaviors, or promiscuous relationships. Contrary to what is taught in many dysfunctional families, nobody can make us do something against our will. We are the only person to blame if we make unhealthy choices—not our parents, siblings, or spouse.

God, help me to see blaming as destructive, irresponsible behavior.

> *We are hard pressed on every side, yet not crushed;*
> *we are perplexed, but not in despair.*
> —2 COR. 4:8

Sometimes it is very difficult to figure out just when we succeed in setting appropriate boundaries. It isn't uncommon to feel just like Paul when he said, "We are hard pressed."

The problem seems to lie in the old assumptions you held about what success is. For a long time, you felt successful when everyone was happy. You felt good when there was no tension or conflict. Because you did such a good job indoctrinating yourself with these lies, it is now difficult to figure out when you have succeeded in a healthy way because it feels so awkward.

It is helpful to begin to define what healthy success is. One criteria might be when you don't feel taken advantage of. Another criteria might be when you have followed what you know to be right in your relationships with others. Finally, you know you are on the right track when you have been lovingly honest with significant people in your life in spite of the risks.

Lord, help me to find the means to know success when it happens.

Casting all your care upon Him, for He cares for you.
—1 PETER 5:7

One of the biggest struggles a codependent has is worry. When we are in a troubled relationship, we struggle to be overcompetent, and we are usually very anxious. Truthfully, there are many things to be concerned about, but usually the codependent is the one who takes on the brunt of it.

Jeanne's husband was incredibly irresponsible. He would spend entire nights on drinking binges after which there was little money to meet expenses. He viewed these problems from an alcoholic haze. When she confronted him he would become aggressive and frighten the whole family. The anxiety she felt paralyzed her, making it difficult to arrive at any decisions. Then she would worry because no decision was made.

She certainly was powerless in the face of the chaos caused by her husband's drinking, powerless to make him change, and powerless to deal with the anxiety she felt. These feelings gave rise to a despair and hopelessness. Jeanne needed a higher power to whom she could give the feelings, a caring someone upon whom she could cast her worries and know they would be well cared for.

God, teach me to stop being handicapped by my inability to control my anxiety. I give my worries to you, knowing that you will do a much better job handling them than I could.

Your ears shall hear a word behind you, saying,
"This is the way, walk in it,"
Whenever you turn to the right hand
Or whenever you turn to the left. —ISA. 30:21

Melinda began attending Al-Anon because her son, age twenty-eight, was alcoholic and still living at home. He was not paying rent and was chronically unemployed. Melinda's support groups and her counselor explained to Melinda that she was actually enabling her son to stay sick by allowing him to live in her home. Her son was not required to be responsible for his actions as long as Melinda was there to "clean up his mess." Melinda's counselor and her sponsor recommended that she ask her son to find his own apartment. She finally began to realize that she was hurting her son, not helping him.

After several months had gone by without any action on Melinda's part, she was confronted by her counselor. She said, "I intend to do it, but I need some time." Several more months elapsed, and Melinda was still noncommittal. It was soon obvious to all who knew her that Melinda was not going to do what was right.

We are often like Melinda. We know the right choice but fail to make it, making excuses instead. True recovery means we must match our actions to our words. As the saying goes, "We need to walk the walk, not just talk the talk."

God, help me to walk the walk in my recovery program.

*Let your speech always be with grace, seasoned
with salt, that you may know how you ought to
answer each one.*
                                        —COL. 4:6

Grace is a word in the English language that conveys
acceptance. But for the codependent, giving grace to
others is much easier than giving grace to himself. He
may have come to the conclusion that it is wrong to be
gracious with himself. He may believe that he's being
too easy on himself.

How do you give grace to yourself? The answer lies
in how you talk and evaluate your performance in the
activities of living. You can be very critical and unfor-
giving or you can be gracious and tolerant. You're at
the critical end of the spectrum when you say to yourself, "You dummy, you *should* have known better."
When our language to ourselves is littered with
shoulds, oughts, and have tos, you know that you are
not being very gracious with yourself.

The other end of the spectrum is tolerance and acceptance. There you recognize your humanity. You
know that making a mistake isn't the worst thing that
can happen to you. You give grace to yourself and accept your limitations.

Be gracious to yourself and accept your human limitations.

> *For if anyone thinks himself to be something, when*
> *he is nothing, he deceives himself.* —GAL. 6:3

The most difficult person to reach in a codependent family is the know-it-all. He believes that he has all the answers, so help is not needed. Therefore alternative views that address the whole picture are disregarded and progress is blocked.

One such husband sabotaged every intervention attempted with his family. The family's feelings of hopelessness were quite evident as he announced, "We already know that—I don't think you really understand." In reality everyone involved did understand; his belief in his omniscience was the problem. This proud man kept his family blocked from progressing through the steps of change.

When you have viewed the problem from your vantage point for a long time, it is hard to change perspective. But by letting go of your mistaken beliefs, new views of the situation become possible. Be careful of believing that your knowledge is better than others. Your pride can stop your progress.

Help me, all knowing God, to let go of my mistaken notions about my dysfunction.

> *"The heart is deceitful above all things,*
> *And desperately wicked;*
> *Who can know it?"*
> —JER. 17:9

A young lady in early recovery from codependency blurted out this statement in a support group meeting: "Why is it so hard for me to see my shortcomings?" She was confused, frustrated, and adamant about getting an answer. After the meeting, several group members approached her and gave their personal recovery stories. The stories were similar in that they all contained one common thread. Each person struggled when he or she was asked to acknowledge and accept personal shortcomings. One person stated, "I was stubborn and arrogant. I didn't want to believe I had deficiencies in my character which I needed to improve."

Accepting the fact that we all have shortcomings in character is a major step in our recovery. Although we may believe we are practically flawless, the real truth rests in our track record. We have demonstrated a consistent struggle with our ability to make healthy choices, and we have hurt others and ourselves in the process.

When we realize our potential to do harm to ourselves and to others, we can be open enough to evaluate our individual character flaws. We must realize, as the verse above states, that our hearts are deceitful. Personal deceit can keep us from viewing ourselves and our actions honestly.

Lord, please break through my deceitful heart and help me to see myself clearly.

> *"O our God, will You not judge them? For we have*
> *no power against this great multitude that is*
> *coming against us; nor do we know what to do, but*
> *our eyes are upon You."* —2 CHRON. 20:12

As you begin to recognize the limits of what you can and cannot control, you will have to decide what or who you are going to rely on. In a sense, it is deciding how to shift your dependence from people to God. That is easier said than done. How does one shift his dependence from something touchable (people) to something intangible (God)?

Dependence on God can take many forms. Sometimes it means waiting to see what God in his infinite wisdom will provide for you in a time of crisis and trouble. On the other hand, it may mean moving ahead aggressively in faith because you feel assured that God will indeed reward your boldness.

How does one know when to act? The more you know about God, the more confident you can become. It is easier to act in accordance with his will if you know what his will is. The more you can know of God, the more you will know of his will for everyone, including yourself. Then, it will be easier to know when to act and when not to.

Father, help me to develop a deeper dependence on you.

"If your brother sins against you, rebuke him; and if he repents, forgive him. And if he sins against you seven times in a day, and seven times in a day returns to you, saying, 'I repent,' you shall forgive him."

—LUKE 17:3–4

This seems like a pretty bizarre concept. Conventional wisdom says that if someone is determined to wrong you repeatedly, forgiveness is definitely inferior to revenge. This is especially true of those locked into dysfunctional relationships. How can one possibly forgive the same wrong seven times in one day?

The key is responsibility. Codependents tend to be overresponsible. When wronged they will take on the responsibility of making the other person change. Sometimes this is done by not forgiving, believing that the other does not deserve forgiveness. While this may be true, only God can judge another person fairly since only God can truly see what is on the inside.

Allow God to do his job. Your part is first to confront the other on his wrongs. If he repents, then forgive. Remember the tendency to take on responsibility for things beyond your control. Don't try to determine whether or not the repentance or guilt he expresses is true or honest. God will do that for you.

Are there people in your life you feel do not deserve forgiveness? Give them to God, who does a much better job taking care of such things.

> *Cast your burden on the Lord,*
> *And He shall sustain you;*
> *He shall never permit the righteous to be moved.*
> —PS. 55:22

Casting our cares on God may seem like a welcome relief, but for some of us it is a frightening experience. Giving our anxieties to God means we allow God to be in control instead of ourselves. This can be threatening for those of us who find our security in being in control at all times.

Sandra was a perfectionist. Everything had to be done right. If the project couldn't be completed without error, then Sandra didn't do it at all. Not surprisingly, Sandra struggled with anxiety attacks because she could not live up to her own unrealistic expectations. She did not give herself the latitude to finish a project behind schedule or to do the best she could with the time given to her.

Are you a lot like Sandra? Do you need to be in control no matter what? Casting our anxieties on God allows us the freedom to do the best we can and feel good about ourselves even if a project is not done perfectly. God tells us that it is wise to give him control because he loves us and wants good things for us. We can trust him with significant concerns. He invites you and me to let him bear the load of our worries.

When we give our anxieties to God we are choosing to let go of control.

*But as you abound in everything—in faith, in
speech, in knowledge, in all diligence, and in your
love for us—see that you abound in this grace also.*
—2 COR. 8:7

Giving is one of those areas that you will always have
to be on the watch for during maintenance. This is because in the past you have given in an unhealthy way,
giving all of yourself and surrendering your rights. You
help no one by this type of giving. As a matter of fact,
you hurt yourself and others more by not maintaining
healthy boundaries.

So where is the balance? We are called upon to excel
in the grace of giving. How does one do this without
giving their boundaries too? A lot of this has to do with
motives which only you can examine. Ask yourself,
"Am I giving this to keep the peace, or am I giving to
the person because I love her and want her to have
what I can give?" The first part shows blurred boundaries and attempts to influence the person to stay
close. The second part reflects healthy boundaries and
giving to a person out of the purity of love. That is the
essence of healthy giving—giving out of unselfish love
without demanding something in return.

*It is important to give in a healthy way by maintaining your bound-
aries.*

*Therefore a man shall leave his father and mother
and be joined to his wife, and they shall become
one flesh.*
—GEN. 2:24

The transition from adolescent living at home to independent adult is one of society's hardest rites of passage. On numerous occasions marital relationships suffer because one or both of the partners have not separated successfully from their family of origin. The result is a marriage involving parents *and* spouses as heads of the house with a chaotic chain of command.

Cecil was still very attached to his mother. When he and his wife Jean would argue he would leave and stay with his mother. Disagreements were rarely fully resolved, and Jean had become bitter. There was little she could say about the matter because Cecil would leave when the discussion became slightly heated. Jean felt like she was arguing not only with him, but also with his mother.

Cecil rationalized his dependency on his mother by citing her health, her age, or her impending death. He saw the problem as Jean's jealousy of his mother. However, he was actually having difficulty becoming an independent adult.

Have you made the transition from your childhood to independence?

*Then Jacob tore his clothes, put sackcloth on his
waist, and mourned for his son many days. And all
his sons and all his daughters arose to comfort
him; but he refused to be comforted, and he said,
"For I shall go down into the grave to my son in
mourning." Thus his father wept for him.*
                                        —GEN. 37:34–35

Losses in life can leave us feeling isolated, scared, and
out of control. We may even feel spiritually and emotionally weak because we feel distressed and angry.
Others say things like "Look at the bright side," "It's all
in God's plan," or "Don't let it get you down." Although
people usually say these things with good intentions,
they deny our feelings. These words can also produce
feelings of guilt and shame when we do experience
feelings of sadness.

In general, our society does not allow for the open
expression of genuine grief. It can be squelched even
further in families where the expression of emotion is
prohibited altogether. Unfortunately, if we do not acknowledge the pain related to loss and express this
pain openly, we may find ourselves going to great
lengths to avoid our feelings. In addition, angry outbursts and deep-seated bitterness may develop.

We are not spiritually or emotionally weak for having intense feelings of sadness, sorrow, or even anger
when we lose something or someone that is significant
to us. We need to give ourselves permission to grieve
our losses on our own time schedule.

God, please give me the strength to grieve my losses honestly.

> *When I kept silent, my bones grew old*
> *Through my groaning all the day long.*
> —PS. 32:3

When people come into treatment, they are typically very quiet and stay pretty much to themselves. Before long, though, the silence is broken, and it seems as if a floodgate of feelings, thoughts, and regrets has been opened. Many times part of the problem was their insistence to keep their problems to themselves and not burden anyone else with them. They gradually began to realize that they felt more and more alone. Keeping silent wasn't working. No doubt they felt very much like David in this passage above.

This same process can occur during maintenance, but the reason is sometimes different. You may begin to think that you have a better handle on your problems, and you *should* be able to handle them. So, instead of talking when you need to, you keep silent and work alone. That isn't the solution either. Even if you *have* the handle on the problem, it is important to go to others for support and encouragement.

It is important to remain accountable to someone in failure as well as success.

The LORD God is my strength;
He will make my feet like deer's feet,
And He will make me walk on my high hills.
—HAB. 3:19

Have you ever seen a deer in the wild? In addition to being pretty animals, they are very nimble and agile. Even in rough terrain deer are capable of rapidly eluding danger with a grace and ease uncommon to most other animals. Imagine a dairy cow attempting to gracefully scamper through the woods or rocky heights. Seems ludicrous, doesn't it?

At times, however, when starting the recovery process one can feel more like a large, encumbered animal than a deer. With the magnitude of unresolved issues and the seemingly long journey facing you, it may feel entirely impossible. From the base, a mountain can appear to be a great distance, and the weight of your concerns adds an additional hindrance. Giving up certainly may seem easier than taking the first step.

This is why you need your higher power as a fellow traveler on your climb. Your fear that the journey is impossible might be quite correct, if you rely only on your own strength. With God's strength, on the other hand, you can be more like the deer, and the climb will be much easier.

God, give me your strength as I begin my climb through difficult terrain.

> *Train up a child in the way he should go,*
> *And when he is old he will not depart from it.*
> —PROV. 22:6

Parenting is an awesome responsibility. It requires self-sacrificing, patience, and maturity. For many of us, these ingredients were missing in our parents as they raised us. Their parenting skills were likely based on the way their parents raised them. Sincere support, nurture, and appropriate discipline may have been missing in their childhoods and subsequently missing in yours.

Lyle was raised in a family with parents who had few parenting skills and little desire to be appropriate parents. Neither parent took time to teach Lyle age-appropriate tasks while he was growing up. As a result of the emotional neglect, Lyle had a great deal of difficulty coping in life.

Lyle eventually attended counseling for depression at the age of twenty-five. He was startled by the counselor's sincere desire to pay attention to his needs. Lyle soon learned that although his parents were non-nurturing, he could choose to reparent himself. He did so by attending counseling, being involved with support groups, and having a personal relationship with God—someone who always cares for him. Lyle did not have to be "stuck" emotionally because his parents neglected their responsibilities. Lyle could use other options.

***

Choosing to reparent ourselves may be the best choice we can make.

When my spirit was overwhelmed within me,
Then You knew my path.
In the way in which I walk
They have secretly set a snare for me.
—PS. 142:3

Have you ever been to a national monument with a guide to show you around? Maybe you have been on a camping trip where you needed someone who knew the territory to guide you. When you are on a strenuous journey, it is consoling to know that you have someone with you who has been there before. He or she can encourage you to keep going because the end is coming soon.

The same is true of your journey to health. You have a traveling companion who knows the trials you face. God truly knows what is ahead, and he can encourage us to keep going. We can find many different kinds of encouragement along our journey that God in his mercy provides for us. It could come in the form of a support person who calls just when you need her to so that you can talk about your trials. Or God may give you the courage to call your support person to talk and get the encouragement you need right then. It is a tremendous encouragement and consolation that he knows the way!

When we grow faint, God knows the way and will encourage us.

> *Let patience have its perfect work, that you may be*
> *perfect and complete, lacking nothing.*
> —JAMES 1:4

If you come from a dysfunctional family, follow-through is something foreign. You have a tendency to take on new tasks but never finish any. Often this characteristic is one that makes recovery most difficult.

When you come from a family where little you do is valued or nothing is ever enough, it becomes easy to give up before completion. You are especially sensitive to any hint of disapproval from others, and you tend to quit rather than face rejection. Thus there is a lot of unfinished business and many loose threads in your life. When you reach a difficult portion of recovery, there will be a strong urge to quit.

Remember that difficulty and adversity ultimately build true strength. Quitting too soon means strength never has time to develop. Be ready for these difficult times and recognize your tendency to give up before completion. Recovery will be hard, but the strength you develop will be worth the investment.

God, help me to see the strength you are developing in me before I give up.

Do not let the sun go down on your wrath.
—EPH. 4:26

Feeling and expressing our anger is not a pleasant experience. In fact, many of us avoid dealing with our anger at all costs. Experts say anger is the most frequently avoided emotion. Professional therapists agree that a lot of therapy time is spent getting in touch with anger that has been avoided for years.

Unfortunately, the more we avoid anger, the worse it gets. Anger does not go away as we attempt to ignore it; in fact, it builds up like steam pressure in a closed container—sooner or later it will blow. The sudden explosion of anger is referred to as the volcano syndrome. Unfortunately, some unsuspecting person usually receives the brunt of our anger in a distorted and exaggerated manner. Someone usually ends up hurt, and relationships may be irreparably damaged.

To escape the volcano syndrome, we must do as the verse states above. We need to address our anger before it builds up and explodes. This means we need to deal with it as it occurs, which is often on a daily basis. God is aware of the dangerous consequences which result from anger that is ignored or allowed to fester.

Resolving our anger begins with facing it, not avoiding it.

Therefore, my beloved brethren, be steadfast, immovable,
always abounding in the work of the Lord, knowing
that your labor is not in vain in the Lord.

—1 COR. 15:58

Have you ever been in a bathroom where the water cuts off after being on awhile? In order to keep the water running you have to keep pushing the knob down. If you're not careful, you will get halfway through washing your hands, and not have any water!

That is exactly what maintenance of the new behavior is like. You have to watch and gauge when the supply of support is waning so that you can replenish it. The maintenance of healthy behavior requires ongoing vigilance and perseverance to facilitate the growth process. You cannot assume that others will be as watchful as you about your supply of energy and motivation. Even those in a support group with you are not as sensitive to your needs as you will be if you maintain such vigilance.

Your labor will not be in vain—it will produce growth and change toward healthier behaviors. This may not always translate into happiness and a continuous sense of well-being, but it will produce growth.

Stand firm and keep vigilant for the lessening of motivation to change.

But Martha was distracted with much serving, and she approached Him and said, "Lord, do You not care that my sister has left me to serve alone? Therefore tell her to help me." —LUKE 10:40

Upset that she was doing all the work by herself, Martha became angry at her sister. Mary's priorities were quite different, she was satisfied to listen to Christ talk, she was busy having her spiritual needs met. This was infuriating to Martha, who was anxiously taking care of everyone.

Martha was clearly codependent. Her value was firmly set in the work she was doing, and she became increasingly angry at her sister who did not do the same thing. Furthermore, she did not confront her sister directly; she angrily went to someone else.

Rather than support her dysfunctional behavior, Jesus confronted her. She was neglecting the important thing, her spiritual growth, while furiously trying to care for others. Like Martha, codependents spend far too much time neglecting their own important needs, while trying to please others. In the long run, this never brings happiness, only frustration and anger.

Help me, Lord, to get my priorities straight. Rather than constantly caring for others teach me to care for my own needs, spiritual and physical.

> *"But they all with one accord began to make excuses. The first said to him, 'I have bought a piece of ground, and I must go and see it. I ask you to have me excused.' And another said, 'I have bought five yoke of oxen, and I am going to test them. I ask you to have me excused.' Still another said, 'I have married a wife and therefore I can't come.'"*
>
> —LUKE 14:18–20

This verse describes three men who gave several excuses for not being able to attend a banquet. Their various personal activities took precedence. Jesus explained this parable in reference to his kingdom. Some people will simply choose other interests in life over God. Individuals who are tied to compulsive behaviors are excellent examples of those who do not make Christ's kingdom their first priority.

Compulsive behaviors consume our time, energy, and thoughts. In fact, they can appear to become our sole purpose for living. They become the center of our lives and keep our lives out of balance. Because we become so consumed by our compulsions and addictions, we lose our perspectives in life. God is easily forgotten in the process.

Forgetting God is the alarming consequence of being caught in the cycle of compulsive behavior. A recovering codependent once stated that the only way he made it from day to day was to acknowledge God several times throughout the day. By choosing to acknowledge and trust God each day, he was able to keep his life in the proper balance.

God, help me to keep my relationship with you my first priority.

> *"Give ear, Job, and listen to me;*
> *Hold your peace, and I will speak."*
> —JOB 33:31

My daughter and I would often go for a walk in the woods near our home. She would chatter on and on about the things that were important in her life at the time. Before long I would tell her to be quiet so that we could hear the sounds of the forest. It was only after we stopped walking, sat down, and stayed quiet that we began to hear the many sounds and rustlings that characterize the woods in fall. I believe this is what God meant when he said, "Be still and know that I am God."

Stillness is a very important quality to develop in ourselves. We can often drown out the voice of God by our chattering. Sometimes we don't like the silence. Perhaps we keep the noise level up to distract ourselves from the turmoil that is brewing inside us. It may also be a way to not hear God guide us in a direction we don't want to go.

I think this is what God had in mind when he told Job to keep quiet. He wanted Job to listen without distraction. In his silence Job could fully comprehend what God had to say to him. We must develop that ability as well—to quiet ourselves so that we might know God more fully.

It is important to be still so that you can listen more closely to God.

> [*Moses chose*] *rather to suffer affliction with the*
> *people of God than to enjoy the passing pleasures*
> *of sin.*
> —HEB. 11:25

Cindy entered therapy because she knew she had difficulty choosing healthy patterns. For her it was easier to go for the short-term benefits rather than to wait for the long-term good. She knew this was counterproductive. She had experienced pain and fear as a result of her impulsive decision-making, but she continued to focus on immediate satisfaction.

It was understandable. She saw herself as a victim, being controlled by outside forces, rather than as a survivor who was able to exert influence on people and things in her life. Because of this view she made choices for her life that gave her as much temporary pleasure as possible. These choices often had negative consequences weeks and months later.

Cindy feared that if she began to live with a long-term perspective, she would have to give up her personal happiness altogether. In her eyes, life was so difficult anyway she didn't wish to try new behaviors, so she resisted facing her pain. Sometimes change can be hard at first, but like Moses knew, this is a necessary part of establishing healthy patterns for the future.

Is your temporary focus on immediate happiness impairing opportunities for future health?

So let each one give as he purposes in his heart, not grudgingly or of necessity; for God loves a cheerful giver. —2 COR. 9:7

Today someone might ask you to do something for them. It may be your child, spouse, friend, or employer. Perhaps you will be asked to do something you really should say no to because of time constraints, feelings of uneasiness, or inability to complete the task. Will you respond with yes instead of no simply because you feel obligated to do so?

Unfortunately, many of us make our decisions based on a perceived obligation. We believe that it is our responsibility to perform for others, take care of others, or solve the problems of others. Internally, we fear rejection or abandonment if we choose to say no. By failing to set our limits, we inevitably set ourselves up to be resentful and bitter.

The verse above uses the word *grudgingly* to describe our attitude when we do something out of guilt or obligation, rather than from a true desire to give. When we agree to the requests of others, we need to assess our motives for what we are doing. Are we saying yes to avoid rejection or gain approval, or out of obligation to keep others happy? These are the wrong motives. When we agree to help others out of real care and concern, we are giving in a way that pleases God.

Lord, help me to respond honestly to the requests of others.

> *Stand fast therefore in the liberty by which Christ*
> *has made us free, and do not be entangled again*
> *with a yoke of bondage.*
> —GAL. 5:1

The year 1990 was a momentous year in the history of the world. We saw millions of people freed who had been enslaved behind the Iron Curtain. I will never forget seeing people knocking holes in the Berlin Wall, the same wall that people had been killed for climbing over.

The year may have been momentous for you as well. Some walls of your own may have been breached and broken down. But your job has just begun. It is important not to let yourself be taken captive again by the old ways. You need a firm foundation to stand on. That is what treatment has been for you—a firm foundation from which to withstand the influences that would push you back into your old way of life.

You also need to establish the necessary reinforcements that will assure continued progress and growth. These might be support groups, personal journaling, or meeting with someone for accountability. Any of these would serve to reinforce healthy patterns of thinking and behaving. The key is that you plan to stand firm and be free!

Father, help me to stand firm and be free.

He who keeps you will not slumber.
—PS. 121:3

The first three of the twelve steps of recovery from dysfunctional patterns provide the basis for the rest of the process. Succinctly stated they are: "I can't, he can, so here goes!" All recovery hinges on the ability to give up our need to control while allowing an all-powerful God to be in charge of our recovery. While many acknowledge this to be true in principle, in practice it is hard to loosen the grip on old, reliable controlling patterns.

Behind this often is our fear that God cannot do the trick. We fear that God will desert us if we give up control to him. Rather than take this risk, we continue patterns that are not helpful, and usually we contribute to the problem rather than fix it.

Not only is God all-powerful, he does not sleep. He is busy watching out for you twenty-four hours every day, making certain that you are safe always as you trust him throughout the entire recovery process. It is safe to take the plunge because God is always there.

Do you fear that God will not be there when you need him? How does this impede your ability to let him be in charge of your recovery?

When my father and mother forsake me,
Then the LORD will take care of me.
—PS. 27:10

One of the biggest myths in life is that parents are always dependable, trustworthy, and loving. Sometimes we tend to put parents on a pedestal, thinking they are the closest thing to God. We may think parents can do no wrong, and if they make a mistake, we rationalize that they meant well.

Some of us reading this know from personal experience that parents are not perfect. Parents do make mistakes. Unfortunately, parents can disappoint us and sometimes hurt us. Also, their intentions may not always be admirable when they harm us in some way.

Some of us have difficulty accepting the fact that our parents made mistakes and, in some cases, abused us. Subsequently, we continue to put them on a pedestal and pursue a relationship with them, even when they continue to abuse us or reject us.

Parents make mistakes because they are human. The verse above indicates our need to realize two principles. The first is that our parents will forsake us at times in our lives; we can count on it. The second is that God is there for us, consistently and willingly. Unlike our human parents, God is always trustworthy, dependable, and loving. We need to pursue our relationship with God, instead of trying to force our parents to change.

Lord, help me to let go of any distorted view I have of my parents, and accept your love and caring for me.

*Looking diligently lest anyone fall short of the
grace of God; lest any root of bitterness springing
up cause trouble, and by this many become defiled.*
—HEB. 12:15

Imagine that you look out onto your yard and see a
sea of dandelions. They seem to multiply in a matter of
hours. This weed has an incredible tenacity to survive
the most toxic chemicals, and we are told this is mostly
because of its root system.

Many of our old habits of codependency are much
like the dandelion. They, too, are incredibly resilient to
any attempts to change them. Even after we have identified where they are and made changes, they are still
there waiting for the next opportunity to spring up
again. Their roots run deep. Even after the flower has
been destroyed, the danger still awaits.

Begin to deal with the roots of these habits. Then
after the initial attack on these habits, expect a second
wave to occur. If you expect it, you will then be able to
respond effectively. Don't panic just because the roots
aren't all gone the first time. Be patient, expect more
to come, and respond with deliberateness.

The key to effective weed control is effective root control.

> *The authorities that exist are appointed by God.*
> *Therefore whoever resists the authority resists the*
> *ordinance of God.*
> —ROM. 13:1–2

Don took pride in bucking authority. A boss could expect a long litany of questions when asking him to do even a relatively straightforward task as well as reasons why the task was stupid. Friends knew that Don would aggressively pursue any topic until it became an argument. Frankly, it was a chore to have Don around.

Questioning the reasons behind things is not always wrong; often it can result in new solutions to old problems. For Don, however, the motivation was not always correct. His constant challenges resulted from feelings that he was not as good as those around him. Instead of acknowledging this to himself directly, he tried to bring people down to the level at which he perceived himself to be.

Naturally this initially made change difficult for him. His poor attitude toward authority figures also made it hard to surrender his will and compulsions to God. Submission to God's power and intervention means a simultaneous recognition that God has placed some people in authority over you. Therefore, rebelling against them is like rebelling against God.

Help me, God, to recognize the legitimacy of those you have placed in authority over me.

For since the creation of the world His invisible attributes are clearly seen, being understood by the things that are made, even His eternal power and Godhead, so that they are without excuse.
—ROM. 1:20

A significant aspect of recovery is based on developing our understanding of God. This understanding can be especially difficult when we grow up in chaotic homes. In many of these homes, hypocritical parents pretend to be great moral people in public and then fight with each other and abuse the children in private. If these same parents are faithful church attenders, we children may make statements like the following. "If that is what their God is all about, I don't want anything to do with him!" We may doubt the existence of God because we prayed so many times as children. After not perceiving any response, we incorrectly concluded that God didn't exist.

Unfortunately, some of us carry our childish conclusions into adulthood. When we do this, we limit our ability to reach toward God, who can free us from past unhealthy choices. Although we may deny or ignore the concept of God because of our family background, the verse above challenges us to look at other evidence that points toward his existence. As we begin to see God in his created world, we can begin to accept the idea that he is able to help us make positive decisions.

God, help me to distinguish between my emotional pain and your eternal existence:

> *But also for this very reason, giving all diligence,*
> *add to your faith virtue, to virtue knowledge.*
>   2 PETER 1:5

Putting oneself in a position to learn requires some degree of humility. We have to swallow our pride and admit that someone may know something we don't, and we must listen to what that person has to say.

One of the healthiest qualities of a strong maintenance program is the ongoing thirst for knowledge about the recovery process and about yourself. The more you can learn in this way, the better your recovery program becomes. With knowledge one is able to assess more accurately, react more effectively, and follow through with more balance.

These qualities show in any endeavor. Think about the student who is a beginning medical student and the doctor who has been in practice for many years. The difference is striking. The doctor who has learned through practice is more adept. His rate of error is much lower simply because of the accumulation of knowledge over the years. The same is true with your maintenance program. If you are willing to be a student of your experiences, you will be in a better position to take action when you need to.

Be a student of your recovery and use your experiences to add to your knowledge of recovery and maintenance.

> *"Ask and it will be given to you; seek, and you will find; knock, and it will be opened to you. For everyone who asks receives, and he who seeks finds, and to him who knocks it will be opened."*
> —MATT. 7:7–8

One healthy behavior that many codependents need to discover is assertiveness. You may feel that rejection will occur if you stand up for what you believe. Asking for your needs to be met is out of the question, so you simply meet everyone else's needs but neglect your own.

This can lead to anger and frustration. But, due to a lack of assertiveness, you may only express your anger indirectly. Your needs are important, having them met will result in happiness. However, the only way this will happen is if you take the initiative and ask for this.

At first you may experience guilt when asking for what you need. On the other hand, not asking makes certain that you continue feeling angry and neglected. See the guilt as it is, an impediment to avoiding a dysfunctional pattern of always caring for others while neglecting yourself.

In the past twenty-four hours, were there times you neglected yourself but became angry and frustrated taking care of others? What could you have done differently?

> *A soft answer turns away wrath,*
> *But a harsh word stirs up anger.*
> —PROV. 15:1

Resolving our anger in a healthy manner promotes growth in ourselves and in our relationships. On the other hand, attempting to resolve our anger by attacking another person often stirs up more animosity.

John learned that a healthy way to deal with his anger was to first take ownership of it. In the past, John accused his wife of *making* him angry. Therefore, if he followed his logic through, it was his wife's responsibility to undo John's anger.

When John began to take responsibility for his anger, he realized he needed to learn new skills to resolve it. What worked the best for him was to identify and verbalize his anger as soon as he felt it. This meant he began to use "I" statements instead of "you" accusations. He said, "I feel angry and hurt," instead of "You make me angry." Next, John learned to describe the behavior that was affecting him instead of attacking the person doing the behavior. He also learned to offer a solution to the problem instead of demanding that the other person change.

John's new communication skills proved to be very beneficial in helping him manage his anger. The steps outlined above are healthy ones to use because they lead to conflict resolution.

Dear God, help me to talk about my anger in ways that lead to restored relationships.

"Then the master of that servant was moved with compassion, released him, and forgave him the debt."
—MATT. 18:27

What is the hardest thing about forgiveness for you? Is it that you can't be sure that the person is going to change? Are there times that you have withheld your forgiveness in order to use it as a tool to get somebody to ask for forgiveness?

Many of my clients have been abused in one way or another. One client told me she couldn't forgive a man for what he had done to her because if she did, that meant that she approved of what he had done. So, she held on to her rage in the vain hope that someday he would beg for forgiveness and she would be finally vindicated.

Forgiveness continues to be an issue throughout treatment and recovery. We tend to want revenge and the satisfaction of seeing our abuser crawling to us for forgiveness. If we were to look closely at our *real* motives, I think we would find that there are times when we don't trust God to be a righteous judge. So we take the law into our own hands, and we pronounce judgment and verdict. We desire justice, and sometimes we feel we are the only ones who know what justice really is. We should leave justice to a judge who can be truly fair and righteous.

―――――――

Father, help me to forgive others like you have forgiven me.

> *But godliness with contentment is great gain.*
> 1 TIM. 6:6

Having grown up poor, William vowed not to let poverty ever affect his family in the way it did him. He had attributed the conflict during his childhood to the fact that there was never enough money. He set out as an adult to earn enough to keep his family living in comfortable style.

The rest of the family was feeling tremendous resentment toward the workaholic William had become. He felt hurt and somewhat bitter that no one appreciated the way he provided for their needs. Actually, they didn't have the one thing they all felt they needed—a father.

In resolving past hurts and conflicts, people often go to the other extreme from childhood. In this case William had fought so hard to avoid poverty that he had become almost a nonexistent member of the family.

In order to resolve the problem that had arisen, William needed to balance the need of his family for money with the need of his family for a father. Then he could begin the process of recovery by setting limits on his workaholic tendencies.

Lord, help me to be content with the things I do have, rather than allowing myself to strive for things I don't need.

The young man said to Him, "All these things I have kept from my youth. What do I still lack?" Jesus said to him, "If you want to be perfect, go, sell what you have and give to the poor, and you will have treasure in heaven; and come, follow Me." But when the young man heard that saying, he went away sorrowful, for he had great possessions.
—MATT. 19:20–22

These verses give us insight into the true nature of man. The rich man described above displayed a desire to have God be the center of his life. But Jesus could see that he was holding onto a significant source of personal security, his money. The young man's unwillingness to surrender this revealed his true character.

As a counselor, I have learned to anticipate what I term "surprise secrets." Surprise secrets are new and important pieces of information being confessed by an individual after he has been in counseling for some time. These revelations often involve being entangled in chemical, food, or sexual addictions. If kept hidden, the individual cannot make healthy choices in the future.

Tom came to counseling complaining of depression. He seemed open and willing to address his issues, but when Tom did not respond to therapy, his counselor suspected Tom was hiding something. When confronted, Tom admitted to being involved in an affair during the past two years. He was promptly asked to end the affair. Tom refused to do so and left counseling prematurely.

God, give me the courage to surrender every area of my life to you.

*And my God shall supply all your need according
to His riches in glory by Christ Jesus.*

—PHIL. 4:19

To whom are you looking to meet *all* your needs? Is it your spouse, your best friend, your children, your fiancé? Maybe it's your job, hobby, or even your status. Whatever it is, we will slowly get out of balance if we seek one thing or person to meet all our needs.

People who struggle with boundary issues are people who are trying to control others to meet their needs. They do all that is within their power to guarantee that another person likes them, needs them, and wants them. They do this by submitting their every desire and want to the other person. If there is any conflict whatsoever, the other person's desires win out. So, if in the presence of this significant person they are asked for an opinion, they might say, "What do you think?" Upon hearing the response, they will promptly agree.

The person who does this is saying to God, "I don't trust you to meet my needs. Therefore, I will do what I must to get these overwhelming needs met for myself." Remember to trust God to meet *all* your needs according to the riches he has.

Dear God, help me to trust you to meet my needs through many instead of only one person in my life.

*Do not lie to one another, since you have put off
the old man with his deeds, and have put on the
new man.* —COL. 3:9–10

The goal of recovery is to become a new you. Had you
been satisfied with the old self, you would not have
embarked on this journey. Letting go of old practices is
certainly hard; being completely honest is even harder.
There are so many things to cover up: guilt, vulnerability, fear, irresponsibility, and control. To admit these is
difficult, especially when it requires telling others.

For many years you have covered up underlying
feelings and tried to be independent. This did not lead
to freedom and is now obsolete. Recovery requires you
to be honest about yourself and accountable to others.
When confronted with hard times you will tend to be
less than honest. This is an old habit, one of the compulsive patterns from the past.

Watch out! Old habits die hard. When you begin
practicing even the most benign behaviors of the past
you are in danger of slipping in your recovery. Be honest not only with yourself, but with others. Tell several
people you trust. If they confront you when these old
patterns occur, listen to them. Dishonesty means you
have begun to give up on the change process.

Keep me truthful even when I feel afraid to be honest.

> *Therefore gird up the loins of your mind, be sober,*
> *and rest your hope fully upon the grace that is to*
> *be brought to you at the revelation of Jesus Christ.*
> 1 PETER 1:13

The difference between where we want to be in life and where we are is usually determined by a lot of hard work. It takes more than a creative thought or a good idea to accomplish our goals—it takes action. The same applies to those of us desiring to make healthy choices. We may clearly know what we want to do, but we may choose not to follow through for a variety of reasons.

Often, with codependents talk is cheap and action is rare. Usually an individual comes into a treatment program in desperation. He is often anxious about his poor physical health or about losing his job or family. At the beginning of treatment he makes several promises to change his behaviors and make healthier choices in the future. Within a couple of weeks or so the pain of his desperation has subsided. Then he takes back the promises he made earlier, saying, "It was not that bad."

We need to search our own lives and ask the question, "Do we prepare our minds for talk or for action?" It's essential to have a determined attitude that our actions will demonstrate healthy choices. Some of us may be afraid of actually following through with healthy choices and boundaries. The verse above gives comfort for us as we put our hope in God's grace, not our fears.

Remember, talk is cheap if it is not followed by action.

Indeed we count them blessed who endure. You have heard of the perseverance of Job and seen the end intended by the Lord—that the Lord is very compassionate and merciful.   —JAMES 5:11

Perseverance is certainly the key to maintaining healthy patterns of behavior. But perseverance is hard and sometimes unglamorous. We have a great example of perseverance in Job. He persevered in his faithfulness to God in spite of his impatience for justice. There is much that we have in common with Job throughout recovery, but particularly during the maintenance phase.

First of all, we will always have our detractors who will make life pretty difficult for us. They will find every reason to give us some of their most qualified advice as to how we could do better. They aren't like Job's counselors who did their best work during the first seven days when they kept quiet!

Second, we will sometimes question God's justice and faithfulness. Will he reward the work that I am doing? Does he see what hard work this is to change? Like Job, we must hang on to God's character and remember his compassion and mercy. Those are the qualities that we can depend on, just like Job, to help us persevere.

———

Lord, help me to persevere as I maintain my healthy behaviors.

> *"When they had pasture, they were filled;*
> *They were filled and their heart was exalted;*
> *Therefore they forgot Me."* —HOS. 13:6

Angie entered therapy seeking fulfillment. She was motivated and accomplished a lot in a short period of time. Her progress was satisfying to not only her, but also to her family, friends, and therapists. She felt so good that she decided she was strong enough to quit.

Now, Angie had reason to be excited. Indeed, she was quite successful at grasping a new way of life. It wasn't long, however, before she was back. It had been too soon for lasting change; she experienced spontaneous remission, a temporary cessation of symptoms early in treatment.

Most people find quick relief having someone care and listen to them. If you mistake this for lasting change, you stop looking to God and can become satisfied with what seems to be strength. Don't stop acknowledging God as your power source. Recognize spontaneous remission and keep working until long-term change has occurred.

Keep me humble enough to recognize you as the true source of lasting change. Keep me from relying on my own feeble power as I successfully accomplish my goals.

For I will declare my iniquity;
I will be in anguish over my sin.
—PS. 38:18

Confession plays a significant role in the healing process of recovery. The act of confession was especially emphasized in the early church. Unfortunately, some individuals seeking forgiveness through confession do so only to seek immediate relief from guilt. Since these same people are not truly troubled by the impact of their actions on others, a change of behavior does not follow.

A retired man attended Mass daily at his church. During this time he made confessions for his actions of the previous day. When he returned home, he began to drink his vodka and tonic. As usual, he eventually began to fight with his family. Each day of fighting usually ended with him pushing and bruising his wife. The next morning he returned to confession and began the cycle again.

When this man finally received professional help for his alcoholism, he thought that if he just confessed everything he did wrong, he would be free to go home. Of course, he became very angry with the staff when they wanted more from him than just his confession. This man had to learn to take the time to examine his actions closely and to be aware of the intense pain he had inflicted on his family. The knowledge of this pain would lead to a sincere confession and a change in action.

Lord, help me to heal from confession rather than hide behind it.

> *Finally, my brethren, be strong in the Lord and in the power of His might.*
> —EPH. 6:10

It takes a great deal of courage to be a mountain climber. Few mountain climbers make their ascent alone. They are always in groups, and they take a ton of equipment. Actually, though, they have meticulously prepared for their ascent and there is little they are carrying that they won't use. It is all very calculated.

Every one of us is a mountain climber. We all have mountains to face, but some of you make it tougher on yourselves than it needs to be. Imagine for a moment the mountain climber who begins to climb and realizes that the top of the mountain is getting farther away. What a discouraging realization! How many would give up in complete despair?

You might be one of those who unknowingly does that to yourself. The measure of your success is never reached, because with each success you raise the standard higher. There is no sense of reaching a goal because the goal is always changing! If this sounds familiar you may have to work with friends and support people to set goals, leave them be, and allow yourself to enjoy it when you attain your goal.

Set a goal, work toward it, and celebrate the success once you achieve it.

> *"For if you forgive men their trespasses, your
> heavenly Father will also forgive you."*
> —MATT. 6:14

I feel like I must have committed the unforgivable sin.
I constantly feel guilty even though I have asked hundreds of times for forgiveness from God." This is a common sentiment expressed in therapy. Many individuals have felt that they are too bad to merit God's grace. Frankly, God quickly forgives the first time someone asks. However, often the guilt feelings linger.

For some the cause is projection. They feel they cannot forgive certain individuals, so they hold on to bitterness and anger over past wrongs far too long. Then they project this onto God, mistakenly perceiving God to be like themselves, unable to forgive them.

To combat this kind of projection, one needs to begin practicing forgiveness of others. As one begins to let go of the bitterness, granting forgiveness, a feeling of tremendous relief may result. Forgiving others has an added side effect: often forgiveness will begin to flow inward to oneself.

Begin making a list of people you have difficulty forgiving and start asking God for assistance in granting forgiveness to them as well as to yourself.

> *Do not hasten in your spirit to be angry,*
> *For anger rests in the bosom of fools.*
> —ECCL. 7:9

Take a moment and think of the last time you became angry. What did you do with your anger? How did you express it? Was it resolved or are you still angry about it? If you struggle with anger, as many people do, you are probably grimacing at your responses to these questions.

A young man named Mitch had a terrible time dealing with his anger. It seemed that as soon as he felt slighted in any way by another person, he became extremely angry. He expressed his anger by attacking the other person verbally. Mitch eventually sought counseling after losing his eighth job in two years.

In counseling, Mitch realized that much of his anger could have been avoided if he had only asked a few clarifying questions. Also, he realized that he needed to be a more patient listener. Most important of all, Mitch began to understand that the way he handled his anger was causing him to make unhealthy choices in his life. He could now see the damage it caused himself and others.

We need to learn the same lessons Mitch learned. Instead of allowing our anger to control us, we need to control it by being better listeners and choosing our words carefully.

Lord, help me to develop patience in my listening and my speech.

But if you have bitter envy and self-seeking in your
hearts, do not boast and lie against the truth.
—JAMES 3:14

Bitterness is one of the hardest issues to overcome in counseling people struggling with boundary issues. It is always shrouded by denial and defensiveness. Any single hurt or disappointment in how others have treated you has the potential to make you bitter.

Why is this such a difficult issue to address in counseling? One of the reasons is that it is often cloaked in self-righteousness and justification. People defend themselves, saying, "Well, I have a good right to be angry." This process is a formula for relapse. Suddenly, you are back to making your actions dependent on someone else. Instead of going to that person directly, you attempt to draw her into an interaction so that you can extract your pound of flesh for her insensitivity.

The solution? Grace. Grace does not mean that you must become a doormat. Instead it means that you offer the transgressing person an opportunity to heal the relationship and approach her with your concern. In so doing, you will also be continuing your progress toward recovery.

Father, help me to offer myself and others grace to prevent bitterness.

> *And those who know Your name will put*
> *their trust in You;*
> *For You, LORD, have not forsaken those*
> *who seek You.*   —PS. 9:10

Celia looked at the twelve steps of recovery with dismay. Change for her would mean risking something she greatly feared: rejection. It was much easier to play it safe, to continue isolating herself from God and others. She was afraid to chance the possibility that after she made changes, she would come up empty. She would rather be certain that it would work before jumping into something that could hurt.

One of the most important parts of recovery for Celia would be trusting God, but this was frightening for her. In her past, trust almost always meant being abandoned and then feeling the hurt of loneliness. It was like jumping into a safety net that she feared would be pulled away at the last moment.

Celia was not alone. Many who first enter recovery face this fear of abandonment. But you need not fear rejection. If you seek God you will find him, and you will not be left to face your pain alone. God does not abandon those who ask for his help.

Tell God that you are holding him responsible to be true to the promise that he will not leave as you place your trust in his healing power.

I will instruct you and teach you in the way you should go;
I will guide you with My eye. —PS. 32:8

God cares about the choices we make in life. In fact, he cares so much that he promises to instruct us, teach us, counsel us, and watch over us when we need to make decisions. Some of us have a perception that God is distant and removed from our day-to-day problems. If we believe God is impersonal and distant, we have chosen to eliminate the one resource we have to give us guidance and courage to make healthy choices on a daily basis.

Ginger did not believe God would guide her in her codependency recovery program on a daily basis. Her idea of God was distant and impersonal. Ginger thought God would only help her with major problems, and that if she wanted God's guidance, she would have to pray very hard, do penance often, and watch for a miraculous sign. Fortunately for us, God is not limited to working in our lives by only doing the miraculous.

As Ginger grew in her understanding of God's guidance, she began to believe that he truly wanted to help her daily. Her eyes opened up to a new understanding of how God works. She learned that God wanted to instruct her through his words in the Bible, through prayer, and through her involvement in her church and support groups.

We need to allow God to help us on his terms and not on our own.

> *"And now I urge you to take heart, for there will be no loss of life among you."*
> —ACTS 27:22

Sometimes it is hard to be encouraged. We feel so down on ourselves and our situation that any words of encouragement seem to be useless. For us to encourage others is no problem, because that is what we are good at. But for us to *be encouraged* doesn't work somehow.

Somewhere along the line, we have come to believe that we don't deserve to be encouraged. It doesn't feel right. To be encouraged by someone else would mean being indebted to them, and that would mean that we are worthy of that debt. We don't believe that, though. So, we do what we can to stay out of debt. The result is that we continually seek to keep others in need of us, as a hedge against the future.

Encouragement is a vital part of the recovery maintenance process. We need to be willing to be encouraged by others in order to remember just how precious we are to others as well as to God. That may mean allowing ourselves to feel indebted to others and their love for us. We are not necessarily at a disadvantage just because we allow ourselves to be encouraged.

Lord, help me to accept your love and others' love for me.

*And when they had mocked Him, they took the
purple off Him, put His own clothes on Him, and
led Him out to crucify Him.* —MARK 15:20

A scapegoat is a very difficult role to play. In dysfunctional families, often one child is identified as the problem and is singled out to be blamed for the craziness of the entire system. As a therapist, I recognize this as a form of denial whereby the family assuages their own pain by giving it away.

This especially is true with children and adolescents. They easily fall into the role, blaming themselves and trying to hold the family together by their problematic behavior. They have a strong sense of purpose: if the role is relinquished then the family will fall apart. They also have a sense of isolation in this role, because they believe that something is fundamentally wrong with them that no one else can understand.

God, however, can understand. He gave his only son to serve this role for all humanity. Jesus was shamed, falsely accused, rejected, and ultimately killed as a scapegoat for evil he was not a part of creating. With God's help you no longer have to be isolated in this role.

———

Thanks, God, for understanding the craziness of my family's dysfunction. Help me find the freedom from roles that add further to the dysfunction.

> *And Moses said to Aaron, "What did this people do*
> *to you that you have brought so great a sin upon*
> *them?" So Aaron said, "Do not let the anger of my*
> *lord become hot. You know the people, that they*
> *are set on evil."*   —EX. 32:21–22

A sad story was told one night in a church support-group meeting for battered wives. A petite, older lady explained her involvement in three physically abusive marriages. At the end of the story, the lady made a surprising statement. She told the group not to feel angry at her husbands because they had been abused as children by their fathers. She said, "That's just the way they are. They did not know any better. I can't be angry with them."

How many times have we made the same excuse for our own actions? Of course, we may use different words. We may make statements such as, "You can't teach an old dog new tricks," or "I'm stubborn and hot-headed. I'll never change." No matter how it is said, the idea remains the same. We convince ourselves it's acceptable to act and react the way we always do, because we've done it the same way in the past.

This is, of course, dangerous and irrational thinking. When we want to rely on the excuse, "That's the way I've always been," we need to stop ourselves and realize we do have choices as to how we want to behave.

Our past behaviors can serve either as an excuse not to change or as motivation to change.

> *In God I have put my trust;*
> *I will not be afraid.*
> *What can man do to me?*
> —PS. 56:11

What is the worst thing that can happen?" is a question that I ask my clients. The question is designed to get them to look at their fears realistically. It is also designed to force them to come up with solutions for the *worst* that could happen. Presumably, if they can solve the worst, then they can deal with anything less.

People struggling to define new boundaries are running from their worst fears. One of those fears is connected with what someone can do to them. A person can withdraw attention and care from them, and to them this is the worst thing that can happen. They wouldn't be able to survive. Catastrophic? Maybe, but real all the same.

So, what *can* a person do to me? A person can hurt me, reject me, and create a great deal of emotional pain. However, if I can find a place where I am safe and feel secure, then no matter what the worst is, I can handle it. It can be someone who has demonstrated reliability as a friend and confidant; better yet, it can be found in our relationship with God. Look at the psalmist's solution—trust in God. There is my safe haven of rest.

Courage is fear that has said its prayers.

> *"And God will wipe away every tear from their eyes; there shall be no more death, nor sorrow, nor crying; and there shall be no more pain, for the former things have passed away."* —REV. 21:4

I once heard a prominent Christian musician sing a song about being a stranger on the earth, "This world is not my home," he sang, "I'm just passin' through." Our world has more than its share of problems, which can be experienced as pain. Sometimes this pain becomes so intense that escape seems to be the only solution.

Lucy was an escape-oriented person. She had married young to escape her family, believing her dynamic and handsome boyfriend would fulfill the needs her family had failed to meet. It soon became apparent that she had married someone much like her father, and her fantasy of "happily ever after" was shattered. Since she did not believe in divorce, she could not escape. Lucy was stuck, and she had no other options at her disposal. She fell deep into a depressive quagmire.

Escape is a temporary solution to a problem that relies on one's own power to elude pain. Pain is part of our existence and an inescapable part of our reality. As Lucy began to realize this, she began to look beyond the current situation to the place where all pain would be gone and all tears would be wiped from her eyes.

Is this land your home, or are you "just passin' through"?

*Yes, we had the sentence of death in ourselves, that
we should not trust in ourselves but in God who
raises the dead.*　　　　　　　　　—2 COR. 1:9

Most people attempt to remedy a cold or other minor
illness without seeking professional assistance. However, these same individuals will ask for medical attention when they are in severe pain or are close to death.
Similarly, people such as addicts, alcoholics, and codependents often don't seek help from others until the
actual fear of death is present.

Most addicts, alcoholics and codependents enter
treatment after a suicide attempt, talk of suicide, or a
belief that their choices in life will soon lead to death.
Typical statements on the first day in treatment are, "I
feel so out of control," "Death seems like an option to
end the chaos and pain in my life," or "I can't handle it
anymore." They realize that they cannot rely on themselves alone to change their choices in life. They need
others and they need God.

If you feel your life is out of control, turn to God and
rely on him. If you try to change patterns of unhealthy
choices on your own, you will simply be *on your own*.

*God, help me to use my feelings of desperation as a signal that I need
to turn to you.*

> *"These things I have spoken to you, that in Me you may have peace. In the world you will have tribulation; but be of good cheer, I have overcome the world."*
> —JOHN 16:33

I just want to be happy and have a little peace!" a woman yelled as if she were in a gymnasium. It was in my office, and I waited for her anger to lessen before we began once again to look at her inability to stay on top of changes in her family. She had been doing a good job of setting limits on others' behavior toward her. She also seemed to be making strides in understanding how she was protecting others to protect herself. It seemed as if the timer had finally gone off. Her agenda was out of the bag.

She had mistakenly set her agenda to be happiness and peace in a given amount of time. When that didn't happen, she got instantly frustrated and very angry over a seemingly incidental issue.

So what is wrong with peace and happiness? Well, nothing, but that isn't necessarily what you are after in the long run. What you are after is recovery and growth in your spiritual walk. This may not always mean peace and happiness.

Set your sights on growth and recovery instead of happiness.

> *"I will be a Father to you,*
> *And you shall be My sons and daughters,*
> *Says the Lord Almighty."*
> —2 COR. 6:18

Peter's anger hinged on the rejection he felt from his parents. Both had been so invested in their own lives during his childhood that they had little time for him. In many ways he had raised himself, and he had done a fairly poor job. Few children are up to the task of adequately caring for themselves.

As an adolescent and young adult, he had become quite self-destructive. At one point he even shot himself in the stomach to attract his parents' attention. But when the crisis he created calmed down, his father again distanced himself. No matter what he tried, he could not make his parents meet his needs.

Peter needed a new parent, one who would pay attention before he had to take such drastic action. His deeply-rooted needs had to be met by someone who would not reject him. God has promised to be such a parent. His resources are more than adequate to meet neglected needs, and he will receive someone whose own parents have forsaken him.

Heavenly Father, free me from frustration with parents who did not do an adequate job parenting me. Be the parent I so strongly desire.

> *Let no one deceive you with empty words, for*
> *because of these things the wrath of God comes*
> *upon the sons of disobedience.* —EPH. 5:6

We all love attention, especially complimentary remarks. For some of us, these enticing words can present a real trap in terms of inappropriate boundaries. When we hear a number of flattering statements, we may believe that the speaker will provide us with positive interaction. As a result, we fail to investigate the healthiness of the relationship.

Jennette was recovering from a recent divorce. Her former husband was an alcoholic who left her for another woman. Jennette was devastated by the turn of events in her life. Within two months after her divorce, she met a friendly and outgoing man who lavished her with compliments about her looks, personality, and wit. Instead of taking time to get to know him more objectively, she became engaged and married within six months. During their first year of marriage, her husband's charm turned into abuse. Once again, Jennette found herself in a destructive marriage.

Some of us are like Jennette. We fall in love with anyone who reaches out to us. If we want to establish healthy boundaries, however, it's essential that we examine relationships carefully as they develop. In addition, we need to give ourselves permission to discontinue a relationship if we feel uncomfortable or if it is influencing us to make unwise, unhealthy choices.

Lord, give me discernment as I evaluate new relationships.

He heals the brokenhearted
And binds up their wounds.
—PS. 147:3

Have you ever seen a child come to her parent after she has hurt herself? The parent will ask to see the wound and the child will stretch out her wounded limb slowly, only to snatch it back before the parent can touch it! Isn't that the same way with us as we begin to let ourselves feel all the emotions that we have so carefully hidden from others?

As you maintain your progress in making new decisions, don't forget to do all the things you have learned so far. Allow yourself to feel. It is in the feeling that you can begin to experience not only the comfort from others but also the comfort from God himself. He promises to bind up your wounds, both past and present!

We are like children, who have just been hurt, our reflex is to retreat in order to control the hurt. That will be the case when you are confronted with a hurtful situation. Will you retreat, or will you be willing to stretch out your "wounded limb" and feel the comfort that is waiting?

Don't retreat—you will be cutting yourself off from the comfort of others and God.

There is no fear in love; but perfect love casts out fear.

—1 JOHN 4:18

Fearful people tend to be lonely people. It is difficult to engage in healthy love relationships when afraid. To one who was raised in a chaotic family where love really meant feeling guilt, enduring abuse, or keeping frightening secrets, the image of love is something to be avoided rather than sought.

Such individuals are trapped in a desperate cycle. They deeply need to be loved but have never had this need met safely. They engage in unsafe relationships, reasoning that at least physical closeness is better than nothing. When this becomes uncomfortable, they run from the situation, feeling empty since the need for love has not been met. Then the cycle begins again.

If you are trying to disengage from this dysfunctional cycle, first define what your need is and why your efforts have failed based on this definition. Then a new definition of "perfect love" can be substituted based on God's love which drives out fear. With this in mind, you will be free to explore new relationships that are based upon the liberating knowledge that love can be safe and free from fear.

Aid me, God, to see that love doesn't have to be a fearful and unfulfilling thing.

"For wrath kills a foolish man."
—JOB 5:2

Anger left unresolved becomes resentment; and resentment leads to bitterness, hatred, and often a relapse. Nobody knows this better than Brad. Brad is an alcoholic attempting recovery. He is married to a "nagging and controlling wife," at least in his opinion. Brad attempted to stop drinking several times in his marriage, but he failed to do so because of his inability to resolve his anger. Brad would only succeed in his abstinence for two to three months at a time. When he relapsed, his excuse sounded like this: "I might as well drink if I have to put up with her nagging." Brad's unresolved resentment became an easy excuse to drink.

Finally, Brad attended an Alcoholics Anonymous meeting whose topic for the evening discussion was resentment. The speaker gave testimony as to how his resentments fueled several relapses in his recovery. At the end of his talk, the speaker made a brief but invaluable comment for Brad to use in his own recovery program: "Remember, resentments are the number one reason to relapse."

Brad knew that if he was serious about not drinking, he had to resolve his anger before it built up into resentment. This meant he had to address issues with his wife as they occurred. He knew that if he continued to avoid or ignore the issues it would ultimately lead to his own demise.

Are you harboring any resentments?

Beloved, do not avenge yourselves, but rather give place to wrath; for it is written, "Vengeance is Mine, I will repay," says the Lord.

—ROM. 12:19

How does revenge fit into your maintenance plan? Have you taken into account the strength of this emotion? There are few things that threaten maintenance like revenge. The threat exists each time someone wrongs us, we choose not to pursue it and we reconcile with that person as best we can. As soon as we decide not to keep our emotional accounts short, we are opening the door for the nurturing of revenge.

It is easy to fall into the feeling that we know better than God how to deal with wrongdoing. We are convinced that the injustice we see is an indication that God has chosen not to do anything in this situation. Then we decide that God is indeed uncaring and unjust. Based on that conclusion, we can justify just about any behavior.

God will avenge all wrongdoing; we can count on it as surely as we can count on him. The only thing we cannot count on is that his timing is the same as ours. It is truly an act of trust when we say, "I have been wronged, but it is not my job to be the judge and jury. That I will leave to a truly righteous judge."

Father, help me to avoid revenge by trusting in your promises for justice.

*"They will fight against you,
But they shall not prevail against you,
For I am with you," says the LORD, "to deliver you."*
—JER. 1:19

Confronting others around you can be hard. Certainly it is much easier to only communicate the positive emotions. Karen, a fifteen-year-old anorexic, had dieted until her skin had a yellowish tint and her hair had begun to fall out. She had started dieting because she was overweight, but by the time she was hospitalized she looked like a concentration camp victim.

Both her parents were incredibly controlling, eager to change their daughter, but very unwilling to own their part of the problem. In the early sessions Karen harbored tremendous resentment for the way they focused on her and ignored their futile marriage. Her father was alcoholic, and both he and Karen's mom knew this was an untouchable issue.

The key to Karen's recovery was the day she decided to confront her parents for their double standard. She began to realize that starving herself would not give her control of her life, instead it added to her out of control feeling. Once she was able to talk about her anger, her need to maintain rigid control of her food intake diminished.

Help me, God, to rely on you when I deal with forces that seem beyond my control.

A hot-tempered man must pay the penalty;
if you rescue him, you will have to do it again.

PROV. 19:19 (NIV)

In a hospital, to rescue means to save a person from injury or harm. Ironically, in a codependency or addiction treatment program, rescuing means to actually cause further harm to an individual. Rescuing causes additional harm because the rescuer prevents another individual from experiencing the natural consequences of his behaviors. Therefore, the person develops little desire to change his behaviors, no matter how destructive they are.

Valerie did a great deal of rescuing in her family. Her husband had a quick and often abusive temper. When he became angry, he verbally assaulted the children and became physically rough. Instead of confronting her husband's behaviors, Valerie told her children, "Your daddy didn't mean to be so hard on you. He really loves you." Because of Valerie's rescuing, her husband encountered few natural consequences to his abusive outbursts. Each episode seemed to get worse, until one day he broke the oldest child's leg. At this point Valerie realized that her rescuing was assisting her husband to get worse, not better.

Many of us rescue because we mistakenly believe it will bring peace to conflicts. Although rescuing may bring temporary relief, we need to look at the long-term impact of this behavior.

Lord, give me the wisdom to choose non-rescuing behaviors.

> *"Yet the righteous will hold to his way,*
> *And he who has clean hands will be*
> *stronger and stronger."*
> —JOB 17:9

It is hard not to coast after a lot of progress has been made in any area. I see it everywhere to such an extent that I can almost predict it before it happens. I see it when parents have worked so hard to begin to discipline in a consistent and appropriate manner, and their children begin to respond positively to such consistency. I also see it when people who have worked hard to change the way they draw their boundaries.

We have the mistaken belief that once we have gained ground on our problems, they will continue to disappear on their own. Think about it. Once you have gotten your car fixed does it automatically maintain itself from that point on? Of course not. That same principle applies in your recovery as well. You will have to go back to the basics once in a while to refocus your efforts and further define areas that need your attention. That is what good maintenance is all about. It isn't sitting back on your laurels and taking in the applause. Rather it is keeping up with all that you have already learned and continuing to adjust to keep the progress moving.

It is important to maintain your progress "aggressively."

> *Reject a divisive man after the first and second admonition.*
> —TITUS 3:10

Chris had tried several times to explain his new feelings to a friend, being direct and honest. Unfortunately the friend continued to pressure him to be the way he was before the change process. This was a close friend, one Chris did not wish to lose, but also one he recognized was holding him back.

Chris knew that not everyone would accept the changes that came with recovery. He was beginning to feel that this individual was one of those who would not. He wisely had begun to feel that his recovery was more important than holding fast to relationships that could be potentially destructive.

First, Chris needed to share honestly his fears with this friend and ask for support in his recovery. Then Chris needed to share with this individual that his recovery was more important than the friendship if it continued to be destructive and then ask again for support. If Chris was still being held back, it was time to draw new boundaries that excluded this individual.

There probably are relationships in your life not conducive to recovery. Have you begun to confront the problems there?

The righteous should choose his friends carefully,
For the way of the wicked leads them astray.
—PROV. 12:26

Establishing healthy friendships can be a difficult experience for some of us. Our tendency may be to be unbalanced in our approach to getting to know others. Sometimes we may keep ourselves withdrawn and distant, inviting only superficiality from others. We avoid close relationships because we fear rejection. We are afraid that once people get to know us, they really won't like us.

On the other hand, some of us naively throw ourselves into relationships without taking time to check out the other person. We do this for several reasons. One reason may be because it takes less work. Developing a healthy friendship takes time and energy. Another reason stems from guilt feelings. We may feel our mission in life is to make others happy, no matter who they are. Also, we may feel that everyone we meet we must take care of. Finally, we may simply fear being alone—anyone is better than no one.

Having healthy friendships directly affects the choices we make in life. It's important to search our motives for the relationships we have and be willing to demonstrate patience and sound judgment in choosing our friends.

Lord, give me patience and wisdom in the friendships I choose.

> *"Is not the whole land before you? Please separate from me. If you take the left, then I will go to the right; or, if you go to the right, then I will go to the left."*
> —GEN. 13:9

One day a father sat on the couch in my office and announced to his son, "I have finally come to realize that we are different people, and I can't expect you to feel and think the way I do. I am committed to allow you to be different from me." It seems obvious on the surface, but many parents feel that something is wrong if their children don't see things the way they do. Some even feel their children are disobeying when the kids honestly disagree with them, even in a respectful fashion. This is one of the biggest challenges to redefining boundaries in relation to feelings.

Your behavior will tell you whether or not you expect your kids to think and feel the way you do. Ask yourself, "Do I get upset when my child disagrees or feels differently than me?" If you answered yes you may need to reevaluate what you are *really* expecting of your child. You may need to make the same speech this father made to his son. Be willing to admit that you may have seen things wrong, and decide that you are willing to allow your son or daughter to be different from you.

Lord, give me the strength to let go of expecting my children to think and feel like me.

Be kind to one another, tenderhearted, forgiving
one another, just as God in Christ also forgave you.
—EPH. 4:32

Kindness and compassion are very hard concepts to grasp when struggling with hurt. When someone has deeply wronged you, it's hard to forgive. A natural first feeling is wanting to take revenge, wanting to see the other suffer as you have.

Ralph was full of bitterness. He had suffered many wrongs in his marriage and felt he had a legitimate right to feel bitter. At times, the bitterness consumed him and was the only thing on which he could focus. Work suffered, he stopped having fun, he couldn't sleep at night, food was no longer appetizing. Even when he succeeded in getting revenge the victory was short-lived and unsatisfying. There was nothing he could do in the way of vengeance that made things better.

When I broached the idea of forgiveness with Ralph, his initial impression was that he was being told he had to give up and be a doormat. This, he feared, would leave him vulnerable to further hurt by his wife. When finally he understood that this forgiveness was a choice that only he could make, he began to see the power he had in the situation. Ralph was then free to move on in his recovery.

Are there relationships in your life where bitterness is in control?

> *Let no corrupt communication proceed out of your
> mouth, but what is good for necessary edification,
> that it may impart grace to the hearers.*
> —EPH. 4:29

Gossip destroys relationships. When we engage in it,
we demonstrate inappropriate boundaries because we
look for other people to give us value. Unfortunately,
gossip and backbiting occur with great frequency in
family relationships. Typically, a sibling or parent becomes the central focus of family discussion. Family
members use words that are demeaning and degrad-
ing, not supportive. In clinical terms, this negative focus is called scapegoating.

Do you live in a family where one person receives
nothing but negative attention from other family members? Perhaps in your family, the focus of gossip
changes depending on the circumstances. At some
family gatherings, every family member will be gos-
siped about in one way or another. Sadly, families like
the ones described above seem to thrive on criticism.
Helpful, supportive communication is rare.

If these descriptions of family gossip sound familiar,
you need to carefully set limits on your own speech.
When you say something about a family member who
is not present, you should evaluate your motives: Are
you seeking to build up or tear down?

*Usually, something that can't be said directly to another is not worth
saying at all.*

*Be kindly affectionate to one another with brotherly
love, in honor giving preference to one another.*
—ROM. 12:10

Can you imagine what our churches and world would
be like if we learned to honor one another? Often
when I propose this principle in a family, they are often
to quick to remind me that if they were to do that, they
would get walked on.

What does honor mean? For the purpose of our understanding, honoring someone is treating them in
such a way that is consistent with their worth. If our
worth is based on our creation by God himself, what
does that say about the honor we should accord one
another?

Honor does not mean subjugating our every desire
to another person with the intent of not losing them.
That is neither love nor honor. That is manipulation.
Honor means treating someone with the respect they
deserve and not demeaning them by not respecting
their boundaries. It also means treating someone with
the respect they deserve without letting them walk all
over your boundaries as well. Honor means holding
someone in esteem and respecting them enough to
stand your own boundaries while respecting theirs as
well.

*Father, help me to honor others around me by maintaining my own
boundaries.*

> *Today, if you will hear His voice:*
> *"Do not harden your hearts."*
> —PS. 95:7–8

When a person denies a problem long enough, they can no longer see the situation clearly. They become hardened to others who care and who attempt to help them see reality.

Sheila's children had become uncontrollable. She was quite frustrated at their antics which caused her great embarrassment, and wanted her therapist to "fix" them so that she could lead a normal life. In sessions, when her children tried to tell her their feelings of anger and resentment at the family's dysfunction, she would berate them for not taking responsibility for their actions and trying to slow the process of change.

Sheila failed to grasp that the process of change *was* their expression of frustration. Growing up, she was told "bite the bullet" when she was angry and not express her feelings openly. Therefore, Sheila had learned to not tolerate this from her own children. It was hard for her to see that she had begun to do the same for her children, and rather than face this pain, she maintained a rigid stance that the children had the problems, not her. This hardness would prove to be a major stumbling block in the progress of her family in therapy.

_____

Grant me a new openness to face my situation as it really is and help me to recognize my denial.

"Your wisdom and your knowledge have warped you;
And you have said in your heart,
'I am, and there is no one else besides me.'"
—ISA. 47:10

Trusting in ourselves alone can be a disastrous choice to make in our recovery programs. We need input from others and from God, through his Word, to keep our reality accurate. This truth is illustrated in the lives of recovering addicts and codependents.

Before recovery, the addict and codependent often view life through a narrow tunnel, eliminating others and God from their peripheral vision. They usually make their decisions based only on their own experiences in life. They not only avoid input from others, they usually detest it. In recovery, however, addicts and codependents are encouraged to stop isolating themselves and to start reaching out to others for input and advice.

Those in recovery learn to reach out, in part, by attending support group meetings. They are able to strategize with others on how best to handle difficult situations in their lives. Given frequent feedback from others, they are able to make healthy choices on a consistent basis.

Reading God's Word and taking advantage of positive relationships with others through support groups, church activities, social functions, and close friends are all ways to check out our reality.

Lord, keep me from thinking too highly of myself that I avoid input from others and from you.

Teach me to do Your will,
For You are my God;
Your Spirit is good.
Lead me in the land of uprightness.
—PS. 143:10

It is not unusual to find our perspective to be very different from God's perspective about what we need to come into a closer relationship with him.

We often define our "level ground" in terms of peace, prosperity, and good fortune. But like a patient teacher, God knows what we need and very often leads us through a valley of unrest, emotional poverty, and misfortune. For him, that is the level ground we *need,* not the level ground we want. We are often quick to seek a solution to life's problems instead of seeking to obey him.

As you move through your maintenance you may want to be careful how you define your "level ground." It is through adversity and trials that we often grow and learn instead of through peace and prosperity. As a matter of fact, we usually learn more through the adversity because our skills and knowledge are tested. Strive for obedience of God's word, and not for immediate solutions.

Father, help me to seek the level ground I need.

Rest in the LORD, and wait patiently for Him.
—PS. 37:7

One young woman became upset when change did not occur quickly enough for her. Angrily she asked, "I've been working for two months, what does it take?" My answer was, "It takes time." She wanted things to be different, but she felt frustrated that it did not happen at the pace she expected.

Patience is important to the recovery process. After grasping that a higher power can and will help, we tend to want him to work rapidly. God, however, recognizes that true change takes time. It is necessary to be certain that the new changes are not temporary, that they are fully part of the new you.

We cannot control God's timing. As with all the other individuals in our lives, we need to avoid trying to control God. True surrender to our higher power means that we also give up our notions of how quickly recovery must occur. We should just do our part and trust God to do his.

———————

Grant me the patience to recover within the time scheme you see best.

> *"Judge not, and you shall not be judged. Condemn not, and you shall not be condemned. Forgive, and you will be forgiven."*
> —LUKE 6:37

A healthy concept of forgiveness eludes many of us, especially when we have poor boundaries. One problem area is believing that we are only forgiven when others forgive us. Roger had this belief when he entered an alcohol and drug treatment program. Roger had been involved in a car accident which killed his ten-year-old daughter. His feelings of guilt and remorse for his behavior overwhelmed him. Fortunately, Roger took responsibility for his actions this time by working a twelve-step recovery program and fulfilling his legal obligations.

A year into his recovery, Roger became seriously depressed. He even considered suicide. His family still struggled with forgiving him. Roger felt this meant his actions were unforgivable. The obstacle he faced in recovery was his belief that he was not a worthy person until his family forgave him. He allowed their withholding of forgiveness to affect his ability to forgive himself.

Roger's predicament is just another example of inappropriate boundaries. We need to be responsible for ourselves and not allow what others do or don't do determine our outlook on life.

Are you allowing someone else's lack of forgiveness to affect your choices?

Wait on the LORD;
Be of good courage,
And He shall strengthen your heart;
Wait, I say, on the LORD!
—PS. 27:14

Probably the hardest part of maintaining progress in recovery is knowing when to wait. After dealing with your boundary issues and trying to make new choices, you are ready to act. But sometimes the best act is to decide to wait.

There is a time and place for patience and waiting to see what the Lord has in store for us. The best strategist in any field of play is the one who is willing to wait for the right time to act. All the newfound knowledge you have gained may best be used in recognizing situations when it is best to hold your tongue.

It is interesting that God doesn't intend for us to wait and do nothing. Rather he encourages us to be strong and take heart. This isn't a passive sitting-back-and-twiddling-your-thumbs-waiting. No, it is an active process of growing strong and being encouraged while you wait for the best time to act.

Wait on the Lord and grow strong!

> *"He sets on high those who are lowly,*
> *And those who mourn are lifted to safety."*
> —JOB 5:11

Dorothy is a housekeeper in the hospital where I work. For over fifteen years she has made beds, cleaned toilets, emptied trash cans, and done other very "menial" tasks, at least by the standards of the society in which she works. Around her are the various mental health professionals who pride themselves on their prestige and status, while she quietly performs her less noticeable duties.

There is something special about Dorothy. As she works, she smiles. There is an inner peace and tranquility about her, a quality therapists attempt to teach to those who occupy the rooms she is cleaning. Her secret is her personal belief in a God who sustains life and keeps her safe, giving her joy even if her job is the lowest on the hospital totem pole.

Often I will use Dorothy as an example of a truly satisfied life, not just for those with whom I work, but for myself as well. You see, Dorothy has learned that it is not how others see her that makes her special. It is the knowledge that God loves her that keeps a smile on her face and an encouraging word on her lips. Dorothy's greatness comes not from her accomplishments but from her reliance on her higher power.,

It is not the mighty by the standards of the world who will ultimately be elevated, but those who quietly believe that God keeps them safe.

"Be angry, and do not sin."
—EPH. 4:26

It has been said that of all the emotions, anger is the most perverted and distorted. When a group of people was asked to give one-word thoughts on the emotion of anger, the following list was given: rage, resentment, hate, vengeance, revenge, violence, abuse, yelling, loss, hurt, fear, isolation, and death. These words are obviously quite negative.

Most of us learned to associate these words with anger because they describe the way we experienced the expression of anger. Some of us grew up in homes where anger and violence were synonymous. Frank was raised to believe that if he felt angry it was all right to yell, call names, and even physically abuse others. When his father became angry, Frank frequently heard this excuse for the violence which followed, "It's your fault that I'm angry, so now you're going to get it."

Frank learned to confuse the emotion of anger with the way it was expressed in his family. Regardless of how we have learned to express anger, we need to realize that anger itself is just another emotion, neither good nor bad. The moral issue becomes involved only in the way we choose to express our anger. The verse above does not state, "Don't get angry." Instead, it tells us that when we get angry, we are not to sin. Sin becomes a factor when we do or say things that are destructive to others and to ourselves.

Lord, help me to deal with my anger appropriately.

> *Endeavoring to keep the unity of the Spirit in the bond of peace.*
> —EPH. 4:3

Have you ever noticed that when someone talks about unity they often mean uniformity? What's the difference? What has it got to do with boundaries and decision-making?

Unity means that two people agree on the same goal (for example, healthy relationships), but they allow each other the freedom to pursue this goal in different ways. In a condition of unity there are solid boundaries, and decisions are made based on whether or not the two people get closer to their goal.

Uniformity, on the other hand, demands that each person look, think, and feel the same way about their goal. Uniformity blurs boundaries, and decisions are often made by only one person. Disagreement is seen as disloyalty rather than something healthy from which the relationship could grow strong.

Do you see yourself striving for unity or uniformity? If you are striving for unity, you are allowing others to have the freedom to pursue the same thing you are but differently. If you are striving for uniformity, you will get angry when others disagree with you. Keep your sights on unity. That will build healthy boundaries, not tear them down.

Father, help me to pursue unity in my relationships with others.

Set your mind on things above, not on things on the earth.

—COL. 3:2

When one judges oneself in comparison to others, it is easy to fall short. Most of the time the comparison is based on only the positive outward qualities of the other, while the shortcomings are overlooked. We look at earthly standards of success such as prestige, power, and looks, while missing heavenly standards of love, concern, and compassion.

Jim did this often, usually finding that he did not measure up. While he was able to acknowledge that he had many good traits, he felt that none of these set him apart as someone who had arrived. Thus, he constantly felt as if something was missing. Perhaps, by society's standards, something was, but nothing that kept him from being the whole person he was capable of being.

As a result of his negative, self-judgment Jim believed he was a nothing, so he struggled for the approval of those he perceived to be better than himself. Jim needed to begin focusing on himself from a different set of standards, heavenly ones, that recognized that God had made him special regardless of whether or not his peers saw him that way.

Are there positive attributes about yourself you overlook in striving to meet the approval of those around you?

> *Then said I:*
> *"Ah, Lord GOD!*
> *Behold, I cannot speak, for I am a youth."*
> *But the LORD said to me:*
> *"Do not say, 'I am a youth,'*
> *For you shall go to all to whom I send you,*
> *And whatever I command you, you shall speak."*
> —JER. 1:6–7

A forty-one-year-old married woman sat in her counselor's office talking about her involvement in several extramarital affairs. Suddenly, she switched the topic to her childhood and described being sexually abused by her father and uncle. When she finished describing the sexual abuse, she calmly stated, "You see, that's why I'm promiscuous and can't have a healthy marriage. I am really acting out my childhood abuse."

Although this woman's abuse was a tragic and painful event in her life, she used it as an excuse to continue her destructive behaviors. This use of excuses is similar to the alcoholic who states that because alcoholism is a disease, he cannot be held responsible for his drinking.

The verse above shows us that God wants our obedience in action. He does not want our excuses; he does not want us to blame others. Responsibility rests on our shoulders alone.

Lord, help me to grieve my childhood losses and not to use them as an excuse for my present actions.

Now as he reasoned about righteousness, self-control, and the judgment to come, Felix was afraid and answered, "Go away for now; when I have a convenient time I will call for you."

—ACTS 24:25

Throughout maintenance you will inevitably meet people who cannot understand the things you have learned. As a matter of fact, it will be very threatening to them to hear some of the things you talk about. For example, some family members don't know what you have been through and don't understand what codependency is all about. To explain to them some of the insights you have gained could be a very frustrating experience. They might not want to hear what you have to say.

Remember to maintain a "big-picture" focus. You didn't learn these new insights instantly; it was a slow, sometimes painful, process. You will need to give people permission to not understand at first. As you talk with them, chances are they will begin to understand. They will eventually be able to put what you are saying into a context that makes sense to them. You can also refer back to different things you have said and connect them to actual things that have happened.

There will be many times that you will be called upon to educate your family and friends about what has happened to you. You will need to be as patient as others have been to you.

Father, help me to be patient and allow people to learn what I have learned at their own pace.

> *My little children, let us not love in word or in*
> *tongue, but in deed and in truth.*
> —1 JOHN 3:18

The words "I love you" are very important to any relationship. If one does not say them enough the other begins to wonder if they are true. When spoken often but not followed with caring and concerned behavior, they are empty and meaningless.

Seventeen-year-old Candy saw her new boyfriend as her savior. She had a rotten home life, an uncaring stepfather, and a mentally ill mother. She saw this new relationship as her chance to escape her family and become an independent adult. He said he loved her, and in her neediness, she believed it. Because she wanted so badly to escape, she overlooked the times he hit her, the times he stood her up, and the fact that he had infected her with a sexually-transmitted disease.

Clearly, Candy was about to make a big mistake. But when confronted with this, she became angry and sullen. Her need for love brought about denial, which unless stopped, would result in a repetition of the problems she was trying to escape. Her focus on the words "I love you" aided her in overlooking the fact that the actions simply were not there.

God of love, teach me to recognize that real love is action, not just an empty phrase.

> *"'For this reason a man shall leave his father and*
> *mother and be joined to his wife.'"*
> —MARK 10:7

Experiencing change in relationships is a normal and healthy part of the growth process. Changes occur as we encounter new responsibilities and challenges in life. This is certainly the case when we become adults and take on new responsibilities such as a career or marriage. The relationships we had with our parents when we were children and adolescents dramatically changed as we became adults.

Edward had difficulty making necessary changes in his relationship with his parents once he got married. His wife complained that he spent too much time with his parents and gave them money that she and Edward needed to raise their own family. In essence, his wife believed she was in competition with his parents for his attention, time, and money. Edward thought his wife was being too demanding of him. His parents were elderly and had some chronic medical problems. Also, being a regular church attender, Edward felt it was his spiritual duty to care for his parents. After Edward spent a week with his parents and neglected his own responsibilities at home, his wife asked him to pursue marital therapy with her.

Are you allowing your relationships to change as your responsibilities change, or are you hanging onto the past?

———————

God, help me to accept necessary changes in relationships as I take on new responsibilities.

> *In humility correcting those who are in opposition,*
> *if God perhaps will grant them repentance, so that*
> *they may know the truth.*   —2 TIM. 2:25

What kind of teacher do you learn from best? The taskmaster who is rigid and exacting in his instruction? Or one who is patient and gentle, willing to stick with you no matter what? Obviously, we learn best from the gentle, patient teacher who conveys respect and warmth to us.

As you travel through your struggles to maintain your new behavior, you may be called upon to instruct those who are not as far down the road to recovery as you. You may want to fill them in on all the necessary information even before they actually need it. On the other hand, it would also be easy to become impatient with them for not seeing even the most obvious points.

Gentleness carries with it an understanding of the needs of the person you are dealing with, whether that is yourself or someone else. We can get caught up in the information to be mastered instead of the nurturance which needs to be conveyed. When you are in the position of helping others learn what you already know, remember that gentleness will foster more independence than an insistence on doing things just right.

Father, help me to be gentle in my instruction with others on the road to recovery.

Be sober, be vigilant; because your adversary the devil walks about like a roaring lion, seeking whom he may devour. —1 PETER 5:8

In therapy, we expect answers. The answers we get, however, usually are not the kind we expected, instant knowledge of what to do in every situation. In fact, it is better to obtain warning signs, red flags that alert us of upcoming danger so that internal controls can be used to prevent relapsing.

June came to a session upset. After plunging headlong into an angry shouting match with her husband because of a misunderstanding on her part, the old feelings of defeat and hopelessness came rushing back. Initially she took her frustration out on her therapist for not warning her that such situations would occur. She felt that she should be getting better and should be able to avoid these old feelings.

This session provided an opportunity to show June a red flag in her life. There were some indications that the argument was about to happen, road signs that when read correctly could have prevented her loss of control with her husband. Recovery requires that we be aware of signals warning of hazardous conditions ahead; then we can use self-control to avoid a mishap.

God, before I react impulsively, remind me to use my self-control.

> *"'You shall not hate your brother in your heart.*
> *You shall surely rebuke your neighbor, and not*
> *bear sin because of him.'"* —LEV. 19:17

Joann was a bitter woman. She was bitter because she avoided dealing with her feelings, especially anger. As a child she was taught, "Be a nice person; don't make waves." This meant if she expressed her anger and someone else became angry as a result, it was her fault. Therefore, Joann stuffed her feelings inside and avoided expressing them if at all possible. Because she had so many unresolved issues building up inside her, she became bitter and resentful toward others.

One of the healthiest choices we can make is to deal with our feelings up front, instead of avoiding them. This is especially true with the feeling of anger. If we avoid addressing our anger as Joann did, often feelings of bitterness, resentment, and even hatred result. The verse above instructs us that hatred can be avoided by directly confronting those with whom we have a grievance.

Although Joann thought she was responsible for the other person's emotional reaction, this was certainly not true. She was responsible, however, for her willingness to address her issues with others and not to hold onto feelings of bitterness or hatred.

If we attempt to avoid small waves now, a tidal wave of bitterness and hatred may result.

For thus says the Lord GOD, the Holy One of Israel:
"In returning and rest you shall be saved;
In quietness and confidence shall be your
*   strength."*
But you would not.

—ISA. 30:15

There are times when we seem to be bent on asserting our independence even when it may hurt us. We know all the things we *should* be doing, but we ignore those things and just go on doing what we want. You can probably expect that to happen to you at one point or another during your maintenance. You quit keeping watch over your behavior just to assert your independence, and in the same fashion you begin to lose ground.

We have an intense desire for independence. It is a part of us from birth. There are times, though, that in our strivings for independence we make ourselves more dependent. This is because we strive for our independence *in reaction* to something that has happened to us. This reaction is what ties us to more dependent behavior. Instead of making a decision based on the facts of the situation, we make our decision and actions in the opposite direction of what has happened to us. At times like these, we need to assess the situation and act in accordance with the biblical principles we know are healthy.

Father, help me to resist being stubborn just to show that I am independent.

> *"You have heard that it was said to those of old,*
> *'You shall not commit adultery.' But I say to you*
> *that whoever looks at a woman to lust for her has*
> *already committed adultery with her in his heart."*
> —MATT. 5:27–28

Look, I'm not *that* bad a person, I haven't had affairs or anything," said a young man early in therapy. He was trying to convince me that basically he was a good person, that he had not done anything so terribly wrong to merit the problems in his relationship with his wife. While his logic made sense to him, it missed the point.

Basically all people are sinful, all have wished ill upon other people, all have had lustful thoughts, all have believed themselves to be better than others at times. While the acts you conceive in your mind may not have actually been committed, the thought is as much the problem as the act. When you think and envision the act mentally, it is as good as done.

Trying to justify yourself is a dangerous habit. You may tend to rationalize your behavior, to make yourselves believe you are not really as bad as if you had done the things others have. Perhaps it is true that others have done things that pale in comparison to yourself, but that doesn't make you better than them. Be careful of this tendency. It is possible you may begin to minimize the wrongs you actually *have* done.

Are there areas of your life you have minimized by comparing yourself to others?

The words of his mouth are wickedness and deceit;
He has ceased to be wise and to do good. . . .
He sets himself in a way that is not good;
He does not abhor evil.   —PS. 36:3–4

Sometimes when we don't get what we want, we may be tempted to resort to different kinds of manipulation. At times, getting angry seems to work well, while at other times being cold and distant seems to get us what we want. If we don't get the desired response from these first two methods, we may try to nag, threaten, or even cajole.

Brittany struggled with codependency. She derived her self-worth from her family. If they were doing well, she felt happy. When Brittany's family struggled, she felt miserable. To avoid the miserable feelings, she found herself pushing her husband and children to do better. She nagged and scolded them until their performances improved. At times, she threw tantrums. Brittany and her family would have benefited greatly if they had been aware of the nature of her manipulative actions.

Like Brittany, we can benefit from being aware of our own manipulations. Instead of manipulating, we need to let go of control when others are not doing or saying what we would like. We are deceptive when our behavior is backed by ulterior motives.

A desire to control often breeds deceitfulness and manipulation.

> *"But those things which proceed out of the mouth
> come from the heart, and they defile a man."*
> —MATT. 15:18

We are really very good at identifying problems in our behavior that are overt and obvious. It's the less obvious with which we have trouble. As a matter of fact, we would much prefer to stick to the obvious because we don't enjoy making mistakes and being uncomfortable. But remember, the process of recovery wasn't painless, and neither will be the maintaining of healthy behavior.

There will be times that even the best-looking behavior has behind it the motivation of keeping people close so that you don't feel any more pain. This motivation is the same seed that reaped a harvest of poor decisions and blurred boundaries. It is important to remember that we all have the ability to "look" really good, and at the same time have motivations behind this good behavior that are truly selfish and self-serving.

Be skeptical of your motivations when you feel wishy-washy about making decisions or setting limits. This kind of skepticism is healthy; after all, we underestimate our ability to fool ourselves.

Father, help me to be realistic about my ability to fool myself.

*On the contrary, you ought rather to forgive and
comfort him, lest perhaps such a one be swallowed
up with too much sorrow.* —2 COR. 2:7

Underlying much of the anger individuals feel is a
tremendous sense of hurt. Their anger is a protective
shield used to keep further hurt from entering their
lives. It keeps others distant, since no one likes to be
close to an angry person.

The response these individuals seek, and yet regret,
is rejection. While rejection is safe it also hurts and
contributes to feelings of sadness and alienation. You
probably know such angry people; usually their words
resulted in pain as they lashed out to keep you distant.
Probably you complied by becoming angry, rejecting
them, and feeling bitterness.

There is only one way to get through to these individuals. Let them know you forgive them and offer
them your empathy. Wisely avoid allowing their anger
to control you by keeping you distant and defensive.
And most of all, don't try to take revenge by not forgiving. Distance is exactly what their angry actions were
designed to produce.

------

*Are there people in your life you have rejected because you could not
see the hurt and fear behind their anger?*

> *Then she came and worshiped Him, saying, "Lord,*
> *help me!"*
> —MATT. 15:25

Rita had a difficult time communicating her needs. In her marriage she generally expected her husband to read her nonverbal communication and respond to her accordingly. Of course, this often failed and Rita found herself frustrated and angry. Her conclusion was, "If you loved me, you would know what I want!"

Some of us communicate indirectly like Rita. We may have learned as a child that pouting works well to get people to ask us what is wrong. Or perhaps we have learned to use our anger to intimidate others into asking us what we want. The silent treatment can also be used as an attempt to communicate indirectly. In all these cases, we are expecting others to be responsible to understand our needs, even if we do not verbalize them.

Healthy communication requires us to be direct, not indirect. We need to be like the woman in the verse above. She is direct and to the point, "Lord, help me." By being direct, we take the guesswork out of our communication. We therefore increase the ability of our listener to truly understand our needs, which increases the probability that we will receive a helpful and supportive response.

Lord, help me to be direct in my communication.

> *But exhort one another daily, while it is called
> "Today," lest any of you be hardened through the
> deceitfulness of sin.*   —HEB. 3:13

Many clients come into my office and complain that in their quest for healthier behavior they feel alone and isolated. Often these people are afraid to extend themselves in relationships again because they feel they will set themselves up for more codependent behavior. Basically, they are trying to hedge their bets against future failure in relationships.

This is the wrong approach. It is essential to allow yourself to be encouraged by important people in your life. How can you feel encouraged and supported if you don't allow yourself to risk new behavior in significant relationships? The solution is not withdrawing from these relationships. Seeing it in black and white ("Either I have a relationship or I don't have a relationship") will not help you develop the skill of setting appropriate boundaries. You have to begin to take some risks in order to learn these new behaviors. You should also expect mistakes. Mistakes are unavoidable, expected, and an opportunity to learn healthier behaviors.

———

Take appropriate risks to continue to develop healthy boundary-setting behaviors.

> *"When I say to the wicked, 'O wicked man, you*
> *shall surely die!' and you do not speak to warn the*
> *wicked from his way, that wicked man shall die in*
> *his iniquity; but his blood I will require at your*
> *hand."*
> —EZEK. 33:8

Isolation from people in pain is common among children of dysfunctional families. When you have experienced tremendous pain you may feel that any more would be devastating. You may attempt to insulate yourself from the anguish that others feel; thus you fail to share the insights they are beginning to have.

This can be irresponsible. When you are entrusted with great truth there is an obligation to share it. If you fail to do so, that person may not have the opportunities that were available to you.

Part of your recovery process is an open and honest sharing of your personal struggles and triumphs. This aids you in the process of being humble, and it can bring you great satisfaction knowing that your personal recovery has assisted others. As you gain awareness of your limitations, be willing to use these to help others in need of your knowledge. This sharing is the cornerstone of any twelve-step recovery group.

Are there individuals in your life who could benefit from the knowledge you have gained through your recovery thus far?

In the multitude of my anxieties within me,
Your comforts delight my soul.

—PS. 94:19

Anxiety will certainly be present as we begin the process of making new, healthier decisions in life. As you experience anxiety, keep in mind an often-used expression: "Easy does it." This phrase reminds us to slow down and reflect on the fact that God is in control. When we hear it, it may prevent us from making impulsive decisions. Impulsive decisions can lead to relapse. This is almost what happened to John.

John was the diplomat in his family. He played mediator between siblings and parents in order to keep peace. When the family was happy, so was John. However, when there was fighting, John felt terrible about himself. He interpreted family conflict as proof that he had failed.

After receiving counseling, John learned about his codependency. Soon, he realized that in order to establish healthy boundaries with his family, he would have to allow family members to take care of themselves. When John was with his family during the holidays, he found himself feeling anxious, guilty, and overwhelmed as he struggled not to intervene in a sibling dispute. Then he remembered what his counselor had told him. "Easy does it, John. Take time to pray. Ask God for guidance, courage, and strength to do what is healthy."

Lord, remind me to slow down when things feel out of control.

> *"I still have many things to say to you, but you cannot bear them now."* —JOHN 16:12

As you continue on the path of recovery, you will sometimes come into contact with people who know you from old times. This situation presents new challenges that you probably haven't faced.

It is important to realize that your friends' understanding is significantly hampered by their past memories of you and your behavior. They probably will not be ready to accept the changes in you right from the start. Timing is critical.

There will be times when it is better to withhold certain information about the changes you have made because these old friends simply wouldn't understand. This just means that you will have to be patient and wait for their understanding to increase. If you want them to understand the significance of your new insights, you should let their understanding increase slowly.

Christ knew this better than anyone. He had much to tell his disciples, but he also knew that there was just so much they could take in. So he waited. The same is true for you and your friends. Waiting is worth it to help your friends understand how significant these changes are.

――――――――

Father, help me wait for people to understand the changes I have made.

*Let us therefore come boldly to the throne of grace,
that we may obtain mercy and find grace to help in
time of need.*   —HEB. 4:16

Seventeen-year-old Wanda had a dilemma. She recognized that she needed a higher power in her life. However, despite a commitment to turn her dysfunctional patterns over to God, at times she did not know where to find him. There were times she felt God was far away from the crises she experienced in her daily life.

Wanda knew from her past that when she failed to live up to her parents' standards they had a tendency to reject her, and she feared God would do the same. When she engaged in old behaviors there was an underlying worry that God would desert her, rejecting her like her parents. It was difficult for her to believe in the concept of grace and forgiveness even though she did not fully deserve it.

Prayer immediately brings one into the presence of God. Wanda needed to approach that presence with confidence, knowing that mercy and grace would be given her whether or not she deserved it. There was immense relief when she began to understand that God would accept her despite the fact that she failed at times in her recovery.

In times of need, even if you have failed, remember that grace is available to you and approach God with confidence that it will be granted.

> *Repay no one evil for evil. Have regard for good*
> *things in the sight of all men.* —ROM. 12:17

Revenge destroys lives. Ironically, the lives it destroys are not so much the ones who receive the revenge, but those who are seeking it. When we spend an enormous amount of time, energy, and thought obsessed with "getting even," we lose sight of our own responsibilities and soon find ourselves trapped on a path of destruction.

Mike entered a rehab program for his drug addiction because his wife threatened separation if he refused to get help. Although Mike encountered various obstacles in his treatment, the largest occurred as he attempted to prepare a list on how he hurt others due to his drug usage. During his presentation of the list, Mike frequently digressed into how his wife had hurt him. He became determined to get her back for sending him to treatment when she needed it as badly as he did. Mike left treatment prematurely, and he resumed his drug usage immediately.

As we evaluate our own wrongdoings in life, we can easily become sidetracked and focus on how our brother, spouse, or parent has slighted us. When the wrongdoings of others become our focus and we concentrate our energy on ways of getting back at them, we disobey God and only end up destroying ourselves.

God, help me to let go of the hurts others have caused me, so I can concentrate on my own responsibilities.

Then He came to the disciples and found them asleep, and said to Peter, "What, could you not watch with Me one hour?" —MATT. 26:40

As you maintain your new behavior, you will meet people who will make you angry because of their lack of insight into the importance of the changes you have made. Even if they do notice, they might be apathetic about it and minimize the significance of what you have accomplished.

More than anything, it is disappointing that people close to you don't notice or try to understand the significance of what you have done. I'm sure Jesus must have felt that as well when he returned from praying. Maybe he had hoped that these three disciples would have seen the importance of this night for him and would have prayed for him instead of sleeping.

It is part of the constant reminder we all have that everyone at one time or another will let us down. This fact is not something to get depressed about. Just because they let us down by not seeing things as being as important as we do does not mean that they are any less concerned or interested in us. It just means that they are still lacking in the understanding, and that can be changed.

Father, help me to remember that people are just as human as I am.

> *Because the foolishness of God is wiser than men,*
> *and the weakness of God is stronger than men.*
> —1 COR. 1:25

Some people in your life will never change. Try as you may to make them be different, it will not occur until they decide it is time. Begging, yelling, worrying, even threatening won't work—some things are just beyond the limits of your power.

Randi's husband was an alcoholic and had created enormous tension in the household. Naturally he blamed his drinking on her nagging, and she blamed her ulcer on the chaos his drinking created. Despite every coercive method she attempted, he refused to quit drinking. And, unfortunately, Randi refused to quit threatening. They had reached an impasse and Randi felt like she was falling apart.

Randi's mistaken notion that change would happen based on her tactics had created a tremendous sense of helplessness on her part. She desperately needed to recognize that certain things are better left to God to change, while she changed things within herself that were within her power. She needed to accept the peace that comes from leaving something in God's capable hands.

Begin to recognize that some things are outside your power to change.

And the next day we landed at Sidon. And Julius treated Paul kindly and gave him liberty to go to his friends and receive care. —ACTS 27:3

Asking others for help can be extremely difficult. Many of us are great at giving help but are clumsy at accepting it. When we allow others to provide for our needs, we may feel awkward and uncomfortable. We may believe we are being selfish in accepting others' help. Or we may think we really shouldn't ask for help unless we experience an emergency. Still another reason for not requesting assistance is to avoid having a lot of attention focused on us. We may fear that when people get to know us, they may not like what they see.

Doug entered a hospital setting after becoming depressed and suicidal. His therapist immediately focused on Doug's past relationships. Unfortunately, Doug had been raised to believe that only the weak accept help. Therefore, he felt extremely embarrassed when someone offered him assistance. Since Doug refused help when it was offered, his own needs went unmet. Subsequently, feelings of worthlessness and hopelessness began to fuel his depression.

We need to balance our giving with receiving. It is essential that we learn to let others provide for our needs when we are unable to do so. If we choose to refuse help from others, we choose to isolate.

Lord, give me courage to tear down my pride and accept help from others.

Happy is the man who is always reverent,
But he who hardens his heart will fall into calamity.
—PROV. 28:14

Are you one of those who cries at a sad movie? You have a "soft heart," one that is moved and touched by the human condition. Throughout recovery, keep the softness in your heart. Without it, there will be a callousness that preserves you from feeling the pain of disappointment or unbridled anger.

A woman once commented to me that she felt that she had lost sensitivity in her recovery. She had been very distracted by the holidays and hadn't been able to keep her focus on the changes she needed to maintain. The measure of her callousness was her response to certain songs she had listened to weeks earlier. These songs had touched her quite deeply as they captured her feelings and pain. When she listened to them again there was no response. She realized then that she needed to reestablish her usual routine of journaling and meeting with a friend to help her get back on track.

Do you have a measure or barometer to tell you the level of your "softness"? If you are getting too hard, reestablish some routines to regain your focus.

Father, help me to remain soft and sensitive to my recovery.

> *"Those who regard worthless idols*
> *Forsake their own Mercy."*
> —JONAH 2:8

When we put anything ahead of God, our higher power, we make that object our god. Our energies become spent pursuing avenues of hope that are devoid of real power. Relief from pain can be one of those pursuits.

Caroline had been abused sexually as a child. She entered therapy to seek relief from the painful memories that kept cropping up in her mind. Every conversation with her would ultimately come back to her pain. She did believe that God could remove the hurt, but her whole mission in life was to escape the pain. Without the pain, she would have nothing on which to focus.

Caroline had become so focused on the pain that it replaced anything else in her life. She revolted at any suggestion of this, feeling attacked and defensive. Her pain had become a worthless idol for her, and real relief would mean giving up something which had become part of her. Recovery for Caroline ultimately would require changing a major focus of her life, from pain to God.

Are there things in your life which have kept you from committing control of your life and recovery to God?

*Therefore comfort each other and edify one
another, just as you also are doing.*
—1 THESS. 5:11

Andrew grew up in a nonsupportive home. His parents' idea of encouragement was to criticize and threaten severe punishment if the children didn't do as they were told. The concept of building each other up was unheard of in his family. His family practiced tearing each other down to the point of causing a great deal of emotional and psychological damage. Several times his parents stated that they wished he had never been born because of the trouble he caused them. For Andrew, a tragic consequence of being raised in this environment was his negative self-esteem.

Fortunately, Andrew received therapy to counter these messages. He learned that his parents had displayed very poor boundaries because they attacked him, rather than his behaviors. He also learned that if he wanted to practice appropriate boundaries himself, he would have to focus on building others up instead of tearing them down.

Are you involved in relationships which tear you down or in which you're tearing someone else down? If you are, it is very likely that your relationships are destructive to yourself and to others. Practice using words that build other people up. This type of language is respectful of God's creation.

Lord, give me wisdom to select words that are helpful, not hurtful.

*"I am not able to bear all these people alone,
because the burden is too heavy for me."*
—NUM. 11:14

Even after struggling with the issues of boundaries and decision-making, you will always have to be aware of your uncanny ability to take on others' burdens. There are at least a couple of things that fuel this tendency.

The first is pride. It was pride that Satan used to lure Eve into eating the apple ("you will be like gods"). It was pride that made it difficult for you to admit there was a problem in your life. Now pride lures you into thinking that you are strong enough to take on others' burdens. Moses was in the same mindset until he realized his limitations and admitted his need.

The second aspect that hinders your ability to stay on top of this problem is need. You cannot strip yourself of the need for people and their attention. You *can* learn to live without some people. This same need, if underestimated, will encourage you to bear everyone's burden just as before.

So be careful not to underestimate the power of your pride and your neediness. If you learn to question your motives in a healthy way, you will be able to keep your maintenance on the right track.

It is important to know your limits and stick to them.

> *For I consider that the sufferings of this present*
> *time are not worthy to be compared with the glory*
> *which shall be revealed in us.* —ROM. 8:18

When we are depressed, we can only see the misery around us. The future becomes something frightening, to be avoided at all costs, even to the point of considering suicide. In contrast, when we are hopeful we are able to see richness and beauty, recognizing the possibilities for the future.

Eugene described his life as very dark and dismal and felt he had no reason to live. Granted, his life had been difficult. Adopted when he was twenty-two months old, he had been severely neglected and even abused as a young child. He had then been raised by a workaholic father and a very anxious mother. Despite having a number of very positive qualities, he had difficulty understanding how anything would ever be different.

It *is* hard to see light at the end of the tunnel when all you can see is the tunnel. Eugene needed to grasp the concept of a future hope and glory that transcended his present suffering. While the present *did* seem bleak, those around him could see much more for his future. The key to his success in therapy was grasping this hope.

Is your outlook so current that you fail to recognize the possibilities for the future?

*And though I bestow all my goods to feed the poor,
and though I give my body to be burned, but have
not love, it profits me nothing.* —1 COR. 13:3

In evaluating the healthiness of our choices, we need to examine not only our actions, but also the motives behind them. Some of us get caught up with pleasing others and wanting their approval, so we make choices to gain the acceptance of others. In essence, our motives are actually selfish in nature, rather than godly.

Actions based on selfish motives violate healthy boundaries. Gloria's actions within her family demonstrate this principle. Gloria was raised in a family environment where acceptance was gained by achievements. She was a straight "A" student and was active in many school activities as an adolescent. After she married, she thought the only way she could get approval and acceptance was to be the perfect spouse and mother. To her, this meant taking care of others to the point of sacrificing her own needs. To the casual observer, Gloria would seem like a devoted and committed wife and mother. Unfortunately, Gloria suffered greatly in the long run. Because it was impossible to be perfect in these roles, Gloria ended up in counseling to treat a serious depression.

What are your motives behind the choices you make? Are they to gain approval, or to control a situation? Are you gaining your self-worth from others or from God?

God, help the motives behind my actions be pleasing to you.

Catch us the foxes,
The little foxes that spoil the vines,
For our vines have tender grapes.
—SONG 2:15

What are the little foxes in your process of recovery? Most farmers can tell you that despite their size, foxes can wreak havoc with livestock and poultry on their farms. That is exactly the kind of danger you are in if you don't pay attention to the small stuff.

It is our nature to overlook the small stuff to pay attention to the more pressing and urgent things in our lives. The problem is that the big, pressing things in life are often made up of many minute things that have built up over time. It isn't the big, catastrophic things that cause major problems. It is the small, seemingly insignificant, daily irritations that have gone unattended that cause such calamity. So we focus on the small, irritating interactions we have with each other in order to restore healthy relationships.

The same is true in the recovery process and maintaining the growth that has already occurred. You must continue to "sweat the small stuff." If you don't, you will once again find yourself in the same predicaments you were in before.

Father, help me to pay attention to the "small stuff."

> *I have learned in whatever state I am, to be
> content.*
> —PHIL. 4:11

When was the last time you felt content when physical needs went unmet? It is possible to feel that way. Many times, however, it is not the physical needs that cause us to feel discontent, but rather a deep yearning for something else. Not understanding these needs, we seek to fill them with physical things, believing that these will assuage the discontentment.

There is a moment in therapy when an individual comes to an understanding of this principle. The urgency with which she has pursued the external things to meet internal needs dissipates. She realizes that physical objects are far less important in the long run than taking care of herself and the relationships in her life, both of which will be important long after the temporary excitement of having an object is gone.

It takes some people longer to give up mistaken beliefs than others. However, it is important first to recognize intellectually that the discontentment stems from emotional needs. Then one can move forward in being content regardless of the situation.

Help me to recognize the true source of my discontent.

A sound heart is life to the body,
But envy is rottenness to the bones.
—PROV. 14:30

A severely destructive boundary issue lies within the attitude of envy. When we act out of envy, we attempt to get what others have, and we may do so at any cost. We no longer focus on being responsible for what we do have, we just want more. We complain life isn't fair, and we attempt to make it fair by our own means.

Phil always envied his youngest brother, Mark, for receiving so much attention from their parents. According to Phil, his parents thought Mark could do no wrong; they praised Mark for everything he did. Instead of being angry at his parents' behaviors, Phil attempted to win their approval by putting Mark down and pointing out Mark's faults in front of his parents whenever possible. After several more years of trying without success to get approval from his parents, Phil became depressed.

In therapy, Phil realized how his whole life had become centered on his envy for the attention Mark received so easily from his parents. Phil began his own healing process by changing his attitude from envy to contentment. He became content when he counted his blessings. When he let go of his envy, Phil described feeling a peace in his heart—something he hadn't felt in a long time.

Are you hanging onto envy in your life? If so, let it go before it destroys you.

Rooted and built up in Him and established in the faith, as you have been taught, abounding in it with thanksgiving.
　　　　　　　　　　　　　　—COL. 2:7

As we near Thanksgiving, our thoughts are often centered on the things for which we are thankful. Family, friends, material possessions, and jobs are on the list of things for which we are eternally grateful. Maybe during this Thanksgiving you can begin to be thankful for the work God has wrought in you. It is indeed his empowering that has brought you this far and will carry you farther.

It is worth remembering the pivotal points in your odyssey that God has orchestrated to help you farther down the road of change. The person who holds you accountable, the support group you are in, the therapist who helped you gain the focus you so badly needed to begin your recovery, the changes made by family members and their support could all be considered turning points in your recovery. It is easy to lose sight of the eternal. We are so easily bound by our material experience that we fail to see God's hand in shaping our circumstances and our lives. It is important to remember that in spite of the fact that we may not see God's hand at work, we know and can depend on his faithfulness and his heartfelt love for us.

Father, help me to be thankful for the recovery you have brought about in me.

> *So rend your heart, and not your garments;*
> *Return to the LORD your God,*
> *For He is gracious and merciful,*
> *Slow to anger, and of great kindness;*
> *And He relents from doing harm.*
>
> —JOEL 2:13

Suddenly, when you least want it, old angry feelings begin churning! You know the feeling: that dangerous desire to show the other person just how it felt. Often we follow through, acting out aggressive impulses. Those impulses rarely satisfy and leave us with a stronger resolve to really show them next time.

It is common to attribute such human traits to God. We expect that because of all the wrongs we've done, a payback from an angry, vengeful God will soon follow. So each time another calamity occurs in life, it gets attributed to a punishment from this almighty being who wants to make our life miserable or execute payment-in-kind.

Fortunately, God is quite reticent to show anger and chooses instead to substitute love, graciousness, and compassion. Most often, calamity occurs as a natural consequence of our own actions.

Thanks, God, for your levelheadedness and for not being quick-tempered and vengeful.

Faithful are the wounds of a friend,
But the kisses of an enemy are deceitful.
—PROV. 27:6

Patty returned home to her family after attending a treatment program for her eating disorder. Part of her aftercare plan included getting involved in friendships that would provide help for her in her recovery. Patty was frightened of the kind of friendships she would need to stay healthy. She knew real friends would confront her if she began to slip back into old patterns.

Patty allowed her fear to influence her decision making. Instead of choosing friends who would provide true support, she surrounded herself with old friends who were more than willing to tell her anything she wanted to hear. Three weeks after leaving the hospital, Patty found herself returning to her old behavior of compulsive overeating.

Just like Patty, we need to beware of friends that are willing to say whatever we want to hear. Their flattery and compliments will undoubtedly enable our unhealthy choices. Of course, a friend who enables us does so for selfish reasons. A true friend's confrontations can be trusted because she speaks the truth with our best interests in mind. We need to surround ourselves with friends who will be willing to challenge our unhealthy choices.

Lord, give me the wisdom and courage to choose healthy friendships.

> *"Now everyone who hears these sayings of Mine,*
> *and does not do them, will be like a foolish man*
> *who built his house on the sand."*
>
> —MATT. 7:26

How much of your maintenance program is built on solid rock and how much is built on sand? Much like what Jesus said here, if you are not putting the principles you learned during treatment into practice, there is a part of your maintenance program that is built on sand.

It is unlikely that you will use all the principles you learned all the time. That would be impossible and impractical. But, the "house" you have built (the process of change and recovery) needs to be on a firm foundation. If it isn't kept firm, before too long, a part of your house will begin to crumble.

It is a good idea to have a "book of principles" you have learned along the path to recovery. That way you can review and keep your focus on the changes you are after. This is one effective way to tend to your foundation. It gets you in the practice of ongoing evaluation and attention.

Father, help me to maintain the foundation of my recovery.

> *"And whoever exalts himself will be abased, and*
> *he who humbles himself will be exalted."*
> —MATT. 23:12

The key to success in recovering from dysfunctional patterns is humility. This can be difficult when you have struggled for many years to make something of yourself in order to gain the approval of others. Approval seeking means calling attention to yourself and the good things you have done in order to combat feelings of inferiority.

It rarely makes you feel better because it doesn't really fill the emptiness you feel. After each new accomplishment, you feel more emptiness, which means another achievement is sought until the pattern is completely ingrained and then compulsively repeated. Meanwhile you still suffer from feelings of low self-worth.

Rather than fighting poor feelings about yourself, it is better to admit the truth. Trying to obtain value from exalting yourself doesn't work. Usually it leaves you in a worse place because you experience no success. Recognizing that you are powerless will bypass this problem. Being truly humble means admitting that accomplishments and success make a person no better or worse. Your source of value is not what you do, but the God that you serve.

Great God, you are my source of value; help me keep my achievements in perspective.

> *Ponder the path of your feet,*
> *And let all your ways be established.*
> —PROV. 4:26

The holiday season is approaching rapidly with all its promises of excitement and festive events. Unfortunately, for most of us the holidays can also be a time of disappointment and pain. Ironically, much of the pain and disappointment results from our own choices and actions.

One of the most common ways to set ourselves up for disappointment occurs when we have unrealistic expectations of others and ourselves during the holidays. We may anticipate this season hoping this is the year the family will finally be united and together, seeing eye to eye with each other. Or perhaps we hope that this year will make up for all the disappointing holidays of the past.

Each year Frank hoped his family would resolve their issues and get along with each other like "normal" families do. After each holiday season, Frank became upset because his expectations were not met. In fact, the holidays generally brought out the worst in his family.

We set ourselves up for disappointment and even rejection if we approach the holidays with unrealistic expectations, especially concerning our families. Frank experienced the "holiday magical-thinking trap," hoping the season would change his family. Are you doing the same?

God, help me to have healthy, realistic expectations this holiday season.

A little sleep, a little slumber,
A little folding of the hands to sleep.
—PROV. 6:10

I'm sure you have heard that a little bit of something goes a long way. What does that mean to you? I think the idea is that whatever it was you were doing was annoying enough that only a small amount was necessary to gain someone's attention. It is also like a very strong spice. You only need a little to affect the taste of the dish you are making.

The same is true of allowing dysfunctional behavior to creep into our behavior patterns during maintenance. It only takes a little bit to begin to affect more and more of our behavior. Much like a strong odor that spreads through an entire room, it begins to work its way through more and more of your interactions with others. As the author of Proverbs makes clear, it is when we begin to waffle on inappropriate behavior that we will begin to find ourselves slipping.

So beware of little signs of dysfunctional behavior creeping back. Act immediately to deal with it and re-establish healthier behaviors. In that way, you will avoid having to deal with a huge crisis in the future.

Father, help me to attend to the little things that threaten to sidetrack me.

For God is not the author of confusion but of peace.
                                            —1 COR. 14:33

As therapists, the people we see in our daily practice are people with intense problems. This is especially true with individuals who struggle with codependency. Their lives have become so problem-focused that all seems terribly chaotic. In the midst of this is a tremendous anger at God. Have you ever said to yourself or someone else, "How can God allow this to happen to me?" Such a statement assumes that God is somehow responsible for the chaos we allow in our existence.

According to this passage, however, God is not the author of chaos or disorder; he is a God of peace. While we make choices that maximize unhappy results, God is looking to maximize our serenity, and he has an eye toward our long-term good. Sometimes we fail to realize this and cut ourselves off from the true source of joy in the midst of our pain. How much better life could be for us if we took responsibility for our unhappiness and gave God the credit for the peaceful times we experience.

_____

God, help me to grasp your peace even when I create turmoil for myself.

He who is slow to wrath has great understanding.
—PROV. 14:29

Carrie described her mother as being a "basket case." Apparently, her mother's only method for coping with difficult people and situations was to create a crisis. Carrie copied her mother's method of coping and repeated this pattern with her own family. Carrie could see how she reacted to everything and everyone around her. She lacked patience and sound judgment.

Carrie felt controlled by her outside environment. She became panic-stricken with every event that appeared to be outside of her control. Her frantic reactions interfered with her marriage and adversely affected her parenting skills.

With counseling, Carrie learned to act on situations, rather than to react in crisis fashion. She learned to give herself time to make decisions. She learned to delay her responses in order to allow herself to think carefully and objectively. This extra time enabled her to request input and support from others. It also allowed her to ask God for guidance.

Like Carrie, many of us instantly react in times of pressure and stress. When we react to situations without careful thought and consideration, we often make poor choices and violate appropriate boundaries. We need to practice patience and ask God for help before we say or do anything.

Take time to act, not react.

And he said, "How can I, unless someone guides me?" And he asked Philip to come up and sit with him.
—ACTS 8:31

It is pretty easy to become smug after going through treatment and struggling with so much. Before long, you may begin to think that you have all the knowledge there is to acquire about changing behavior. Obviously, this is overstated, but it is important to remain a student of boundary issues and poor decision making. No doubt the eunuch who invited Philip into his chariot was a learned man. Here he was studying Isaiah but not understanding what he was reading. He was willing, though, to seek knowledge even from someone along the side of the road. That is motivation to learn!

The same must be true of you as well, as you maintain your boundaries. You are surrounded with opportunities for learning. Whether or not you are looking for them will make the difference between benefiting from or missing a valuable opportunity. Strive to remain teachable and pliable as you seek to learn as much as you can of how to continue the *process* of growth. If you quit learning, you will find that you will quit growing as well.

Father, help me to remain teachable and look for opportunities to learn and grow.

> *"And why do you look at the speck in your*
> *brother's eye, but do not consider the plank in your*
> *own eye?"*
> —MATT. 7:3

We often hear children say, "but he did it first," as if the other's behavior was really responsible for their own. It is much easier to blame than to take responsibility.

When I think of this passage a mental picture comes to mind. If you envision the plank and the sawdust speck literally, a sort of Laurel-and-Hardy type tragicomedy becomes possible. There's Dr. Hardy with a two-by-four board extending from his head, trying to perform delicate eye surgery on patient Laurel who has a stubborn speck lodged near his tear duct. Each time Dr. Hardy makes a move the board gets in the way, until poor Laurel has not only a stubborn speck of dust but also an assortment of black-and-blue marks all over.

Often we try to perform eye surgery on those close to us, while ignoring the fact that we contribute even more to the problem. Our desire to rectify our own dysfunction gets taken out on others as we try to fix their problems.

How clearly do you see your plank? Be careful not to judge others more harshly than yourself—your vision might be clouded.

God, grant me 20/20 vision before I try to fix others' insufficiencies.

> *If the foot should say, "Because I am not a hand, I*
> *am not of the body," is it therefore not of the body?*
> *And if the ear should say, "Because I am not an*
> *eye, I am not of the body," is it therefore not of the*
> *body?*
> —1 COR. 12:15–16

Randy, a thirty-year-old marijuana user, entered inpatient treatment after his wife threatened to leave him. Randy had been using marijuana daily since the age of fourteen. He had all the physical symptoms of long-term use, such as premature aging, memory problems, and poor concentration. Randy was asked how his drug usage affected his three children. He emphatically stated, "It didn't affect them at all! When I used, I became more mellow, not mean like some other drug users I know." With the help of therapy and support group meetings, Randy developed a list of one hundred ways his family and friends had been affected by his use. The making of this list was the most painful task he encountered in treatment. However, because he was able to identify the damage his drug use caused his family and friends, he made the healthy choice to stop.

Randy's fantasy was to believe that he could somehow use marijuana and not affect those around him. When he realized his illogical thinking, he was able to make healthier choices for himself.

Lord, help me to see how my choices affect others.

*"But I say to you, love your enemies, bless those
who curse you."*
—MATT. 5:44

I bet there is at least one person in your life who seems
to have the capacity to "push all your buttons." A
mother once told me that when she was talking to her
son, she was so hooked into keeping him happy that
she couldn't even think straight. She would approach
him to confront him about some inappropriate behavior, and she would walk away feeling that she was stupid to even think there was a problem! Now, that's
power!

We might be apt to look at people like this as our
worse nightmare. We may even see them as an enemy
to our recovery because of their incredible power over
our emotions. It is important to remember that they
have such power because we have somewhere in time
given them the right to have such power. You might
ask yourself, "What is it about this person that I am so
worried about?" Or, "Why is it so important to me that
this person not get angry?"

The button-pushers in our lives are always going to
be around. We can't get rid of them all (as much as we
would like to). Since you can't get rid of them, you may
want to turn this situation into a learning opportunity
to make more progress.

_____

Father, help me to learn from the button-pushers in my life.

> *"Those who are well have no need of a physician,*
> *but those who are sick. I did not come to call the*
> *righteous, but sinners, to repentance."*
> —MARK 2:17

I'm not good enough for God. Once I get it all together, then I'll let God be a part of my life." Ever hear this statement? The underlying belief is that God is like a parent who will not accept us until we meet some standard too high to attain. And so we wait.

If we approached medicine this way, there would be no need for doctors. Let's imagine a person thinking to himself, "Boy, I sure feel ill today. My doctor would never accept me in this condition, so I'll just wait until I'm better before I ask for my doctor's help." Clearly, this would be ludicrous! We need medical attention when we are sick, not after we have recovered.

Likewise, God recognizes us in our fallen state. The time we need God most is when we are at our weakest. If we believe we have it all together, a totally mistaken belief, we have no need for God. Don't wait until you are "good enough." Help from a higher power is available now when you need it most.

What areas of your life have you hidden from God, believing they are too bad?

Thus says the LORD, your Redeemer,
The Holy One of Israel:
"I am the LORD your God,
Who teaches you to profit,
Who leads you by the way you should go."
—ISA. 48:17

After making many changes, how do you now maintain the consistency necessary to assure success? One way to accomplish this is practice living according to principles rather than others' reactions to what you do and say.

It takes diligence to develop a consistent set of principles to deal with others. You have already begun this process, though, when you make new boundaries and choices. If you begin to judge your actions according to the principles, then your actions will become more consistent because you are using the same measure each time you judge your behavior. On the other hand, if you are constantly adjusting your actions and thoughts according to the reaction you receive, you will never find consistency in your behavior.

Therefore, it is important to decide the measure you are going to use to judge your behavior. The Golden Rule? The guidelines provided in the Bible? By each situation?

It is important to judge our behavior by some set of standards rather than by the reactions of others.

All the ways of a man are pure in his own eyes,
But the LORD weighs the spirits.

—PROV. 16:2

With two weeks before Christmas, it's important to take an inventory of our holiday plans and expectations. We all know the holidays can create an enormous amount of stress as we plan our activities. It's most important to examine our attitude and motives going into the final phase of the holiday season. Are we hoping others will approve of us by the gifts we give them? Are we feeling responsible to make others happy during the season?

Our attitude may indeed be one of making others happy; this is one of the most common areas of unhealthy boundaries during the holiday season. It may start out with the honest desire of having everyone experience the best Christmas of all. However, our desire becomes unhealthy when we begin to feel personally responsible to insure their happiness. The healthiest choice we can make during the holiday season is to decide we will only be responsible for our own happiness. We will plan activities that bring joy and meaning to us and allow others to be responsible for their own appreciation of the holidays. With this attitude, the choices we make concerning gifts, activities, and who we will see will take on a new and healthier meaning. Our choices and actions will be based on love, not on pleasing others or getting our value from others.

Be responsible for your Christmas, not for everyone else's.

> *But those who wait on the LORD*
> *Shall renew their strength.*
> —ISA. 40:31

Hope requires us to look to the future. Hope ceases to exist when the future looks dim and our prospects are bleak. When we become depressed, our ability to look toward a bright future is impaired. Eventually we give up, failing to see the strength that God gives to continue trying despite current discomfort.

Only seventeen years old, Stephanie had been raped twice. Fearing that her highly success-oriented parents would believe her to be a failure, she never told them. Her life had become a shambles due in large part to the big secret she had kept for many years. Although still young, she had become disenchanted with relationships. She feared that she was doomed to a life of continued suffering from abuse with no one to trust to help her.

In the process of this struggle, Stephanie had given up hope. Without help from others, she had begun to believe that she was destined to a dismal future and felt weak and powerless to continue. Stephanie needed to know that even though her own hope was lacking, with God's hope she could have the strength to face tomorrow.

_____

God, help me to hope in you and to become strong enough to face my future, bleak as it may seem today.

It is better to hear the rebuke of the wise
Than for a man to hear the song of fools.
—ECCL. 7:5

We all need others to help us interpret life and make the right choices. Of course, we need to determine who would give us the most accurate advice.

As a therapist in an inpatient setting, I often watch patients refuse the counseling staff's input and instead make their choices on the advice of family or friends. Most of the patients come into the hospital out of a last desperate attempt to get their lives straightened out. They have exhausted all of their own methods and their families' to solve their problems. However, when counseled on healthier choices for the future, they immediately defend themselves and their actions, remarking, "How do you know what I should do—you're not me. Besides, my family thinks otherwise."

William entered treatment because of depression. The initial evaluations revealed William's excessive alcohol consumption was the root cause of the depression. When informed that his drinking behaviors were alcoholic, William called and asked his wife if she thought he drank too much. When she said no, William promptly left treatment.

Who we consult with is important to the choices we make in life. Are we being wise in who we choose, or are we choosing people who will tell us what we want to hear?

The beginning of a healthy choice is choosing the best consultants.

> *"Where were you when I laid the*
> *foundations of the earth?*
> *Tell Me, if you have understanding."*
> —JOB 38:4

I once met with a family in which there were so many different members, the child who was brought in to see me wasn't sure who was in charge. Sometimes she had to listen to her parents; at other times, she had to listen to her siblings or her aunt and uncle. If one watched her behavior, it would appear she had several different parents. So who was she supposed to listen to? Who was the authority? She often would misbehave just to find out who was the authority.

The key to helping this family was to define more clearly who was the ultimate authority for this youngster. It meant that when someone was left in charge of her, they followed the discipline patterns and philosophy of her parents. When the parents returned, they assumed their leadership role. Defining boundaries also means defining roles and responsibilities in a way that makes it clear who is in charge and who isn't.

Lord, sometimes I'm not quick enough to take charge. Help me to be instrumental in defining the roles in my family.

> *He Himself has said, "I will never leave you nor
> forsake you."*
> —HEB. 13:5

Ruby entered into each new relationship with a knowledge that ultimately the other would see her as she saw herself. Then the inevitable would occur—she would be rejected. She was so certain of this that there were times she pushed friends and loved ones away rather than allow them to reject her.

As she talked about her fears of being hurt this way she began to realize what a dysfunctional belief this was. It was Ruby herself who was doing the rejecting in order to protect herself from it. Instead of simply allowing it to happen to her, she tried to control the process by ensuring that it would happen. Naturally this made relationships impossible, and Ruby had become lonely and miserable.

Fear of rejection is common. For one who bases his sense of self-worth on whether or not others like him, it is devastating when rejection occurs. God has promised this will never happen in a relationship with him. This is a fairly safe bet, one relationship risk that is worth taking.

---

*God, show me that I can be safe with you. Let me know that you will
not leave if I trust myself to enter a relationship with you.*

Let us search out and examine our ways,
And turn back to the LORD.

— LAM. 3:40

The biggest symptom of any addiction, including co-dependency, is denial. Counselors, family members, and employers have tried many methods to break through denial. Interventions are conducted solely to break down a person's denial and get the person to admit the need for help. When the person refuses to get help at the end of the intervention, a final step is taken; it is called the "If" contract. The person is told if they relapse or continue their unhealthy behaviors and choices, they will admit themselves for treatment.

Warren's family and employer intervened on Warren for his drinking problems. Of course, after hearing how everyone was affected by his drinking, Warren submitted he'd stop drinking if that's what everyone wanted, but he was not going to get help to do it. The "If" contract was used, and Warren agreed, remarking, "I don't need anyone's help, I can quit on my own." Within three days, Warren was drinking again.

Are you like Warren? Do you need to put your unhealthy choices to the test before you admit you need help from others and God? Hopefully not. But if you are struggling with controlling unhealthy behaviors, put it to the test so you can begin making healthier choices.

Failing this test is the first step to winning.

> *But let all those rejoice who put their trust in You;*
> *Let them ever shout for joy, because You defend them;*
> *Let those also who love Your name*
> *Be joyful in You.*
>
> —PS. 5:11

Have you ever noticed when you are beginning to feel happy that you also begin to feel guilty? This is a typical experience of many who are struggling to making healthier decisions. Have you ever wondered why this happens?

One of the reasons is habit. You have gotten pretty accustomed to making your own happiness secondary to someone else's. It makes sense, then, that when you begin to feel happy you might feel that something is definitely wrong.

Another reason is protection. If you feel happy, the other person must not and therefore something is wrong. You will then feel guilty. That corrects the imbalance of positive emotions, and all is "well" once again.

Be ready to notice when your alarm systems go off at the wrong time—when you are doing the right things. Remember that you are in a process of relearning, and old habits have to be broken. Allow yourself to grow and make mistakes.

It is important to notice when the old alarm system goes off at the wrong time and respond differently this time.

> *"Take heed and beware of covetousness, for one's life does not consist in the abundance of the things he possesses."*
> —LUKE 12:15

The media is full of the latest lottery winners and the lifestyles of billionaires. No wonder some of us feel poor, despite having everything we need. One day, as I ran a therapy group for some of the adolescents in our unit, the kids discussed how people will rob others at gunpoint for a premium pair of name-brand basketball sneakers.

Many of the teens in our program suffer from depression, a tremendous amount of deep emptiness. Depressed individuals will go to great lengths to fill the void in their lives. Some try alcohol; others, money. Still others try relationships, food, work, anger, intense flurries of activity, and even basketball shoes. Unfortunately, none of these things plug the leak, and the emptiness continues.

This verse of scripture is very clear in its warning: Be alert, vigilant, and on your guard against greed. One can never have enough things. That is why billionaire land developers never quit and why kids would literally kill for a pair of shoes.

Help me to keep possessions in perspective.

> *In the multitude of words sin is not lacking,*
> *But he who restrains his lips is wise.*
> —PROV. 10:19

Knowing when to disclose information about ourselves or about others is not always an easy task. A common boundary issue is "telling all," lacking discretion as to who we tell, and how much we tell. We may do this feeling that we need to be honest and transparent to other people. If we don't tell everything, we may conclude we are being dishonest.

Jane had difficulty with this particular boundary issue while in therapy addressing her childhood abuse. Whenever her family asked her what was going on in her therapy, Jane felt obligated to tell them everything. Of course, her parents did not like what they heard, so they began to treat Jane with contempt and scorn. Jane learned her lesson the hard way.

It would be great if we could tell all to everyone, but this is unrealistic. In Jane's case, her parents were not interested in Jane's healing process; they were only interested in protecting themselves. Jane needed to be more discerning about whom she would disclose to and what information she would disclose.

Do you feel the need to tell all in any kind of relationship? Practice healthy boundaries in relationships by using discretion on disclosing personal information.

Lord, give me wisdom to discern how much I disclose about myself in my various relationships.

*Now hope does not disappoint, because the love of
God has been poured out in our hearts by the Holy
Spirit who was given to us.* —ROM. 5:5

Hope is an incredibly powerful emotion. It allows
people to endure amazing trauma. It gives focus to our
endeavors and meaning to our lives. One can never
underestimate the power of hope. Some have said that
a person without hope is a person without life. Samuel
Taylor Coleridge, a great poet and writer, once penned
these words about hope:

> *Work without hope draws nectar with a sieve,
> And hope without an object cannot live."*

We need hope, but not an empty hope. You began
the process of recovery with hope for a change in your
life that would be healthy for you and those around
you. This hope, like Coleridge suggests and Paul makes
clear, needs an object. That object is God and what he
has done and promises to do for us. We need to always
remind ourselves upon whom our hope rests. You
have, no doubt, seen the fruit of this hope. If there is
progress, recovery, and growth, you have seen evidence of the object of your hope. So indeed, hope does
spring eternal because it is based on God. It is truly a
hope that does not disappoint!

Father, thank you for the hope of your continued help in my recovery.

For He shall give His angels charge over you,
To keep you in all your ways. —PS. 91:11

In the movie "It's a Wonderful Life" George Bailey gets so discouraged with the trend his life has taken that he jumps from a bridge in a suicide attempt. He is provided with a guardian angel named Clarence to intervene and keep him safe from further danger. While Hollywood makes it all seem quite simple, the concept is scriptural to some degree.

In fact, God does provide angels to guard over people who trust in and rely upon him. As one begins changing old patterns and gives up defensive strategies that have not effectively worked, he may fear that danger will result. These defenses have provided an illusion of safety, and letting them go means that this false security must go also. The result can be fear.

In reality, however, allowing these defenses to be retired provides new opportunities to trust God for real safety. Certainly God's defenses will do a much better job than the flimsy ones we construct. Like George Bailey in the movie, there will be angels to ensure your safety as you begin to practice healthy new behaviors.

———————

Lord, help me to rely on your vast armies of guardian angels for protection rather than on my obsolete and dysfunctional defenses.

Therefore let us not sleep, as others do, but let us watch and be sober. —1 THESS. 5:6

A popular attitude in life is *Que sera, sera*—"what will be, will be." It's an attitude we might hear from friends wanting us to take it easy. These are the kinds of friends who say "don't worry about it" when something is definitely going wrong in our lives.

As an addictions counselor, I have watched hundreds of people work recovery programs. The key qualities I have observed in the successful ones are alertness and self-control—just the opposite of *Que sera, sera*. Ralph exemplified both of these characteristics. He carefully eliminated any unnecessary risks to relapse. It was not an easy task, because many of his colleagues harassed him to have a drink with them after work. When he did not join them, they remarked he took life too seriously. This is where Ralph demonstrated self-control. Instead of giving in to the peer pressure to gain their approval, he continued his diligence in his recovery program. Ralph realized there will always be people who will never learn from their mistakes; he was not going to be one of them.

Do you give in too easily to friends who say, "Live it up, don't be so serious"? Consider the wisdom of being alert and self-controlled in these situations.

Lord, give me the courage to be alert and self-controlled when others want to pull me down.

> *Be . . . hospitable, a lover of what is good, sober-minded, just, holy, self-controlled.*
>
> —TITUS 1:7–8

Maintenance requires commitment, pursuit, vigilance, and what is good. There is no such thing as passive maintenance. We must push ourselves to grow and to cultivate a desire for what is healthy for us. Somewhere along the line, that may have been lost, but it can be regained.

Loving what is good both spiritually and emotionally requires an understanding and knowledge of just what is good. Do you know what is good for you spiritually and emotionally? Are you pursuing these things? To answer these questions may require time to reflect, consider, and list them for yourself. It takes discipline and self-control to cultivate a love for what is good.

Think of people who set out to become experts in fine art. They study other people's writing about fine art, they study the art itself, and they expose themselves to many artists. They are relentless in their pursuit. Does that characterize your pursuit of what is good? Be relentless to cultivate your love for what is good, both spiritually and emotionally.

Father, help me to cultivate my desire to love what is good.

> *"'For I know the thoughts that I think toward you,'"* says the LORD, *"'thoughts of peace and not of evil, to give you a future and a hope.'"*
> —JER. 29:11

It is very common to fear a higher power. Often the memories of authority figures in one's life are laced with abuse, feelings of powerlessness, and fears of losing control to someone who will ultimately be injurious. One avoids "letting go and letting God" because of fear.

Susan desperately feared allowing God to intervene in the crises she experienced. As a child, her faith had been thwarted by the message that her wrongdoing was being recorded and held against her by a wrathful God. As an adult, she had come to believe that she could never please this higher power that looked with disdain on her life. In fact, she believed that the crises were orchestrated somehow by an all-seeing being who wanted her to fail.

Susan failed to recognize that the very being she was avoiding wanted to see her succeed in a hopeful future. Susan needed desperately to give up the controls to a God who would make her life better than she ever imagined. She also needed to recognize that her facade of personal autonomy was part of the problem leading to a dysfunctional lifestyle.

God, help me to see you as you really are, a God of hope with bright plans for a hopeful future.

> *For unto us a Child is born,*
> *Unto us a Son is given;*
> *And the government will be upon His shoulder.*
> *And His name will be called*
> *Wonderful, Counselor, Mighty God,*
> *Everlasting Father, Prince of Peace.*
>
> —ISA. 9:6

What is the purpose of Christmas for you? What do you hope to leave this day with when it's all over? A present? Approval from others? Lots of laughs with family members?

If we look at the above list carefully, we will notice that they fail to address our relationship with God. That relationship is the most vital part of our recovery program in making healthy choices and establishing healthy boundaries. Unfortunately, if we make this day a time to relax, a time to open presents for ourselves, or a time to eat too much, we ignore the most significant part. God desires us to use this holiday to focus on him and our relationship with him, not to distort it by placing our focus elsewhere.

Does this mean we can't have presents, family get-togethers, or holiday parties? Of course not! It just means that we need to keep in mind the reason for our celebration. Don't allow the distractions of the holiday to overwhelm you. Plan some time to pray and meditate on God's sovereignty. Attend church, sing carols, and read the biblical story of the birth of Jesus. These are all ways to regain a healthy focus on Christmas Day.

Mighty God, wonderful counselor, everlasting father, prince of peace, thank you for this day.

Likewise the Spirit also helps in our weaknesses.
—ROM. 8:26

Are we willing to admit just how weak we really are? It is incredibly difficult to allow people to see the weakness in us. You have probably spent a lot of time and energy protecting yourself, and doing what you had to to keep people from seeing your weaknesses. The problem is that we can't escape the reality of our limitations and weaknesses. The denial mechanism we use is to make people think that we really aren't weak at all. It is important through the entire recovery process to keep in sight one's weakness. In so doing, we are affirming what is *truly real* and keeping a firm grasp of the recovery process. It is when we begin to think that we are strong that we will get smug and arrogant and end up falling into a whole host of old behaviors.

We are not without protection, though, if we are really going to allow people to see our weaknesses. God has promised that his spirit will minister to us in our weakness. It is in our weakness that we can *really* see how much God loves us and protects us.

Father, help me to trust you to minister to me in my weakness.

When pride comes, then comes shame,
But with the humble is wisdom.
—PROV. 11:2

Pride is the main inhibitor of good relationships. The O'Shea family brought their son to our adolescent program because he wasn't "behaving as he should." As we began to explore in family therapy what this meant, it became obvious that he wasn't completely accepting his mother's notion of what a good son should be. Mrs. O'Shea was a rigid and demanding woman who expected perfect compliance with her whims. Her husband, a heart patient, controlled the family by clutching his chest during a conflict.

Mrs. O'Shea was tired of being the one who ran the family, yet she clearly didn't want to let go. She rejected our views of the problem and focused on her child as the source of the problem. Mr. O'Shea refused to challenge her because of his heart—an excellent excuse not to rock the boat.

The son slowly realized that no matter what he did, he could not assuage his mother. Eventually, he left home at age eighteen with the family still believing he was the problem. The failure of this mother to let down her pride and see her part in the problems ensured that change did not occur.

Be humble enough to take responsibility for your part in problem relationships. Humility creates wisdom that will give you better perspectives on solutions.

> *I said, "I will guard my ways,*
> *Lest I sin with my tongue;*
> *I will restrain my mouth with a muzzle,*
> *While the wicked are before me."*
> —PS. 39:1

One of the easiest ways to violate healthy boundaries is to allow ourselves to talk in the presence of someone with whom we are having a major conflict. In these situations, we will be tempted to spice our conversation with direct and indirect jabs at the person. In essence, we are trying to play God by inflicting what we determine is just punishment for his behavior. We are also trying to control that person, thinking that if we put in enough jabs, maybe he will change.

In the verse above, the psalmist knew there are certain people and situations which require him to bind his tongue lest he say something which he would regret later. The healthy choice for him is to say nothing when he is around people he considers corrupt. Is this dishonest or rude behavior? Absolutely not! It would be dishonest and rude if the psalmist allowed himself to say something inappropriate. It is apparent the psalmist knew his limitations.

Are there certain people at work, home, or church with whom you know you should practice silence to avoid making a controlling remark?

Sometimes being silent is the healthiest choice we can make.

> *Therefore submit to God. Resist the devil and he*
> *will flee from you.*
> —JAMES 4:7

Old habits really do die hard. Once you finally are free, there is a feeling of power and strength in the accomplishment. This is the time to really be wary; this pride in your own personal power leaves you vulnerable to relapse.

Usually you do not notice the first signals that relapse is starting. That is because it actually began simultaneously with feelings of pride and power. When you fail to recognize your own powerlessness over destructive patterns and your need for a higher power, you become closed to the reality of the situation. This denial leads to a mistaken belief that finally you are truly in control. Control, of course, is part of the problem in the first place.

Often, this is when you first seek professional help. After a number of episodes of success and failure, you begin to acknowledge that perhaps you are unable to control the destructive patterns that cause so much suffering. While this is a humbling and possibly painful thing to admit, it is necessary for long-term change. When you believe your own power is adequate, you are more likely to fall into old habits.

Help me to rely on you for my strength while resisting the temptation to believe vainly in my own power to handle things beyond my control.

> *So Jesus stood still and called them, and said,*
> *"What do you want Me to do for you?" They said to*
> *Him, "Lord, that our eyes may be opened."*
> —MATT. 20:32–33

An important aspect of having clear boundaries means viewing myself as an individual, separate from others. This means that my needs and emotions are my own, not anyone else's. Since I have my own individual needs and emotions, others cannot know them unless I communicate them directly. This means, for example, that when I am feeling sad, I need to talk about the sadness with another and ask for comfort, if that is what I am seeking. I cannot expect anyone, even a spouse or close friend, to guess how I am feeling without actually telling them.

Numerous people hurt in silence as they hope and wait for loved ones to figure out their needs. Unfortunately, lack of clear communication often results in disappointment and resentment.

Phyllis has experienced several disappointments with her husband's inability to read her mind. She is frequently heard to exclaim, "If he really cared, he would know how I feel. I shouldn't have to tell him." Phyllis expects her husband to read her mind because she views him as an extension of herself, not as the separate person that he is. As a result, Phyllis is a hurting individual who is becoming a lonely and bitter woman.

Take a moment today to examine your own boundaries. Do you expect others to figure out how you're feeling without telling them? If so, it's time to stop the guessing games.

> *And do this, knowing the time, that now it is high*
> *time to awake out of sleep; for now our salvation is*
> *nearer than when we first believed.*
>
> —ROM. 13:11

What a clarion call for the end of a year of toil and labor with your recovery. You have no doubt seen successes, big and small. You have also seen failure and disappointments. There is much to be happy and grateful for and much with which to find fault. All the same, as you stop to evaluate where you are and where you want to go, keep Paul's words in mind—be alert!

Maintenance is tough business. It is tedious and frustrating to keep your energy so focused on this enterprise. What sets you apart is that you haven't fallen asleep. You have set your sights on certain goals and have accomplished at least some. Don't downplay the successes, and don't maximize your failures. That will not help in the planning for the year ahead. The key is to remain realistic about the gains you have made and your hopes for the year ahead. Build into your maintenance plan ways to stay alert. Plan times in the year ahead for further evaluation and planning. Nothing will happen if you don't plan for it. The old saying applies here: "If you shoot for nothing, you are sure to hit it."

Father, help me to set time aside to plan, and help me to stay alert.

ABOUT THE AUTHORS

Mark MacDonald is the director of the dual diagnosis and chemical dependency programs at the Minirth-Meier Clinic in Wheaton, Illinois. He is a certified addiction counselor (CAC) and a licensed clinical social worker (LCSW). MacDonald received his Master of Arts degree in Social Work from the University of Chicago and his B.A. from Wheaton College in Wheaton, Illinois. He lives with his wife, Parvine, in Wheaton.

Kevin Brown is a psychotherapist and program director of the adolescent inpatient hospital program at the Minirth-Meier Clinic in Wheaton. He specializes in the treatment of abusive families and those recovering from traumatic relationships. He received his M.S.W. from the University of Illinois at Chicago and his B.A. from Wheaton College. Brown and his wife, Sandy, live in the Chicago area.

Raymond Mitsch, Ph.D., is a clinical psychologist and the director of the child and adolescent division of the Minirth-Meier Clinic in Wheaton. Dr. Mitsch received his M.A. and Ph.D. in counseling psychology from Indiana State University, and his B.A. from Wabash College in Crawfordsville, Indiana. He served as staff psychologist for Michigan Technological University Counseling Services for two years before moving to the Minirth-Meier Clinic in Wheaton. Dr. Mitsch, his wife, Linda, and their two children, Corrie and Anne, live in Wheaton.